The Public Congress

Contemporary members of Congress routinely use the media to advance their professional goals. Today, virtually every aspect of their professional legislative life unfolds in front of cameras and microphones and, increasingly, online. *The Public Congress* explores how the media moved from being a peripheral to a central force in U.S. congressional politics. The authors show that understanding why this happened allows us to see the constellation of forces that combined over the last fifty years to transform the American political order.

Malecha and Reagan's keen analysis links the new "public" Congress and the forces that are shaping political parties, the Presidency, interest groups and the media. They conclude by asking whether the kind of discourse that this "new media" environment fosters encourages Congress to make its distinctive deliberative contribution to the American polity. This text brings historical depth as well as coverage of the most current cutting-edge trends in the new media environment and provides an exhaustive treatment of how the U.S. Congress uses the media in the governing process today.

Gary Lee Malecha is Associate Professor in the department of Political Science at University of Portland.

Daniel J. Reagan is Associate Professor in the department of Political Science at Ball State University.

The Public Congress

Congressional Deliberation in
a New Media Age

Gary Lee Malecha
Daniel J. Reagan

NEW YORK AND LONDON

First published 2012
by Routledge
711 Third Avenue, New York, NY 10017

Simultaneously published in the UK
by Routledge
2 Park Square, Milton Park, Abingdon, Oxon OX14 4RN

Routledge is an imprint of the Taylor & Francis Group, an informa business

Library of Congress Cataloging in Publication Data
Malecha, Gary Lee, 1955-
   The public Congress : Congressional deliberation in a new media age / Gary Lee Malecha,
   Daniel J. Reagan.
   p. cm.
   1. United States. Congress—Public relations. 2. Press and politics—United States.
   3. Communication in politics—United States. I. Reagan, Daniel J. II. Title.
   JK1131.M35 2011
   328.73—dc23
   2011028569

ISBN13: 978-0-415-89427-2 (hbk)
ISBN13: 978-0-415-89428-9 (pbk)
ISBN13: 978-0-203-80677-7 (ebk)

Typeset in Adobe Garamond
by EvS Communication Networx, Inc.

Printed and bound in the United States of America on acid-free paper
by Edwards Brothers, Inc.

For Linda and

Catherine, Andrew and Jane

Contents

Acknowledgments

As we near the end of this project, it is a pleasure to recall here all those who helped us along the way. We are both fortunate to have colleagues who provide a stimulating and collegial academic environment. The faculty in the Department of Political Science at the University of Portland and those in the Department of Political Science at Ball State University inspire and sustain us by the way they conduct their professional lives. They demonstrate that it is indeed possible for smart and passionate people to explore complicated questions in a friendly way, even when they don't always agree. We have been equally fortunate to have colleagues in other departments who provided support and encouragement on more than one occasion.

We also thank the administrations at both Universities for giving each of us a sabbatical, which allowed us to give sustained attention to our work at critical moments in its development.

The Dirksen Congressional Center and the American Political Science Association granted us awards that gave us the financial resources to complete different parts of our research, and we are grateful for their support and confidence.

Meredith Gard, Kristopher Kritzler, and Max Walling not only provided talented research assistance, but their willingness to engage in conversations about our study sharpened our analysis.

Dr. Jane A. Little and Dr. Thomas H. Hostetter not once, but twice generously opened their home to us when we interviewed congressional communications staff in Washington, DC, and they were gracious enough to act as if there wasn't anything more in the world they wanted to do than to listen to us talk about the changing congressional/media relationship.

We also want to thank our editor Michael Kerns and the staff at Routledge for their support and generous assistance as we brought our project to completion. We are also grateful for the insights provided to us by the anonymous reviewers who read and commented on our manuscript.

We also want to acknowledge those members of congressional staffs and those in the DC press corps who consented to be interviewed for this project and shared with us their insights about congressional communications and DC politics.

Finally, we are both fortunate to have loving families who supported us and who, on more than one occasion, graciously gave up time and accommodated their schedules so that we could complete this work. It is to those loving and generous individuals that we dedicate our work.

1 Introduction

Observers of contemporary American politics frequently underscore the role media and public relations activities play in governance and policymaking. It is not uncommon these days to read about politicians "governing with the news" or "governing by campaigning" and how the strategy of "going public" has displaced conventional bargaining and coalition building activities.[1] As Tim Groeling noted, not only do political actors "believe that 'talk matters,'" they "sometimes behave as if talk were *all* that mattered."[2]

While these accounts usually center on the White House, and how the president tries to advance the administration's goals by strategically mounting public appeals, those at the other end of Pennsylvania Avenue also engage in public relations activities, both to get reelected and to advance their power and policy goals.[3] Many do spots on cable news shows and talk radio, write columns or editorials for Internet news providers and newspapers, speak to members of the press back home, hold tele-town events, and if they are back in their constituencies, host regular town hall meetings. A growing number have turned to newer media platforms to communicate their ideas and strategically advance their positions. "Virtual offices" are ubiquitous on the Hill, the percentage of members boasting YouTube channels and Facebook and Twitter accounts continues to climb, and it is common to hear about lawmakers' digital IQs and read about social media going "viral" on "Capitol Hill."[4] Even leaders like the Speaker of the House now advertise how they use YouTube to receive and answer citizens' questions.[5]

Congressional parties, meanwhile, devote substantial time to honing their messages and proliferating communications plans to shore up what they now commonly refer to as their "brands."[6] They consider it a point of honor to broadcast their own members' prowess for using YouTube, Facebook, and Twitter.[7] Occasionally, they even encourage rank-and file-members to forgo playing "inside baseball" and mount instead an "entrepreneurial insurgency" through a smorgasbord of communications technologies.[8] The result is that it is no longer unusual to see "a proffered policy and its sponsor trashed in the media and disparaged in the blogs before it receives any traction."[9] Indeed, shortly after the opening of the 112th Congress, the *New York Times* reported: "Via news conferences, Web videos, floor speeches, media appearances and a steady stream of critical statements and e-mails,

Democrats have accused the new regime of ignoring the implications of repealing the new health care law, breaking promises to run a more open House and, for good measure, letting lawmakers who were not sworn in cast votes."[10]

It has not always been this way. For much of the first half of the twentieth century, most lawmakers who eagerly sought publicity by getting in front of cameras and overtly pushing themselves in headlines and lead paragraphs of news accounts were disparagingly referred to as "show horses" and "mavericks." More often than not, they were ostracized and treated as marginal players on Capitol Hill. The prevailing normative structure of the institution instead provided members with incentives to labor quietly, and cooperatively, behind closed doors on committees to which they were assigned.[11]

Just how we got from there to where we are today is the complex tale this work addresses. It is a story with many parts, and it is one that continues to unfold. It is also an account that brings to the fore questions concerning Congress's ability to function as a deliberative body and leads us to consider whether today's more public institution reflects and contributes to a political order that is at odds with the regime fashioned by the Framers of the Constitution.

The highly visible role that public communications plays on the Hill, while made possible by a rapidly evolving and increasingly interconnected media world, is actually rooted in transformations that extended from the late 1950s through the early 1980s. These included, among other things, changes in the presidency, political parties, pressure groups, and the media as well as a series of Capitol Hill reforms that decentralized power and opened up the institution. Combined, these eroded the institutional culture that encouraged members to stay behind the scenes as they carried out face-to-face negotiations, prompting more of them to try their hand at "governing with the news."

That, however, is only the first part of the narrative. The next involves the recent ideological sorting out of the electorate that has resulted in more cohesive and polarized congressional parties. Members of Congress now find that their own preferences more often than not align with the policies advocated by the parties to which they belong. As a result, by promoting the performance and public standing of their parties, they incidentally serve their own goals. This, in turn, gives them an incentive to have their congressional parties regularly plan and orchestrate public relations campaigns to advance their collective legislative goals, claim success for their performance, distinguish themselves from their partisan rivals, and thus improve their stature or "brand name" in ways that help them court voters and reassure supporters.[12]

But here the plot thickens. This part of the story brings into sharp relief the considerable collective action challenge confronting congressional parties as they try to execute public relations campaigns.[13] On the one hand, by crafting coherent messages and articulating them in a multitude of different media forums, they can clarify what they are offering voters and other political actors and constituencies, reinforce brand loyalties, and prompt their followers to mobilize on their behalf during critical stages of the legislative process. On the other, the parties find themselves in a fragmented, fluid, real-time 24/7 news world where they need to coordinate the activities of rank-and-file members and other political actors who have their own communication needs and expanded their own communications resources. Moreover, they must address this challenge in an environment in which members' costs in obtaining media access seem to be declining. As one veteran Hill staffer recounted,

> I began working here in the early 80s and I wasn't overtly doing press until later but obviously we were all sort of exposed to that.... In the early 80s you still had...a twenty-four hour news cycle...meant it was twenty-four hours before you were going to interpret.... Now it means something completely different. CNN came in but you still had the big papers, the big networks and not much else. The Internet no one was even thinking about...cable was a fledgling kind of thing. Now I get a call, for the past number of years, I get a call every week from a brand new show or electronic...of some kind that never existed before ... once a week on average.... Even the mainstream press now they have an online thing, too, and so sometimes if they get a little interview and they don't want to put it into an article or if they're going to have to wait until tomorrow or if they're weekly or later in the week they've got their dot com piece also they can put it on....[14]

We will show that in this media world that lowers individual members' costs, which enables them to take a more public posture, congressional parties have tried to adapt to this specific collective action problem in much the same way they have responded to other similar challenges.[15] This, in turn, has implications beyond enabling them to shore up their public standing in ways that serve members' goals. Congressional parties' success in carrying out their "messaging" activities also shapes the context for presidents as they follow a public strategy.[16] Presidents thus now on occasion risk the possibility of confronting a choreographed public opposition capable of creating an echo chamber that can more closely match the breadth and intensity of White House appeals.

These adaptations have important normative consequences as well. In particular, while they serve the immediate interests of the members and the parties to which they belong, they also pose a challenge to the institution as it tries to carry out its responsibilities. After all, many of the Framers believed that the system of government they created would be guided by "the cool and deliberate sense of the community."[17] And they surmised that Congress, which they structured to work in a context that controlled the effects of majority factions and allowed for the refinement of popular opinion, would be instrumental in helping the polity arrive at more informed, reflective decisions. That is not to say that the Founders believed that deliberation would only occur in the legislative branch, since in creating a system of checks and balances they certainly anticipated the other branches of government would be also be involved.[18] Still, following "those politicians and statesmen who have been the most celebrated for the soundness of their principles, and for the justness of their views," they found Congress—a "numerous legislature"—"best adapted to deliberation and wisdom."[19]

The Framers set a stringent standard for what makes for deliberation, what Joseph Bessette describes as *"reasoning on the merits of public policy."* While this may occur in a variety of different ways, it comprises several distinctive yet "essential elements." Deliberative activities start by reflecting on a problem and then amassing information necessary to derive an appropriate policy solution. This educates other actors about a problem and shapes their views and thus mobilizes support for, or opposition to, taking some public action to deal with it. Second, deliberation involves using information to construct a coherent argument that links a preferred alternative course of action with an identified problem. The "final" and "singular mark" of deliberation involves using information and arguments to persuade others and help them develop "reasoned judgments."[20]

It would, of course, be a mistake to assume that the Framers believed Congress would always carry out its responsibilities in a truly deliberative manner. They were, after all, keenly aware, as Madison wrote in *Federalist 51*, that ambitious, self-interested men, not angels, would be at the helm.[21] Jeffrey Tulis reminds us that while the Framers' aspirations included making "deliberation more likely," they were realists enough to anticipate that the legislative process would include more than the occasional instance of "bargaining, logrolling, or nondeliberative rhetorical appeals."[22] The problem, potentially, is that as members of Congress and the parties to which they belong make their cases in public and bring popular sentiment to bear on their chambers' policymaking activities, they diminish the ability of the institution to realize even the more modest deliberative potential expected by those who created it. As today's members on the Hill concentrate more resources and time to helping their parties communicate their messages, they find themselves constrained to perform those information gathering and problem solving tasks necessary to deliberate well. Then again, as they take their case into the public realm and try to score points by repeating carefully scripted arguments to advance more immediate partisan interests, they threaten to drive out the kind of rational, public spirited discussion necessary to promote deliberation.[23]

Our narrative on the rise of public communications on the Hill, the collective action dilemma these operations pose for parties, and the challenges they present to Congress as a deliberative body, is carried out over the rest of this book. Chapter 2 opens with a portrait of a policy-based media battle, of the kind that has become commonplace in today's Washington community. This chapter illustrates the public relations approach to governing that is so dominant and shows how members of Congress have followed the president's lead in using a communications strategy to realize their ambitions. It also argues that in today's more partisan environment individual members find it profitable to team up with their party colleagues to mount public relations campaigns to serve party objectives. As congressional parties have become more internally homogenous and polarized, many representatives and senators have incentives to work with their fellow party members to court the media in carefully constructed public relations campaigns. Working together allows them to attract more media coverage, and this increased visibility gives them the chance to shape policy decisions, claim credit for positive developments, distinguish themselves from their partisan opponents, communicate with attentive publics, provide cues to other political actors, raise money, and secure reelection. The chapter concludes by showing that these strenuous congressional public relations efforts are taking place in a new media world, one that is more dynamic, fluid, fractured, and real-time oriented. This new media world, which brings together more traditional outlets and newer venues, including web-based social media platforms, both gives congressional party members incentives to work together and provides them with ample opportunities to wander off message.

Chapter 3 explores how the public Congress has emerged over time. Here we explain how today's publicity-conscious legislature is a product of pivotal transformations both in the Congress and the larger political system. We begin with an account of what scholars have identified as the "prereform Congress," an institution structured by norms and rules that discouraged members from using publicity to carry out their legislative duties.[24] We trace how internal reforms in the 1960s and 1970s and subsequent changes to Congress's external political environment combined to produce a legislative order that not only links lawmaking and public relations campaigns, but often makes those media efforts a requirement for political success. Some of the changes to its external environment include the growing polarization and cohesiveness of political parties, the expansion of the "public" presidency, and the proliferation and transformation of interest groups. This chapter shows that the new role publicity plays in congressional politics is deeply rooted in some sweeping changes that shaped the American political system in the latter part of the twentieth century. Thus, while it is true that the emergence of a more complicated and fluid media environment—the rise of talk radio, cable television, the Internet, blogs, social media, and niche news providers—facilitated the emergence of a more publicity-oriented Congress, the media alone did not produce it. We discuss how the political changes coalesced with the new media environment to first encourage individual members to become more media conscious in their activities, and later prompt them to join their partisan colleagues to mount public communication campaigns.

Scholars who concentrate on the development of American political institutions have concluded that Congress, notwithstanding the many changes it and the country has witnessed, is, as we show in chapter 3, remarkably resilient. Chapter 4 extends that theme as it explores how individual members on the Hill have adapted to a congressional order that prizes communications activities conducted within a media environment buffeted by multifaceted changes in how information is gathered, evaluated, reported, and received. We show how individual members have adjusted by increasing and deploying their institutional resources in ways that help them craft and disseminate their messages. The first part of the chapter focuses on communications personnel. We show that individual members, chamber leaders, and committee heads have adjusted to the new demands placed on them in a more publicity-conscious institution by continuing to increase the size and elevate the importance of their offices' professional communications staff. We then trace how members have applied and expanded new communications technologies in carrying out their message operations. Expanded communications staff and the application of new communications technologies have increased lawmakers' abilities to widen the breadth, heighten the intensity, target the direction, control the content, and synchronize the timing of the political messages that they seek to communicate to political actors outside of Congress. This, in turn, has left them better positioned to attain their goals.

Just as lawmakers increased their own ability to engage in public relations activities, they discovered greater incentives to coordinate with their partisan colleagues to get out consistent messages that supported their initiatives. If congressional parties can craft coherent messages and articulate them in a multitude of different media forums, they can clarify what they are offering voters and other political actors, reinforce loyalties, and prompt support from followers at critical stages of the legislative process. By claiming credit for their work and accomplishments, and by countering their opponents' assertions, party communication efforts can shore up the public image of their members, reinforce support from their constituencies, and improve members' chances of obtaining their political goals. Yet the need to provide consistent, unambiguous, and well-timed messages across an ever expanding number of forums presents parties with a collective action problem. Not only must they get members to go out in the public realm to carry messages, and do so in ways that reach relevant audiences, but they must also tie their communications campaigns to legislative actions and synchronize their public responses with actions taken by other branches of government as well as with events unfolding on the electoral calendar.[25] Additionally, since every individual member has greater wherewithal and more opportunities to attract news organizations' attention, parties constantly confront, and must address, the challenge of inducing members to stay on message. Chapter 5 explores how in recent years the parties have tried to negotiate this collective action problem. We describe how parties in both chambers have responded to these challenges by adapting institutional structures and evolving organizational strategies to help them get out their messages across a variety of media forums. We show how the parties have worked to synchronize their communications operations and speak with greater unity and clarity as they aim to reach a variety of other political actors in an increasingly fragmented media environment.

Chapters 6 and 7 illustrate the potential and the limitations of the organizational structures and strategies congressional parties enlist as they try to execute coordinated and carefully calibrated public relations responses. Chapter 6 covers three different cases: Prescription drug coverage and Medicare reform; increased funding for the state children's health insurance program (SCHIP); and immigration reform legislation. These cases, while they do not exhaust all possibilities, do provide a good cross-section of recent and significant policy initiatives. They cover instances of both unified and divided government, and they also give us policies on which there are different degrees of unity within the parties.

Communications relations battles that unfold on the Hill also implicate the White House, which has its own incentives for following a public governing strategy. Chapter 7 illustrates these communications campaigns within the context of interbranch relations. Only a few short years ago, when presidents opted to go public to advance their programmatic objectives, they occupied center stage.[26] Isolated congressional leaders then played increasingly important, though nonetheless minor supporting roles in the accompanying publicity battles. That, as we will show in this chapter, has changed. Today's presidents confront a different environment. In particular, while they still command the largest megaphone, they now share the public stage with multiple actors, who, by coordinating or institutionalizing their efforts, can on occasion either significantly advance or hinder the White House as it tries to muster public support on behalf of its positions. It is therefore possible that even the president's limited ability in "exploiting existing opinion" is now constrained in ways it had not been before.[27] To highlight this, we focus on a major domestic initiative of the Obama administration, the American Recovery and Reinvestment Act—the stimulus bill—passed in 2009. We use this to illustrate how the White House and the congressional parties exploit the wide range of new media venues to communicate messages to support their partisan and policy goals, and to underscore the extent to which congressional parties' message operations have perhaps changed the context in which presidents now carry out their strategy of going public.

Scholars sometimes become partisans of their expertise.[28] So in American politics it sometimes happens that imaginative and careful explorations of the Congress give scant attention to the role that the legislature plays in the political system of which it is a part. But that is not how the Congress's creators thought about the institution. While they were keenly interested in its structure and operation, they were primarily concerned with designing it in such a way that it would make distinctive contributions to the new constitutional order they were fashioning. They were not, in other words, interested in Congress as an end in itself, but rather in how it could behave in ways that would supplement and enhance the ends of the regime. And this is what we mean when we say that we want to think constitutionally about the Congress. To what extent does the behavior engendered by today's more publicity-oriented Congress enable or inhibit it from making the kinds of contributions to the American public good that only a legislature can make? This leads us to focus on the Congress's deliberative capacities in our last chapter. Taking a normative turn, we move from giving attention to the role public relations plays on the Hill and in the larger Washington community to considering how an increased emphasis on public and partisan communication impacts Congress's ability to meet its obligations as a deliberative body.

2 Let's Take It Outside

The New Front on the Hill

On February 5, 2001, President George W. Bush's economic advisor, Larry Lindsey, appeared on ABC's *Good Morning America* to present the case for a ten-year, $1.6 trillion package of tax cuts. The president later unveiled his bold "Agenda for Tax Relief," while members of Congress quickly followed with their own communications blitz. Senate Minority Leader Thomas Daschle (D-SD) and Sen. Kent Conrad (D-ND), the Senate Budget Committee's ranking minority member, held a Capitol Hill press conference to raise concerns about the president's initiative. Others fanned out to disparate media outlets. In a CNN news show, House Budget Chair Rep. Jim Nussle (R-IA) defended Bush's proposal; Rep. Robert Matsui (D-CA) countered that it was fiscally irresponsible. Sen. Tim Hutchinson (R-AR) and Rep. Martin Frost (D-TX) took to MSNBC's *Hardball with Chris Matthews,* where Hutchinson pressed for sweeping tax cuts while Frost argued they would wreak havoc with the budget, do little to maintain the solvency of programs like Social Security, and provide few benefits to the working class.[1]

Appearing on CNN the following day, Lindsey again extolled the virtues of Bush's plan, repeating many of the points he had conveyed in a front page story of that morning's *New York Times.* Sympathetic interests and think tanks joined this public fracas. A senior fellow at the Cato Institute, for example, penned a newspaper editorial that pushed tax relief and intimated that the White House's opening move was perhaps too restrained in light of projected budget surpluses. This communications battle even spread to smaller news venues, like the *Worcester Telegram and Gazette*, which ran a story covering Democratic representatives' initial reaction to the president's proposal. There three members—Rep. James P. McGovern (D-MA), Rep. Richard Neal (D-MA), and Rep. John Olver (D-MA)—reiterated their party's message that Bush's proposed cuts were too large, would be phased in too fast, and tilted too much to the very rich.[2]

Publicity campaigns touched off by the president's economic agenda picked up steam over the next several days. Secretary of the Treasury Paul O'Neill advocated the package in a CNBC interview on February 7. That same day a group of high-ranking congressional Republicans, which included House Speaker Dennis Hastert (R-IL) and House Majority Leader Richard Armey (R-TX), held a press conference, broadcast live by CNN, to weigh in on the president's side. House GOP backbenchers amplified their leaders' case. Rep. J. D. Hayworth (R-AZ), for instance, squared off against Rep. Harold Ford (D-TN) on Fox's *Hannity and Colmes* to repeat their parties' talking points.[3]

The president's spokesman, Ari Fleischer, appeared in the White House Briefing Room the next day, February 8, to lay out the administration's case and to tell reporters that an "aggressive outreach program," including "a series of things done with local media, with talk radio, with the Internet" to keep the president's initiative moving on the Hill, was underway. As Fleischer addressed the press corps, Lindsey pushed yet again for tax cuts on National Public Radio's *Talk of the Nation*.[4]

Speaker Hastert joined Senate Majority Leader Trent Lott (R-MS) and Secretary O'Neill that same day at a press briefing to make another pitch for the administration's plan. Not to be overshadowed, Sen. Daschle (D-SD) and House Minority Leader Richard Gephardt (D-MO) convened a press conference where, staging a bit of political theater, they tried to frame the issue to drive the news narrative their party's way. Featuring a $46,000 luxury model Lexus and a run-of-the mill car muffler at the event, they noted that the privileged few who fell into the upper-income tax brackets would be handsomely rewarded by Bush's tax initiative, saving enough money to buy the gleaming new automobile. Most everybody else, they added, would be lucky if out of their tax saving they could scrape together enough to get the muffler.[5]

This public relations skirmish did not let up as the day unfolded. That afternoon O'Neill sat for a "newsmaker" interview on the *Jim Lehrer News Hour*, where he outlined the benefits of what he identified, in light of existing financial data, as a prudent "Goldilocks" economic package. Meanwhile, Majority Leader Armey and Rep. Barney Frank (D-MA) appeared on MSNBC's *Hardball* to discuss the president's tax initiatives. Congressman Frank hewed to his party's talking points; Majority Leader Armey defended the cuts as fair and reasonable, and even held out the possibility that they could even be ratcheted up a bit. Rep. Pat Toomey (R-PA) was interviewed that afternoon on Fox's *Special Report with Brit Hume*, where he departed from the administration's Goldilocks script and pressed for an even more expansive package of cuts. Toomey later appeared on CNN's *Spin Room* and reiterated his preference for more significant tax relief.[6]

This dizzying array of media events represents only a series of snapshots of the first days of a spirited, multifaceted public relations campaign that accompanied the president's introduction of his fiscal plan. An untold number of members of the administration and Congress, as well as leaders of concerned interest groups and think tanks, barnstormed the country and saturated disparate media outlets to disseminate their positions while trying to frame coverage and sway public sentiment. Today, such communications offensives are commonplace. This "political talk," to quote political scientists Tim Groeling and Samuel Kernell, is "purposive behavior in its own right. Modern politicians give speeches, issue news releases, and otherwise conduct the public's business in front of television cameras not from vanity but from strategy."[7] While we certainly do not discount the role vanity plays in prompting politicians to pursue publicity, actors on both ends of Pennsylvania Avenue usually have specific political aims in mind when they take themselves into "public arenas"[8]

As members of Congress have followed the president's lead and taken their cases to the public, they have, as we shall see, adapted an outside strategy to further their power, policy, and reelection goals.[9] This includes, on many occasions, teaming up with colleagues to mount public relations campaigns on their party's behalf. In today's more polarized and ideologically coherent congressional parties, most members now find their personal goals more closely aligned with their partisan interests, thus increasing incentives for them to have their parties orchestrate and mount aggressive public relations campaigns. By coordinating their efforts as they market their political wares, legislators are better able to attract media interest and "strategically" use that greater news visibility to move their partisan agenda, claim credit for their programmatic initiatives and legislative actions, reassure their grassroots supporters and campaign contributors, and sharpen the policy and philosophic differences they have with their opponents, all of which improve their parties' public images and incidentally advance their own interests.[10] At the same time, a muscular collective public relations effort in many instances now not only serves members' goals but it is also well suited to the fractured, rapidly evolving, and complex media world in which the nation's politics is now carried out.[11]

The New Front in Washington Politics

Beginning with the emergence of a partisan press and its contributions to debates surrounding colonial challenges to the British government, the media have played an important role in the American polity and in shaping its development. Still, even when set against a historical backdrop where media have hardly been on the periphery, the position that news media occupy in today's political system stands out. As Timothy Cook has noted, current members of the media are "more central and visible" than their predecessors. It is also the case that "*every* branch of government is more preoccupied with and spends more resources on the news media today than it did forty years ago."[12] Others echo those views, with some even suggesting that calibrated public relations campaigns have supplanted traditional bargaining relations as the principal governing strategy of American politicians. In the words of Shanto Iyengar: "The battleground for control and influence over public policies has shifted from the halls and corridors of government offices to broadcasting studios and editorial offices."[13]

Presidents on the Communications Battleground

This tactic of using the news as a governing tool is most commonly associated with contemporary presidents and the leadership strategy of "going public" on which they routinely rely. This strategy entails making calculated appeals to the public first, to map out the national policy agenda, and second, to pressure those political actors whose support the president needs. The goal is to create expectations that make it easier for presidents to patch together coalitions that will help them secure their initiatives.[14]

For those in the White House, this style of leadership places a premium on attracting the media's attention and then using that publicity to press their administration's case. As Samuel Kernell notes, it is, in part, "a strategic adaptation to the information age."[15] That, of course, does not mean that presidents are able to make news on their own terms or that they are even successful in gaining and holding the public's interest as they attract the media spotlight; indeed, in today's fragmented and fast-paced news environment, where consumers are presented with a cornucopia of choices, it is often the case that presidents are unable to command the kind of attention or audiences that they once did when only a small number of providers dominated the media.[16] Furthermore, even if presidents manage to capture the public's attention, substantial challenges oftentimes prevent them from moving public sentiment in directions they desire.[17] Few, however, would agree that contemporary presidents are less preoccupied with carrying out public relations campaigns; the steady growth and institutionalization of the White House communications operations clearly suggests otherwise.[18] In addition, as presidents have discovered that they no longer command the sorts of broad based news audiences they once did, they have not stood pat. Jeffrey Cohen, for instance, finds recent presidents have adapted by increasing "the attention that they pay to narrow constituencies, while marginally decreasing the attention...[given] to leading the broad mass public."[19]

Presidents employ a public relations governing strategy in multifarious ways. To begin, publicity can help them define and set the agenda of items that will occupy their efforts while in office. They can, for instance, use it to frame the problems they want to address. After all, constructing problems for the nation's agenda is, fundamentally, a political act, what Deborah Stone describes as "the strategic representation of situations."[20] While they contest political adversaries, presidents oftentimes undertake media campaigns to portray certain events or conditions as problems that invite the sort of policy responses they would like to see approved and implemented. President George W. Bush's effort to link Iraq's failure under Saddam Hussein to comply with UN weapons inspections with the U.S. national security problem of world terrorism illustrates this strategy. He calibrated his public portrayal of "terror cells" and Hussein's Iraq as "different faces of the same evil" to make his policy advocacy of unilateral preemptive war for regime change a more palatable option.[21]

Presidents also use the bully pulpit to heighten the visibility of their strategically defined problems to increase the likelihood that the public will perceive them as important, and demanding of attention. Since citizens frequently judge politicians on responses to issues they believe to be salient, presidents who are able to convince the public of the gravity of the problems they are grappling with make it more costly for other political actors to avoid dealing with those issues.[22] Hence, presidents can use news visibility to create a bias toward political action on their agenda items.

Presidents also seek strategic advantages within a governmental system where power is both dispersed and shared, and frequently they and their advisors surmise that media campaigns, as President Bill Clinton once noted, enable them to "create new political capital all the time."[23] That is to say, presidents believe that by "going public" they can strengthen their hand by effecting benign changes in the "context" in which their policy initiatives are considered, debated, decided on, and ultimately carried out.[24] Most often this involves following an aggressive communications strategy to mold public sentiment in ways that "pressure" other political actors, especially those who occupy the other end of Pennsylvania Avenue, to support their programmatic initiatives.[25] President Ronald Reagan highlighted this visceral faith in the efficacy of this sort of public relations strategy when, locked in a standoff with congressional Democrats over one of his budget packages, he confidently noted in his diary that if they did not come around "'then I take to the air [TV] and there will be blood on the floor.'"[26] And close to three decades later, President Barack Obama's public relations blitz on behalf of the massive $787 billion economic stimulus package he pushed through the 111th Congress reflected just how routine this sort of White House strategic response has become. With GOP senators threatening to tie up the bill, Obama took to the airwaves and the Internet to crank up pressure for its swift enactment, warning the American people that "a failure to act, and act now will turn crisis into a catastrophe and guarantee a longer recession, a less robust recovery, and a more uncertain future."[27]

Presidents also use the bully pulpit to stake out their positions and reveal important clues about their "will" to those with whom they have to negotiate and whose own political calculations must include how intensely presidents feel about the specific matter at hand.[28] And in signaling the depth of their policy commitments, presidents incidentally offer reassurances to core constituencies, that is, those key advocacy groups, think tanks, financial contributors, and partisan activists who compose their most loyal supporters.

Lawmakers on the "Battleground": Members of Congress in the Fight

While "going public" to promote their policies and programs is most often a strategy associated with presidents and their surrogates, it is also true that in today's political environment an increasing number of those at the other end of Pennsylvania Avenue carry out publicity campaigns to advance their preferences and careers.[29] That does not mean that members of Congress always gain the magnitude and quality of attention that they seek or are successful in applying it to the goals that animated them to court the media in the first place. Nor is it the case that this ambition to expand news visibility is a universal congressional trait. There are, to be sure, still a handful of an older generation of lawmakers like Rep. John Dingell (D-MI)—who entered the House in 1955, when only slightly more than half of the nation's households had television sets—who prefer legislating by bringing interested parties together and cutting deals behind the scenes.[30] Moreover, even some backbenchers who have come up through the ranks via a more media-centered campaign process have shown that they are not prewired to seek publicity. Take the case of Rep. Darlene Hooley (D-OR), who retired at the end of the 110th Congress. A local Oregon newspaper described her during her last years in office in ways that evoke the image of a representative at ease with the role of low-profile ombudsman: "She's [Hooley's] not leading her party's opposition to the Bush administration. She's not cranking out statements on dozens of issues in a thinly veiled quest for higher office. In fact, she's one of the few members of Congress without a press secretary. Instead, she focuses exclusively on serving her constituents.... 'Some people want to make it on the national news,' Hooley says. 'I just want to take care of my district.'"[31]

Still, while not all on the Hill are tantalized by the prospects of gaining a higher public profile, a large and rather broad cross-section of today's legislators do follow the president's lead and seek publicity to realize their objectives. Behind the scenes dealmakers have found that their legislative skills and accomplishments, and even their seniority, cannot protect them from being toppled from their perches of power by more aggressive, media-savvy members, as Dingell discovered when, shortly before the start of the 111th Congress, he was ousted as chair of the powerful House Energy and Commerce Committee by the more partisan and publicity conscious Rep. Henry A. Waxman (D-CA).[32] And just as there are some junior members who are not preternaturally attracted to the spotlight, others take to it like moths to a flame. Rep. Michelle Bachmann's (D MN) behavior illustrates this. Shortly after getting elected in 2006, Bachmann hired a national press secretary, a local media press secretary, and a staffer to handle her blogs and social media, and then turned her attention to getting on the national cable news shows. She appeared so frequently on the television talk show circuit that a *Politico* profile on her noted that when it came to cable bookings it was "Bachmann, Bachmann everywhere."[33]

Many familiar with the institution have noted legislators' growing affinity for media attention. Already by the end of the 1980s, Rep. Lee Hamilton (D-IN), surmised that "most lawmakers gear all of their messages to TV."[34] Less than a decade later, veteran Washington television reporter Ann Compton wrote that lawmakers' proclivity for "face time" with media increased so much while she was assigned to the congressional beat that Capitol Hill became "short of press conference space, so tiny interview rooms were improvised and the lawns outside the House and Senate became electronic Hyde Park corners."[35] Long-time student of the institution, David Mayhew, more recently observed that representatives and senators "have been shifting the locus of their public commenting, and even their deliberating, from the House and Senate floors to the television talk shows that proliferated during the 1990s."[36] Numerous other congressional scholars and commentators on Washington politics confirm those impressions, as they highlight myriad instances in which lawmakers have taken their case outside congressional chambers and engaged the media to advance their interests.[37] In the contemporary Congress, "being a 'work horse,'" as Timothy Cook found in his own analysis of representatives' Hill behavior, "is no longer distinguishable from being a 'show horse.'"[38]

There are, of course, some members who, as Stephen Hess put it, simply enjoy celebrity status. They find the attention different media shower on them validates their own importance: "I am on TV therefore I am."[39] Nonetheless, most lawmakers have more in mind than simply mugging for the cameras. They believe that getting their names and views into the papers, on the airwaves, and into cyberspace or the blogosphere can help them realize the goals toward which their activities are directed, that is, shaping public policy, increasing their influence on the Hill, building up their campaign war chests, and coaxing their constituents to return them to office.[40]

Like the president, legislators use publicity to expand their leverage over the policy process. Yet members of Congress, including leaders, hardly command the sorts of media attention presidents attract. Speaker Newt Gingrich (R-GA) certainly rivaled President Clinton on the public stage for a short while; however, the visibility he gained, which included giving a prime time address to the nation, is rare.[41] Still, even though most representatives and senators have considerably smaller news profiles than the president and even some in the administration, both backbenchers and leaders believe that national publicity can help them shape and move their legislative initiatives.[42]

First, lawmakers can follow the president's lead and use publicity to determine how a problem or an issue is interpreted so as to make it more appealing for other political actors to join their cause.[43] Rep. Tom Tancredo's (R-CO) congressional career illustrates this. During much of his time in office, Tancredo almost single-mindedly pursued a public relations strategy designed to shape immigration policy outcomes. Once warned by President Bush's political advisor, Karl Rove, that he "should not darken the doorstep of the White House," Tancredo recognized that his tenuous standing with a faction of his own party meant that his "ability to affect change," as he once put it, "is always going to come from the outside."[44] For him, this meant attracting the media spotlight, which he oftentimes used to portray the problem of illegal immigrants in a way that invited his preferred policy initiatives. He appeared on cable television and talk radio shows to mock existing practices and stump for his preferred alternative of sealing the borders, and he frequently leveraged those appearances by posting them on his congressional website.[45] Seen from the perspective of GOP members at odds with Bush's more moderate stance on immigration policy, Tancredo employed his news spots, as Rep. Brian Bilbray (R-CA) once noted, to play the role of "John the Baptist, to wake people up to the crime and sin of illegal immigration."[46] He used his media presence both to represent undocumented workers as criminals and to highlight the failure to secure U.S. borders in a post-September 11 world as an ominous lapse in national security. This prepared the way for him to advance his preference for stricter enforcement of existing laws. Through these efforts he also expanded the House Immigration Reform Caucus and stiffened House GOP resistance to any sort of reform that smacked of "amnesty."[47]

Members of Congress, like the president, also use news visibility to push an issue to the top of the congressional agenda so as to create pressure for some sort of legislative response.[48] Immediately after he shifted his position on Iraq and called for a change in the administration's strategy in dealing with the internecine conflict that ensued after Hussein had been toppled, the late Rep. John Murtha (D-PA) emerged as the leading advocate for extricating U.S. troops from the war. His abrupt and very visible break with a White House he had once supported on the war elevated his public profile. He seemed to be "popping up everywhere."[49] Murtha used this expanding presence in the news cycle to focus legislative attention on the administration's strategy for dealing with a conflict that had metastasized into a full-blown civil war. As he explained: "There wasn't even a debate before, they just went blindly on…. But we're starting to get the attention of the thoughtful people."[50] By speaking out publicly, Murtha "catapulted the debate over the Iraq war to the top of the House agenda."[51] He ultimately used this attention to nudge House Democrats in the direction of turning up the heat on the president and his congressional allies over the administration's superintendence of the war. One foreign affairs columnist described the results of Murtha's publicity campaign this way: "When historians look back at the Iraq war, they will divide it into the pre- and post-Murtha eras."[52]

Lawmakers also use media to communicate their intentions to other political actors. For many, of course, publicity is a way to provide reassurances of their support for policies favored by key advocacy groups or interested partisans and financial contributors. This is what some Democrats aimed to do when they reaffirmed their pro-choice commitments by issuing press statements criticizing the Supreme Court's decision In *Gonzales v. Carhart* (2007) to uphold the congressional ban on partial birth abortion.[53] Yet working the media can also be a handy way to signal or pressure others in the Washington community. Members of Congress, for instance, can use it to try to effect a change in executive branch policy. During the Reagan administration, Sen. Richard Lugar (R-IN) followed an outside strategy to prod the president into withdrawing his support from the Philippine leader, Ferdinand Marcos. This came after he had failed, in private meetings, to convince Reagan that Marcos had most likely stolen the election he claimed to have won. When President Reagan publicly "disputed reports of massive fraud" in an election process that once again brought Marcos out on top, Senator Lugar, as James Lindsay explained, "countered with a media blitz" carried out on the weekend television talk shows *Face the Nation, Meet the Press,* and *This Week With David Brinkley* to encourage the administration to drop its support for the Philippine autocrat. "Lugar's media campaign worked; within days Reagan withdrew his support for Marcos."[54]

Other political actors to whom members direct their attention in their media appearances are oftentimes those on the Hill. Indeed, going public is an expeditious way for lawmakers to communicate with and pressure one another and their staffers. This has perhaps become more important as legislative aides shoulder more responsibilities now that lawmakers spend more time in their districts and states meeting with constituents and raising campaign funds. With fewer opportunities to chat with one another in Hill offices and corridors, they take their cases public to telegraph their intentions or stances or to demonstrate their concerns and the depth of their passion to other lawmakers and their aides. Going "through the media," observed Sen. Charles Schumer (D-NY) while he was still a backbencher in the House, is "one of the ways you reach your colleagues."[55] This is a point that even some of the most senior influential members acknowledge. "Talking to the press," Speaker Tip O'Neill (D-MA) admitted shortly after he had retired from the House, "is one of the best ways to communicate with members."[56]

By deftly employing publicity, members of Congress can also augment their own stature, both within their chambers and the larger Washington community.[57] Heightened visibility, arguably, increases their leverage with other political players. Sheer media exposure, to be sure, guarantees neither influence inside the Beltway nor success in translating greater public stature into preferred congressional outcomes. So, explained Schumer (D-NY): "If you get the reputation for doing media for media's sake, I think it hurts your effectiveness on the Hill."[58] But representatives and senators who have a certain amount of media savvy that they apply strategically can enhance their credibility and, ultimately, expand their own influence in a specific policy area.[59] Rep. Steve Solarz (D-NY), who served in the House from 1975 until his defeat in a Democratic primary election in 1992, illustrates this. Hedrick Smith described him as "one of the sharpest headline hunters" in the Congress.[60] Though somewhat of a "loner," he used his shrewdness with the media to help him surmount, in the words of Burdett Loomis, the "long odds against a House member exerting much influence over foreign policy." Combined, his mastery of the press and his knowledge of foreign affairs gave him a considerable reputation if not always greater clout, and in many respects he "acted" more like one of the iconic "Senate Foreign Relations committee member[s] of the 1960s, such as George McGovern (D-S.Dak.) or Frank Church (D-Idaho), than a typical House policy specialist."[61]

Acuity with the press can also give lawmakers a leg up on their competitors in climbing the ladder of power or advancing to higher office. Indeed, in today's Congress being telegenic and having good media skills are considered prerequisites for leadership positions. A talent for dealing with the press made it possible for less experienced legislators like Sen. George Mitchell (D-ME) and Sen. Thomas Daschle (D-ND) to leapfrog more seasoned lawmakers to their party's position of floor leader.[62] Rep. Newt Gingrich's (R-GA) understanding of partisan communication and his penchant for attracting the interest of the press contributed, at least in part, to his meteoric rise to power in the House.[63] And even when there have been orderly successions through the ranks, as when Majority Leader Jim Wright (D-TX) moved into the Speaker's chair with Rep. Tip O'Neill's (D-MA) retirement in January 1987, concerns about leaders' aptitude for dealing with the media were not far from the surface.[64]

Finally, public relations know-how can help lawmakers shore up constituent support. The right kinds of coverage by different media, along with self-generated information in the form of newsletters, e-newsletters, and materials and links posted on member websites, social networks, and personal YouTube channels, afford lawmakers opportunities to engage in those "credit claiming," "position-taking," and "advertising" activities that improve chances for electoral success.[65] Most lawmakers find local media more strategically suited to these activities, though some discover that even favorable national coverage can help them burnish their image back home.[66] There are also differences between the two chambers when it comes to the value of such publicity for electoral goals. Some surmise that senators have a greater incentive to woo and manage the media. Representatives, after all, generally have to deal with smaller districts and fewer people, putting them in a better position to establish direct, personal ties with their constituents. Moreover, House members' greater concern for things like casework reinforces those connections, and it rarely invites negative media coverage to which representatives have to respond.[67]

These differences notwithstanding, members in both chambers steadfastly work the media to convey favorable impressions to their constituents. Take, for example, the case of Rep. David Dreier (R-CA). According to one account written slightly more than a decade ago, Dreier "presents a skilled example of how self-interest and manipulation of information can merge." It portrays him as one who "pays close attention to the newspapers [in his district] and their reporting.... He visits the newspapers regularly during recesses and engages in discussions with editorial staff representatives, offering additional support for his views. He prepares videotapes in the congressional studio for cable television stations.... [A]nd he solicits editorial endorsements."[68]

By today's standards, such attentiveness to the media would be considered quite tame, if not antiquated. In addition to getting out news releases to media, cajoling editors, and getting video feeds and radio actualities to the local stations, today's lawmakers try to shape news coverage in myriad other ways and on several different fronts. Some submit op-ed pieces to the press on a policy matter in which they are keenly interested or which is of great concern to their constituents. Rep. Earl Blumenauer (D-OR), for instance, responded to voters' growing restiveness over the war in Iraq with an editorial in the local daily that chided the Bush administration for mishandling the conflict and argued that the time had arrived for the administration to adopt a new strategy.[69] Members of Congress also routinely take advantage of the Capitol Hill recording studios, with a growing number of them now using these facilities to do satellite hook-ups to conduct live interviews with local television stations.[70] More and more senators and representatives take time to do a spot on a cable news station or on a talk radio show. Some members in today's Congress are even spurred to turn the tables and host their own call-in radio shows or use Capitol Hill studios to film their own television interview programs that are aired back home. Rep. Loretta Sanchez (D-CA), for example, launched *Loretta Live* several years ago, a cable-access television show that is filmed in the Hill recording facilities and broadcast back in her district.[71]

It is also not unusual to see representatives and senators adapting to the pastiche of emerging venues or technologies of a wired universe to get out their messages. Many members frequently post their views on politics and policy on a host of sites that have popped up on the Internet. As we shall see in chapter 4, congressional web pages have become commonplace, and members have linked them with other venues, including some of the social media that have hit the scene, to broaden and amplify their communications' efforts. Rep. Mike Pence (R-IN), a former broadcaster from the more conservative, activist wing of his party, exemplifies this. Pence, whose ideological credentials, outspokenness, and media and messaging acumen helped get him elected Chair of the House Republican Conference at the start of the 111th Congress, combines a public strategy of tweeting and posting blogs, podcasts, and video clips on the Internet with regularly scheduled appearances on local talk radio and cable news shows.[72] His use of these new technologies and outlets, which he enlists to advance the programmatic cause of his party's conservative bloc, is certainly not out of the ordinary, nor is it something that is confined to younger or more junior backbenchers. Even seasoned senior members have found venues like the Internet, talk radio, cable television, and relatively newer social media like Twitter, YouTube, and Facebook instrumental for disseminating information regarding their local services as well as for communicating their views and explaining their actions to their constituents and other attentive publics. Veteran lawmaker Sen. Charles Grassley's (R-IA) public relations approach aptly illustrates this. First elected to the Senate in 1980, Grassley came of age as a player on the Hill well before the Internet made its presence felt in the political arena. Yet he has adapted. Today, Grassley aggressively employs his website not only to inform his constituents about the sorts of services he provides but also to deliver press releases and to post blogs, podcasts, and radio actualities. There he also includes links to his Facebook page and YouTube channel and even conducts regular webcasts with constituents and Iowa media. Grassley, an avid runner, even gives his page a bit of a human-interest touch by posting webcasts held after some of the races in which he participates.[73] And he caps off all of that with a semiregular tweet to his followers.[74]

Marshaling the Troops for the Communications Fight on the "Battleground"

The tale of individual members' use of publicity to realize their goals, while important on its own, is only part of the story. During the last two decades or so, Capitol Hill has become home to a robust partisan politics not seen since the dawn of the twentieth century.[75] That is not to suggest that within the two parties members march together in lockstep on all issues or policies. Even the more partisan House still has some outliers, like the GOP's socially moderate Tuesday Group and the Democrats' economically conservative and occasionally cantankerous Blue Dog Coalition.[76] Nonetheless, political realignment in the South, an increased partisanship in the electorate, and the design and proliferation of less politically diverse House districts, among other things, have yielded more internally homogenous and polarized congressional parties that rack up extraordinarily high party unity scores on roll-call votes.[77]

This rise of more unified, ideologically opposed parties on the national political scene has had important implications for congressional parties, both inside and outside Capitol Hill chambers. To begin, growing partisanship has prompted members to assign their leaders a more active role in managing and negotiating the legislative process.[78] Because individual and collective partisan interests now more frequently coincide, members find that their own reelection and policy goals are more closely tied to outcomes sought by their parties. Consequently, they prefer leaders who are capable of producing records of achievement that incidentally promote their own interests.[79] At the same time, growing partisanship on Capitol Hill has made members more sensitive to the need to burnish their parties' public images. After all, since members within today's congressional parties are more prone to have common policy preferences, they have incentives to mobilize public sentiment on behalf of party positions and legislative strategies. They likewise have an interest in gaining credit for their party's stances and accomplishments so as to create a positive "brand name" that will help them raise cash and induce voters to select their party's candidates in upcoming elections.[80] Rank-and-file members now find it profitable to mount partisan media campaigns that shape outcomes by framing issues and elevating problems on the agenda and by bringing public pressure to bear on different political actors at critical junctures of the legislative process. They also anticipate that those at the helm will accentuate the bona fides of their party by directing public relations activities that highlight issues of special significance to their supporters and that defend and explain partisan actions to their core constituencies, financial backers, and the voting public.[81] Contemporary congressional leaders consequently now face pressure to mount and choreograph partisan public relations campaigns, and members, who stand to benefit as a consequence of their leaders' efforts, have an interest in joining with them to help the parties carry their battles outside Hill chambers.

Party leaders in both chambers have responded to these expectations and demands. In the House, they have taken up "outside," media-based communications strategies and, especially in the case of the majority party, combined these with tactics employed inside the chamber to advance their political and programmatic interests.[82] On the other side of the Capitol, party leaders also have incentives to mount credible public relations campaigns. Much of this, to be sure, can be attributed to an exercise of leadership that is "typically more muted and constricted than in the House."[83] Senate rules and procedures do not favor leaders; they instead safeguard the prerogatives of individual members and protect the rights of political minorities, thus precluding the rise of strong centralized leadership offices, and in most instances, strict majority rule.[84] Because Senate leaders do not have available to them the procedural mechanisms necessary to control the processes within their chamber, other strategies have taken on greater significance. These include leading and coordinating publicity campaigns on behalf of their partisan colleagues. Indeed, in today's Senate making the public case for their parties' positions is, as Steven Smith described it, "a vital role in parallel to floor duties for the majority and minority leaders."[85]

Although enlisting publicity to promote their political goals and programs is strategically significant for both parties in both chambers, it is most critical for those in the House minority, especially if their party does not control the president's bully pulpit.[86] The institution's rules and procedures, combined with high levels of partisanship, leave the majority holding most of the cards. Their leaders can set the agenda, direct the flow of legislation, craft rules to structure conditions of debate and limit the types of amendments offered to legislative initiatives, control what transpires on the floor, and determine their chamber's representation in conference committees.[87] The House minority's impotence is thrown into bold relief when compared to its Senate counterpart, whose members can employ procedural tactics—holds, filibusters, and the ability to attach nongermane amendments to many types of legislation—to stymie majority initiatives, increase their bargaining position, and even offer proposals advancing their own policy preferences.[88]

Recent political developments have further narrowed the House minority's options. With electoral changes producing more internally cohesive, polarized House parties, they have found it increasingly difficult to pursue the more conciliatory approach that was available when congressional parties were not as coherent and ideological. Growing party unity has made compromise less necessary for those in the House majority, while the ever-widening chasm in policy preferences separating the two parties makes it more difficult to obtain bipartisan consensus. Challenges inherent in negotiating interparty policy agreements perhaps have been further complicated as House majority leaders have applied their institutional prerogatives to promote their party's interests while effectively shutting down their opposition.

The bottom line is that today's House minority is on the periphery of most of what transpires on the Hill. A House Democratic leadership aide captured the House minority's plight when he bluntly protested his party's treatment by the GOP majority: "We're basically getting bitch-slapped around by these guys [House Republicans] because they control everything."[89] Since the minority generally has limited leverage, engaging a wider audience becomes an important political tactic. Specifically, by shaping public sentiment and attracting new allies to their cause they can change the prevailing equilibrium of political forces in ways that help them advance their preferences.[90] The House GOP minority used this strategy in 110th Congress to get Speaker Nancy Pelosi (D-CA) to call the chamber back in session to lift the existing prohibition against off-shore drilling. As Speaker Pelosi dismissed the House for its summer vacation, a coterie of media-savvy House Republicans pulled out all the stops and mounted an aggressive public relations campaign to push this pet policy. They took to the House floor to object to the Democrats' failure to roll back the ban on drilling as gas prices passed the $4 a gallon mark. Using video cameras, Blackberries, and instant messaging services to take their protests to the Internet, they attracted the attention of talk radio, cable television, and scores of bloggers, which amplified their refrain of "drill here, drill now." Their public rebellion even spread to Republican presidential rallies, where crowds erupted into feverish calls to "drill, baby, drill." A phalanx of GOP members gave the story legs by hitting the talk show circuits, writing editorials, blogging on their websites, and posing for Capitol Hill cameras armed with red gas cans. Eventually House Democrats buckled under what they took to be mounting public pressure to tamp down escalating energy costs. At the Speaker's behest, they capitulated and passed legislation ending the twenty-seven-year-old moratorium.[91]

With members expecting congressional parties to advance their legislative goals and enhance their credibility with the electorate by staking out their positions and claiming responsibility for their achievements, there are also now a number of reasons for them to coordinate, within the party, some of their communications activities. First, by partnering their efforts and bringing a broader range of members into the mix, congressional parties can increase their leverage with the media. While individual members can, as we have shown, break through the news barrier, getting a greater number of them to deliver "the same message" increases the likelihood that they will pique the interest of news organizations and bring about the sort of echo chamber required to realize their ends.[92]

Second, mounting organized publicity campaigns also helps parties bring clarity to partisan discourse. "A stable, consistent party image," Groeling and Kernell explain, "is essential if it is to provide a valuable cue for voters and thereby serve politicians."[93] This, in certain respects, is what today's politicians have in mind when they fret about the state of their "brands."[94] Yet, to build a brand name that conveys this valuable information, congressional parties need to be clear about who they are and the policies for which they stand, as well as deliver on what they promise. Those of the president's party, moreover, need to link their messages with positions and views promulgated by the administration so as to avoid sending mixed signals about their party's programmatic and political goals. Letting members off by themselves without an overarching strategy or any kind of coordination frequently results in dissonant messages, creating little more than political noise. Such bumbling confusion hardly shores up, and brings coherence to, the images they want to convey; it also does not serve the party's interest in providing the sort of meaningful information that brings comfort to activists and financial backers and that cues the electorate at large.

Parties' coordination of publicity activities can help them better realize their ends in other ways. The goals of following outside, media-based strategies, after all, are to shape policy outcomes and win elections. To pull that off, congressional parties need to synchronize their communications operations with what happens inside Hill chambers. Institutional procedures and schedules can be manipulated by the party in ways that help it advance its message. Then again, because parties will not find it profitable to push legislation that provokes a fair amount of internal dissent, producing a cacophony of voices in public instead of a clear refrain, parties need to anticipate how their messages will be affected by their legislative agenda and activities.[95] They likewise need to be sensitive to the timing of their communications efforts and undertake such real-time public relations campaigns when they can help move a preferred initiative at some key juncture of the legislative process—committee hearings, floor votes, or conference committee deliberations—or scuttle certain undesirable policy initiatives as they work their way through the congressional labyrinth.[96] This includes calibrating their efforts to gain credit for what they have achieved or to diminish their opponents' accomplishments in the eyes of the electorate.[97]

Finally, orchestrated communications campaigns conducted by parties are especially suited to the media context in which contemporary politicians wage their public relations campaigns. The "revolution" in the nation's "information regime" in these last decades has culminated in a more decentralized, dynamic media environment, one where news is more abundant, accessible, and up to date.[98] This setting has become a more inviting public relations battleground for members and their parties. Today, individual members have available to them more media fronts on which to engage in public relations campaigns. That increase in opportunities is compounded as news organizations come under constant pressure to find material to fill their around-the-clock cycle. Congressional parties, meanwhile, have greater incentives to harness members' communications efforts in ways that promote consistent, timely messages across a wide range of the venues through which contemporary public relations battles are waged.

The New Battleground

The media environment presidents like John F. Kennedy or Jimmy Carter confronted was far different from the one we see today. By the late 1950s, the broadcast networks had made considerable gains in attracting audiences to their nightly newscasts, thereby narrowing the gap with newspapers as one of citizens' principal sources of political information. Surveys conducted during the mid- to late-1960s, for instance, suggested that roughly three-fourths of those over the age of twenty-one read a newspaper every day and that over two-thirds of those over the age of eighteen routinely watched one of the evening commercial television news shows.[99] The three major networks and a handful of newsprint providers had a noticeable impact on coverage in this media environment. Taken together, these organizations offered little variation in the news that they broadcast or printed, as they followed common routines in newsgathering. Frequently this resulted in a disproportionate amount of news attention being given to events surrounding the chief executive.[100] By the early 1970s, television news was so important, and the amount of air time devoted to the president so lopsided, that some legislators lamented that those trends, if left unchecked, would seriously erode their powers vis-à-vis the executive branch.[101]

Today's news environment in which the public relations battles of Washington politics are carried out stands in marked contrast to that earlier context, which some describe as the "golden age of presidential television."[102] The current milieu is much more "decentralized and splintered" than when a handful of "elite news organizations" exercised disproportionate influence over the production of the news.[103] It is also a more dynamic media world, as news accounts are constantly modified, made available in real time, and even personalized. To use W. Lance Bennett's words, "this is the age of information when we want it, how we like it, and automatically updated to suit our tastes, as smart search engines learn our preferences."[104]

Early developments that transformed the media landscape include the rise of cable television news platforms and a simultaneous growth in the number of talk radio shows. These developments, abetted by changes in the regulatory environment and technological advances, made it possible to distribute more content over more venues at a cost that was economically feasible.[105] The growth of the cable television industry in the 1980s and early 1990s brought alternative, real-time news programming from stations like CNN, Fox News, MSNBC, and even more specialized outlets like CNBC, Bloomberg, Fox Business News, Univision, and Telemundo, as well as public service stations like CSPAN. These venues challenged the hegemony of the traditional broadcast networks while fueling a demand for content to fill a 24/7 news cycle.[106] Industry adjustments to the new media market also contributed to the burgeoning number of entertainment programs that provide "soft news" coverage and cable shows devoted to political satire—*The Daily Show*, the *Colbert Report*, and *Real Time With Bill Maher*.[107] At the close of the twentieth century, nearly 80% of the nation's households subscribed to cable or satellite and thus had access to these outlets and the programs they carried. This upward trajectory in the growth of cable outlets and subscribers coincided with an explosion in talk radio forums, many of which took on a political bent in the wake of the Federal Communications Commission's elimination of the Fairness Doctrine in 1987. By the mid-1990s, the number of radio stations with talk programming had increased fourfold over what it had been just a decade earlier, making talk radio the "second most listened to format."[108]

Just as cable news and talk radio were reshaping the news environment, an important, though less noticed change in the composition of the Washington press corps took hold. A 2008 Pew Foundation study found that beginning in the mid-1980s more traditional mainstream news organizations started shrinking their Washington based resources. The quantity of wire and newspaper services accredited to covering Congress dropped from a total of 564 in 1985 to less than 350 in little more than a decade (1997–98). By the end of 2007, the amount had plummeted to 160, a 70% decline from mid-1980s totals. General news magazines and periodicals assigned to the Capitol Hill beat showed a similar secular decline; they plunged roughly 75% over those same decades, falling from 89 to 22. The number of newspapers with Washington bureaus also dropped precipitously. By 2008, the number of newspapers with such bureaus was slightly less than half of what it had been in 1985. Yet that significant diminution in the size of the more traditional DC press corps is only part of the story. While all of this was going on, the number of niche news organizations and more specialized journalists covering Congress and inside-the-Beltway politics actually increased at rather robust rates, as did the number of Washington based foreign correspondents. These niche news groups range from the rather freshly minted information sources that concentrate on following developments that affect different industries and policy sectors like energy, the environment, commerce, agriculture, and countless others to the more venerable, narrowly focused political magazines like *Roll Call*, *The Hill*, and *National Journal*. These outlets provide news to specific elite audiences or issue publics who pay a hefty premium for those informational services.[109] Taken together, this spike in more specialized providers and foreign correspondents and the corresponding decline of press personnel and bureaus attached to more traditional, broad-based news media further contributed to the more conspicuously complex media environment that Washington politicians now have to negotiate.

The development and rapid expansion of the Internet compounded this spate of changes. First, it ushered in an incredibly large and ever expanding smorgasbord of real-time news providers. These include, to name but a few, online publications such as *Salon*, *Slate*, and *Politico*, as well as a rapidly expanding number of popular cybersites and weblogs like the Huffington Post, Crooks and Liars, the Daily Kos, the Daily Beast, Michelle Malkin, the Drudge Report, Real Clear Politics, RedState, TalkingPointsMemo.com, Townhall, and Open Left sponsored by various individuals and political organizations.[110] Second, the Internet's growing popularity has prompted more mainstream media outlets to adapt to a constantly evolving news cycle and adjust to changes in the business model required to survive in this environment. Most now offer websites that supplement their conventional formats and offer up to the minute information and additional commentary.[111] Some, like the *Christian Science Monitor* and *U.S. News and World Report*, have even abandoned the traditional print format to deliver content directly through online sites.

This ongoing upheaval in the news world coincides with shifts in how consumers obtain information. Today, more and more people get their news by surfing the web or by being directed to stories by communications in social networks. Recent survey data show that 40% of Americans routinely use the Internet to get the news, though many of them visit sites maintained by more traditional news organizations, such as newspapers or broadcast networks, and cable television news and political talk shows. As of 2008, the Internet trailed only television as the principal source of news. This upward tick in the number of people who access information online, moreover, has been most pronounced among younger consumers. Currently, close to 60% of those under the age of thirty turn to the Internet for news updates. That number represents a staggering 25% increase over results for that same cohort in a similar poll conducted in September of the previous year.[112] What this trend suggests is that the already sizable percentage of people who turn to the web to learn about political events will only continue to swell over time.

These changes in the distribution and consumption of the news, which have produced an eye-popping number of disparate outlets, brought about a fast-paced, around-the-clock news cycle that has expanded almost exponentially the demand for content, and created more fragmented audiences, have implications for those on the Hill who mount public relations campaigns. First, these developments have multiplied "opportunities" for members of Congress to pursue an outside strategy.[113] That is not to say that all "opportunities" are of equal value. An appearance on a weekend talk show like *Meet the Press* or coverage in a front page story in the *New York Times*, for instance, usually trumps a brief, noontime interview on a niche cable television news show or a blog posted on a website that receives but a few thousand hits. Nor is it the case that these "opportunities," while certainly plentiful, carry the sort of weight that once went with an appearance in a story put out by one of the elite news organizations that dominated the media environment in the preceding era, a time when audiences had fewer programming options available to them.

Nonetheless, these changes have made it easier for members to target their messages to specific elite audiences or core constituencies through appearances or presentations on more specialized media platforms that appeal to a certain niche of news consumers. Members, for instance, can go on cable financial news programs or give an interview to a specialized trade publication or news service to speak directly to Wall Street about the contents of a tax initiative or spending proposal. Likewise, they can appear on a political satire show or employ social media to target a younger, less conventional audience as they lambaste the executive's war policy or announce that they intend to introduce a bill that decriminalizes the use of marijuana. Through web-based media lawmakers can send electronic newsletters or transmit real-time news feeds to representatives of the farming community covering the details of a proposed agriculture appropriations bill. They can even make a case to their partisan "base" on a contentious issue like immigration reform by tweeting their followers, posting a blog on a politically charged website, or by appearing on a television or radio talk show that attracts a devoted following of their party's supporters, and then putting that appearance on their own YouTube channel where it can be accessed and replayed again and again.

At the same time, the more fragmented audience associated with this new media environment reinforces parties' incentives to mount coordinated publicity campaigns. This is especially true as the number of outlets have increased, even if it is the case that their audiences have, as we shall see, grown more polarized as some of these venues have more or less gravitated to one side of the ideological spectrum or the other.[114] Only coordinated efforts by the different parties have the wherewithal to reach across an expanding number of venues to reach their tribes of committed activists. These efforts become even more important as congressional parties seek to go beyond their core constituencies, which on occasion they must, and try to reach a more general, yet nonetheless important attentive citizenry that has less ideological viewing, listening, and reading habits. More specialized groups are easier to target, but it has become more difficult to figure out how to reach broader audiences because of the Balkanization of audiences and because venues offering alternatives to news programs have proliferated.

This dynamic, real-time, and arguably more partisan news context also presents significant challenges for political actors, including those on the Hill who use publicity to govern. While it most certainly enables lawmakers and other interested actors chances to spin or shape interpretations of stories just as they break, the current media environment has "made it all the more difficult for any politician to truly control the flow of information."[115] Political actors now find that they can no longer easily direct, shape, or choke-off stories once they get started. And the acceleration, momentum, and partisan cast news accounts gain as they move through the nation's complex communications grid only compound this.

This highly competitive environment of diffuse providers of instantaneous news, moreover, is studded with potential landmines that an unwary member of Congress can easily detonate. Even the slightest miscues or controversial remarks can now be recorded by any one of an ever expanding number of what, in today's parlance, are known as "citizen journalists." Their video and audio recordings can then be shipped off to an interested television station or radio outlet or even written up in a blog or on a news website and commented on in a tweet. They can be posted on YouTube and linked to Facebook pages, where they can be accessed and continually replayed and ultimately commented on by partisans who populate different regions of the blogosphere. The ensuing chatter that takes place in social networks and on the net, in turn, can also pique and, at times, even sustain the attention of other media—newspapers, talk radio, and cable and network news programs—and drive the story line in ways that can easily spiral out of control, bedevil careers, and complicate parties' messaging activities.

High-profile cases involving veteran politicians, such as Sen. George Allen (R-VA) and Sen. Trent Lott (MS), and even a seasoned radio and television talk show personality such as Don Imus, who became embroiled in controversies given impetus by careless and boorish off-the-cuff remarks, underscore the considerable hazards of a news environment, where stories spread with viral-like intensity that public figures must negotiate.[116] As one newspaper's commentary explained in the wake of Imus's fall from grace: "Words uttered on talk radio and cable TV, once considered almost entirely disposable, are now etched onto servers around the world. They can end up on sites such as YouTube where they are viewed time and again by people well beyond the target audience. They can be redirected to potential critics via e-mail, as happened in this case. In other words, they live on and can come back to haunt the people responsible for them."[117]

Extending the Battle

Employing public strategies to govern is part of the warp and woof of the contemporary political system. While frequently associated with presidents, it is now also important for those at the other end of Pennsylvania Avenue. Today's members of Congress, and the parties to which they belong, enlist publicity to help them advance their goals. Most certainly the news environment as it evolved during the waning years of the twentieth century and beyond has spurred this tendency to mount publicity campaigns and employ media strategies. The rapid growth in the number and diversity of outlets competing to deliver instantaneous news and the proliferation of web-based media that enable members to deliver messages directly present manifold opportunities for lawmakers and parties to take their case outside Capitol Hill chambers. This decentralized, dynamic, and insatiable news setting also brings to the fore a series of rather vexing challenges to which legislators and their parties must be sensitive and respond if they want to realize their goals.

Yet Congress's public relations strategy, while certainly nourished in this new media environment, cannot simply be attributed to this context and the underlying transformations that brought it about. Indeed, as is the case with the presidency, Capitol Hill's routine use of publicity, as we shall see, predates the emergence of this new media battleground on which political actors now find themselves. Thus, this outside approach to governing, while certainly shaped and magnified by changes in the media world, is rooted in the confluence of several mid- to late-twentieth century political transformations and reforms. These moved the Congress from an institution in which governing through publicity activities was frowned upon, even discouraged, to one where such efforts assumed strategic importance, both for individual members and, as the political environment grew ever more partisan and polarized, for congressional parties.

3   A New Washington Community
The Foundation for Congressional
Public Strategies

Hedrick Smith once described a Capitol Hill encounter between a freshman lawmaker, Rep. Tim Wirth (D-CO), and Rep. Jamie Whitten (D-MS), "a Faulknerian figure first elected just before Pearl Harbor." Smith recounted that at a Democratic gathering held shortly before the opening of the 94th Congress in 1975 Whitten sidled up to Congressman-elect Wirth and "muttered with asperity": "Here you've been on national television for the last three days, and you haven't even been sworn in yet!... And in all my thirty-three years in Congress, I've never been on national television once!"[1]

Smith's account juxtaposes two very different congressional orders with two very different attitudes toward the role of publicity. Through the first two-thirds of the twentieth century, most members of Congress, like Whitten, carried out their work by negotiating agreements behind closed doors. They had little incentive to obtain publicity beyond what was required to communicate with their constituents to get themselves reelected. But that, as we have seen, has changed. The story of how all of this came to pass is an encompassing, complex tale that involves pivotal transformations in the Congress and the larger political system. Here we delineate those lines of change and consider the ways they intersected to set the stage for a more outward-looking institution. We commence by drawing a portrait of an older and somewhat closed and clannish order, an institution structured and operated in ways that generally discouraged members' use of publicity. Our narrative then traces how disparate changes in Congress and on the American political landscape converged to produce a legislative order that prizes public relations activities and at certain junctures even makes them a priority for congressional parties. We will show that the public relations activities that are part and parcel of today's Congress, while surely abetted by recent transformations in the media world, are actually rooted in more sweeping changes that shaped the institution and broader political system during the latter part of the twentieth century. As we will see, those changes came together in ways that first encouraged individual members to become more media conscious in their activities and then prompted congressional parties to turn their attention to mounting collective public relations campaigns.

The Old Regime

Although the U.S. Congress has a well-established reputation for stability and continuity, over the course of the last half-century it has experienced significant change.[2] From roughly the 1930s through the 1950s and even on into the early 1960s, the Congress was a place noticeably different from today's open and hyper-partisan legislative body.[3] The Capitol Hill of those years was dominated by small and relatively stable groups of men—party leaders, committee chairmen, and ranking minority members—who frequently and quietly brokered legislative deals behind closed doors.[4]

That Old House (and Senate)

To be sure, members of these Capitol Hill cliques, while powerful, did not always agree with each other. Many of them were ideologically conservative, and in the case of Democrats, disproportionately southern, but they often had divergent views on policy issues.[5] They were also separated by party attachments, and between the two chambers, by institutional loyalties. Needless to say, all of these differences contributed to divisiveness, conflict, and stalemate on more than a few occasions. We should also take care not to overstate their influence. They did not, after all, constitute a "group of men, conspiring together in a secret chamber…pushing the buttons on a nationwide machine."[6] Nor should we ignore important differences between the House and Senate with regard to their internal configurations of power. House committee chairs and ranking minority members, for instance, usually had greater leverage than their opposite numbers in the less hierarchical Senate, and the control they exercised over the chamber in which they sat was somewhat longer lived.[7]

Still, in both chambers these lawmakers had considerable power, and they wielded it in ways that left observers with the impression that Congress resembled an archaic "baronial structure."[8] Committee leaders, the "barons," exercised disproportionate leverage over their panels' jurisdictions. They gained their positions and a fair amount of independence through what was pretty much an ironclad rule of seniority, and they maintained their ascendancy by employing their prerogatives. Chairmen of this era had near dictatorial control over their subcommittees; they almost single-handedly determined if such panels existed, who served on them, who chaired them, what bills they could hear, and how many staffers they were assigned. And if that wasn't enough, many chairs and ranking members were ex-officio voting members of their panels' subcommittees and conference committees, giving them another way "of exerting control" over their committees' recommendations and hence over most final congressional decisions.[9] Yet within this context party leaders who had an aptitude for negotiating deals between, and facilitating the interests of, these formidable and generally autonomous panel chiefs managed to exercise great influence.[10] They maintained control through a strategic use of rewards and threats, gaining leverage by parceling out key institutional resources and patronage, such as office space and staff, and by influencing committee assignments and shaping their chambers' legislative agendas.[11] Together, the power brokers who led their committees and parties knew that between them they usually had the tools necessary to deliver chamber majorities on floor votes or stymie certain initiatives if they so desired. The White House knew that, too.

Their command of institutional resources and procedures afforded them an imposing array of inducements and sanctions they could apply to ensure rank-and-file members' compliance. They could, for instance, block or expedite the passage of bills politically important to their colleagues. They could also advance or hinder careers of more junior legislators with their power to appoint members as floor managers and to other visible posts within Congress.[12] As lawmakers from this era told observers, backbenchers knew that those who comprised "the leadership can single them out as men with a future ... [but] if they lose the confidence of the top leaders, they risk isolation and loss of prestige." They were therefore aware that it was important for them to "seek the approval of those who have command positions."[13] A ditty well known, if not entirely pleasing to congressional members of the Washington community of the 1950s, reflected the extent to which rank-and-file members, especially those in the more hierarchical House, needed to be attuned to their elders' wishes: "I love Speaker Rayburn, his heart is so warm,/And if I love him he'll do me no harm./So I shan't sass the Speaker one least little bitty,/And then I'll wind up on a major committee."[14]

Chamber and party leaders, committee chairs, and ranking minority members thus constituted a kind of congressional "oligarchy," and both scholars and the press corps referred to them with terms that bespoke their privileged position: "the elders," "patriarchs," "emperors, "the Congressional Establishment," "despots," "the powers that be," and the "old bulls."[15] Some of the more expansive commentary even attributed to these so-called oligarchs something approaching superhuman powers: While mere mortals cannot rid themselves of "unpleasant things simply by willing them away, a powerful ... committee chairman very often can do just that."[16] Although such inflated rhetoric most certainly misrepresents their actual powers, few would dispute the more restrained claim that in those days the important congressional decisions of the day were generally "made by a handful of the most powerful legislators."[17]

While the core of this "establishment," the panel chiefs or barons, were not above exercising unilateral authority in dealing with policy matters that fell within their committees' purview, they also personally bargained behind closed doors to work out compromises palatable to contending interests. These negotiations oftentimes involved little more than crafting mutually beneficial agreements between themselves and representatives of concerned governmental agencies and pressure groups.[18] Once they hammered out specifics on a bill, if they could muster the votes to pass it without taking into account the views of the rest of the congressional elite, they did so. But that was not always the case, and in those instances when they needed broader support they quietly negotiated with chamber and party leaders and frequently reached across the aisles to finalize an agreement. Compromises they finessed to break legislative log-jams frequently involved adjusting the language of a bill here, or revising a portion of it there, or agreeing to advance an unrelated bill that was of interest to some of them, or to kill another proposal others in this cohort opposed. As one of this era's members explained to Charles Clapp, "[t]he legislative process is rather like an iceberg. Only the top part, perhaps only the top quarter, of the legislation and the story behind it, shows. What is really important is usually below the surface."[19]

The personal bargaining that produced many of these behind-the-scenes deals defined the parameters of acceptable Hill behavior. Since the congressional elite knew legislative success was dependent on cooperative attitudes and behavior that facilitated negotiations and coalition building, they accentuated "ways" of minimizing "interpersonal friction," habituating members, as one representative told Richard Fenno, to "disagree without being disagreeable."[20] The barons admonished more junior members to speak politely to and about each other, and taught them that collegiality and reciprocity were enormously important for carrying out the Hill's business. Many members recounted, for instance, that "public disparagement of colleagues is strongly discouraged; it is not the way to play the game. Personal attacks are sharply censored." Congressional elders also advised newly elected members that "making friends with [their] colleagues is a most important activity." That included developing relationships with those on the other side of the aisle.[21] Established powers also instructed junior colleagues to carry out their work in ways that, when possible, would accommodate others' legislative interests. As Speaker Sam Rayburn (D-TX) famously advised House newcomers, "If you want to get along you better go along."[22]

Members also arrived at a consensus on acceptable forms of behavior that supported the oligarchs' authority and maintained the benefits of the committee structures at the heart of the congressional decision-making process. This shared understanding included seniority as a criterion of advancement within committees, and it directed backbenchers to tend to their committee's business by specializing, working hard, and deferring to their panel's more informed senior colleagues.[23]

Congressional power brokers maintained institutional stability and also maintained their influence by socializing newly elected members into this byzantine Capitol Hill culture. They instilled in rank-and-file members the value of the norms—apprenticeship, reciprocity, legislative work and specialization, showing deference to leaders, and institutional patriotism—that supported committee dominance and the routine way of doing business.[24] Using leverage over key resources and control of legislative processes, senior members instructed, frequently in not so subtle ways, more junior members about the salience of such norms. Those who flouted these unwritten rules received fewer perquisites, were oftentimes ostracized by colleagues, and frequently saw their political and legislative ambitions thwarted; those who honored them usually gained senior colleagues' respect, generally witnessed an increase in their rate of legislative success, and steadily moved up the congressional ladder of power.[25]

Capitol Hill oligarchs led by example, as well as by applying rewards and sanctions. Except for those occasional moments of extreme party controversy, committee chairs and ranking minority members consulted and cooperated with one another.[26] Not only did such behavior suit their interests, but it was also something for which they were especially well prepared, since "a key criterion" for those who gained positions of authority and plum committee assignments "was a demonstrable record of, or an assumed predisposition toward, legislative give-and-take."[27] Legislators unable to bring a flexible bargaining approach to policy issues, in contrast, were more often than not marginalized.

This era's House and Senate, as the above suggests, were relatively stable, communitarian bodies.[28] Rewards and career advancement flowed in ways to encourage lawmakers to be good or "responsible" members of the Capitol Hill community. "Responsible" lawmakers were those who found the appropriate balance between securing their own preferences and maintaining the collective interest of the institution to which they were elected. Nicholas Masters captured the ideal-typical characteristics of such a member:

> [A] responsible legislator is one whose ability, attitudes, and relationships with his colleagues serve to enhance the prestige and importance of the [Congress]. He has a basic and fundamental respect for the legislative process and understands and appreciates its formal and informal rules.... He does not attempt to manipulate every situation for his own personal advantage…and he is careful to protect the rights of others.... He understands the pressures on members with whom he cannot always agree and avoids pushing an issue to the point where his opponents may suffer personal embarrassment. *On specific issues, no matter how firm his convictions and no matter how great the pressures upon him, he demonstrates a willingness to compromise. He is moderate, not so much in the sense of his voting record and his personal ideology, but rather in the sense of a moderate approach; he is not to be found on the uncompromising extremes of the political spectrum*.... He does not believe that Congress is the proper place to initiate drastic and rapid changes in the direction of public policy. On the contrary, he is more inclined to be a gradualist, and to see public policy as a sort of synthesis of opposing viewpoints. In short, a responsible legislator is politically pliant, but not without conviction.[29]

An Inside Game for Inside Players

The norms that guided "responsible" members encouraged comity in the early post-World War II Congress.[30] The institution placed a premium on members who by dint of hard work developed policy expertise and displayed deference to their chambers' more established senior leaders, and it favored legislators who demonstrated cooperative, nonpartisan behavior. Prizing courtesy, reciprocity, and quiet behind-the-scenes negotiations, it punished contentious, polarizing members who spurned compromise.

Congress's normative foundation and the comity it produced also made for an institution that was, by and large, "inward-looking."[31] Power to move it depended upon leaders' savvy in manipulating congressional procedures in ways that produced floor majorities, maneuvering that often took place behind the closed doors of the offices and hideaways where party elders held court, cut deals, and demanded fealty. Journalists had little first-hand experience of what transpired behind those doors, and most of them were only marginally interested in prying them open to get a look at what they took to be the more mundane aspects of legislative activities.[32] Backbenchers' route to success and ultimately power involved doing serious homework on some policy issue and then winning the favor of the relevant committee chairman, who could broker the deals necessary to move the bill through Congress. Rank-and-file members who wanted to deliver the goods for their constituents and amass influence on the Hill therefore had few incentives to follow an outside strategy and enlist the media to help them muster popular support to realize their goals.

To be sure, even the Congress of that period had its mavericks. They refused to abide by the body's informal rules, and they tended to be less tractable and more strident and ideologically driven than their "responsible" colleagues. Several of them did aggressively seek publicity to advance their policy agendas or effect reforms on the Hill.[33] As long as they did not flagrantly violate existing norms these "outsiders," especially those in the Senate, were indulged.[34] But while such cheeky behavior was occasionally "tolerated," it was most certainly "not rewarded from within."[35] Take, for example, the career of Sen. Estes Kefauver (D-TN). He had an uncanny knack for attracting publicity, which he almost single-mindedly used to fuel his own ambition for higher office. That sort of grandstanding behavior, however, left Kefauver with little influence on the Hill. Douglass Cater, a well-known Washington correspondent of the period, recounted that Sen. Kefauver was "rejected by his more powerful colleagues from membership in the Inner Club [of influential senators]."[36] Others recalled that Majority Leader Lyndon Johnson (D-TX) frequently denied Kefauver the committee assignments he so craved, and that his "colleagues winced every time" he supported "their measures," since his "approval" was tantamount to "the kiss of death."[37]

In light of the reception that congressional mavericks generally received, this era's lawmakers had "a basic decision" to make: they could become "responsible" members and achieve "a position of power and influence within the legislative body" or they could seek publicity by issuing "frequent pronouncements directed at a larger, more national audience" and be confined to the sidelines of the congressional arena. While "theoretically possible to combine the two endeavors," most "perceptive observers" concluded "that the odds are heavily against it."[38] Pressure to remain "responsible" and steer clear of publicity campaigns was strong; indeed, the powers that be frequently reminded junior lawmakers that successful legislators were the workhorses who quietly labored on committee matters, not the show horses whose names popped up in the daily papers' headlines and lead paragraphs.[39]

There were times when congressional workhorses engaged the media. Several of them maintained behind-the-scenes friendships and working relationships with certain correspondents and columnists.[40] Occasionally they used these connections to "leak" important bits of information that aided reporters while incidentally advancing their own political interests.[41] Some were also more visible in the public realm. The Speaker, for instance, did hold daily press conferences.[42] And for a time in the early 1960s, Senate and House minority party leaders—Senator Everett

Dirksen (R-IL) and Representative Charles Halleck (R-IN) and later Representative Gerald R. Ford (R-MI)—teamed up to host their own monthly television show.[43] Some "responsible members," especially in the Senate, quietly negotiated, and subsequently welcomed, favorable headlines they gained by participating in some prominent congressional activity or investigative hearing, something Sen. Lyndon Johnson (D-TX) did while he was making his way up the ladder of power.[44] Moreover, some of the old bulls most steeped in the institution's culture occasionally did a stint under the klieg lights. "Even one like Senator [Richard] Russell, the arch prototype of traditionalism," Cater observed, "can be lured from the Senate cloakroom to dab on the makeup powder and endure the TV director's shouts of 'Take one…. Take Two.'"[45]

Still, using publicity to carry out their Hill responsibilities was hardly a routine occurrence. For most of them most of the time it did not even figure into their calculations as to how to get things done. One of the old bulls, Sen. Carl Hayden (D-AZ), brusquely put it this way when it came to press attention: "When you've got the votes, you don't have to talk."[46]

Most scholarly narratives that detail routine legislative activities in this baronial Congress contain few references to members of the fourth estate.[47] Instances when media do appear in such accounts, apart from the occasional discussion of maverick behavior, usually center on reelection campaigns.[48] Thus, even though the prevailing culture discouraged members from pursuing a public strategy, it did not completely proscribe all forms of exchanges with the media. The costs of conforming to such an expansive prohibition would have been too great. After all, by this time serving in Congress was a professional career.[49] This increased members' incentives for securing their electoral environments, leaving most of them aware that some press coverage was necessary. But the "important thing," as Sen. Joseph Clark (D-PA) observed, was what was "printed and reported on TV and radio back home in…[their] district[s]."[50] Public relations strategies primarily geared to improving electoral fortunes, which included things like issuing press releases, having personal contacts with hometown reporters, and gaining favorable coverage from local and regional media, consequently fell within the range of acceptable behavior.[51]

Although there was a considerable amount of communication with citizens in this electoral arena—"it was a large and constant part of congressional life"—these public conversations had "little to do with other congressional business, carried on in committee or on the floor or in consultation with colleagues and staff." It had little to do, in other words, with "shaping government policy." When the question was explicitly raised, "to what extent" do the interactions between members and journalists "bear on policy," the conclusion was that its impact was at best marginal and idiosyncratic: it was held to be "erratic, partial and subject to variation with the issue."[52]

As the foregoing suggests, the politics of this baronial Congress was very much an inside game for inside players. A public relations strategy of using the media to speak to external audiences to gain their support was of only marginal utility in a system where small groups of power brokers inconspicuously negotiated and cut deals in congressional hideaways, cloakrooms, offices, and closed committee rooms. More importantly, it would have been at odds with the institution's normative foundation and comity. An outside strategy, after all, would have diverted members' energies away from committee work, thus diminishing their ability to serve themselves and the institution by mastering policy and legislative details.[53] It would also have undermined the expectations that more junior lawmakers were to defer to their more senior colleagues. It was, in fact, precisely these two concerns that weighed heavily on Rayburn's mind as he for years stubbornly resisted allowing television cameras into House chambers.[54]

Yet perhaps most responsible for maintaining legislators' resistance to such media strategies were those folkways—courtesy and accommodation—that sustained relations of bargaining and promoted institutional comity. Robert Peabody pointed to this in his analysis of midtwentieth century House leadership contests, where he distinguished between the "different modes of communication" encouraged by "outside" and "inside" strategies. Whereas an "inside strategy is likely to define situations as family matters, and to feature face-to-face interactions among members," an "outside strategy," he noted, "is likely to evoke a more ideological, issue-oriented definition of the situation."[55] This "more ideological, issue-oriented" style of presentation is certainly not conducive to sustaining attitudes and beliefs that encourage different sides to take up bargaining, negotiation, and compromise. More often than not it resembles hard-core partisan debate; it encourages the different sides to espouse positions that will score political points and attract an outside audience's attention. It is a type of communication that highlights political differences and encourages extremism and inflexibility; and it is carried out in the open for all to see, which creates an additional challenge for those involved. The specific problem with the sort of "public posturing" that goes with a public strategy, as Kernell observed, is that it raises the cost of "compromise" for politicians who must overtly trim their demands to reach a deal.[56] Oftentimes, believing that they cannot retreat from their enunciated positions without losing face, politicians who resort to this approach feel constrained to forgo negotiation and compromise.

In the final analysis, because it shaped attitudes and behaviors in ways that kept power in the hands of a few key figures while sustaining more personal bargaining relations, the Congress of this era limited the strategic options available to members who wanted to shape policy and expand their influence. Legislators were usually dissuaded from following an outside strategy like using the media and most adhered to such a stricture. It was therefore not uncommon to find members like Sen. Eugene Millikin (R-CO), chair of the Republican Conference (1947–57) and chair of the Senate Finance Committee (1947–49, 1953–55), who went to great lengths to keep the press from focusing on him in their accounts. Frequently when asked how he intended to deal with some problem or other, he would tell reporters that "I'm going to paint my ass white and run with the antelopes," all the while knowing that journalists could neither print his mischievous off-color response nor report that he had declined to comment.[57]

Yet the norms that discouraged members such as Millikin from seeking public attention, like most of the others implied by the existing order, would not withstand the transformations that altered Capitol Hill and much of the rest of the Washington community. What has emerged over the years as a consequence of these changes is an institution that, instead of being inhospitable to public relations strategies and more media-centered behaviors, actually invites them. Today, a Eugene Millikin would stand out on Capitol Hill, as much for his aversion to press attention as for his colorful language, keen wit, and playful artifice.

Foundations of the Public Congress

The passing of this baronial Congress was due to a series of notable changes that took place both inside and outside the legislature. These developments dramatically altered the environment within which members of Congress operated and increased the salience of outside public relations strategies for the system's most prominent lawmakers as well as its most junior members.

The most important changes in the institution and on the larger political landscape that elevated the status of a public strategy in Capitol Hill politics included congressional reforms, the declining power of political parties, transformations in the pressure group system, the emergence of a new type of member, responses to presidential relations with Congress, and a growing partisanship on Capitol Hill. Our goal in looking at these is not to tell a story whose parts have been told so well by others but rather to sketch, in broad strokes, an account that helps us better understand how the different parts merged to create the structural foundation supporting today's more publicity-centered Congress.

Overthrowing the "Oligarchs"

While it is difficult to get a precise fix on start of the baronial Congress's demise, it appears that the 1958 midterm election was an important historical turning point. That "catalytic event" brought large groups of Democratic freshman to the House (N = 82) and Senate (N = 18).[58] Many of them came from northern and western states, and they were more progressive than a number of the established oligarchs. From their perspective as newcomers, the existing congressional structure and normative order were costly barriers that prevented them from advancing a more liberal agenda.[59] As their ranks grew through subsequent elections, these junior lawmakers joined other similar-minded members, who had been in Congress but had lacked the numbers to challenge the powers that be. Feeling less compunction about violating the unwritten rules that did not serve their policy preferences, they set about dismantling the institutional scaffolding that supported the old bulls' power.[60]

Congressional change started shortly after the class of 1958 arrived on the Hill. Many of these newly elected House Democrats joined other advocates of reform to constitute the Democratic Study Group (DSG). Initially, this body pushed the Democratic Caucus to expand representation of liberals on the House Rules Committee. This panel, especially, drew the ire of reformers like Rep. Richard Bolling (D-MO), who saw it as "a policy committee manned by political primitives" that "functioned as if it were a 'third branch' of the Congress" by frequently stymieing progressive legislation.[61] The DSG, with Speaker Rayburn's support, succeeded in getting the 1961 Caucus to expand the Rules panel and increase the number of its liberal representatives, thus decreasing the conservatives' grip on power. Through subsequent elections the DSG increased its ranks, and by 1965 over half of the Democratic Caucus was attending its events, making the DSG an important forum for liberal reformers to work out proposals and strategies to challenge the institutional underpinnings of the baronial Congress.[62]

Change also came to the Senate when Lyndon Johnson vacated the position of Majority Leader to become vice president in 1961. The growing contingent of liberal, northern, and western Democrats tipped party sentiment in favor of a different style of Senate leadership. No longer willing to brook a heavy-handed leader like Johnson, the party put Sen. Mike Mansfield (D-MT) at the helm. Temperamentally inclined to be less aggressive and power driven than his predecessor, he also was constrained by his party's liberal wing to be more deferential and inclusive, prompting him to spread power around.[63] Though the old bulls retained key committee positions and assignments, this change made the Senate more individualistic.[64]

Momentum for congressional reform picked up over the next several years, as liberal Democrats on the Hill expanded their voting bloc. By 1970, a bipartisan coalition of reformers pushed through Congress the Legislative Reorganization Act, the first in a series of reforms that reined in committee chairs, opened up the institution, and distributed power around the Hill. With prodding from reformers in ensuing years, the two chambers adopted several measures that compounded institutional change. Some of these, like giving the Speaker greater leverage over procedures and committee assignments, promised to strengthen the hands of House leaders; others, like the War Powers Resolution of 1973 and the Budget and Impoundment Control Act of 1974, attempted to increase the capabilities and leverage of Congress in its dealings with the Executive branch.[65]

Most visible and immediate for bringing change to the distribution of power on Capitol Hill, however, were initiatives that curtailed committee chairs' prerogatives, weakened the role of seniority, augmented the influence of the rest of the membership, and brought greater transparency to the legislative process. As a result of these reforms, chairs could no longer act with impunity. The House Democratic caucus first demonstrated this in 1975 when it bounced three imperious committee heads from their positions. The reforms also greatly diminished chairs' abilities to maneuver behind closed doors to control the flow of legislation that their committees considered or to choke-off proposals they opposed. The institutionalization and proliferation of subcommittees that came with the reforms further eroded their power. Reforms that equipped subcommittees with staff, budgets, and other institutional resources empowered more members and buttressed lower-level panels' independence from committee chairs. Individual members of Congress were also provided with handsome increases in allocations for personal staff and travel, further adding to their autonomy.[66]

The early effect of these reforms was a congressional world that had been "turned upside down."[67] The changes spread power *out* from committee chairs to subcommittee chairs and spread it *down* from committee chairs to those in the rank-and-file, thus increasing the number of people on the Hill who had the influence, incentives, and wherewithal to shape congressional policy. As a result, pretty much every Senator "considered himself entitled to participate on any issue that interested him," while in the House, by one estimate, "more than two-fifths of the majority members [were cut] directly into the action."[68]

By the end of the 1970s, the baronial Congress had given way to a more participatory, transparent, and unpredictable institution.[69] The reforms extended the legislative process, pushing it backward to the subcommittees and forward to the floor. Legislators, meanwhile, secured more resources and gained more opportunities to use them. Junior lawmakers thus had a more meaningful role to play, and with fewer sanctions available to their senior colleagues, they had fewer incentives to abide by the old norms. Many more lawmakers used the increased influence the reforms gave them, and they felt freer to shape policy at any stage of the process, including the floor. "Congress" had thus become, as Samuel Patterson concluded at the time, an "unusually democratic" body. "Its aggregate decision making is 'individualistic' in the sense that party or committee influence on members' voting is not compelling."[70]

A Changing Arena

Decentralization within Congress had implications elsewhere on the political landscape. Since subcommittee chairs and even regular members now had an ability to shape congressional policy decisions, they naturally drew the attention of citizen groups or special interests. And members of Congress, in turn, became more receptive to their entreaties as parties continued to lose their grip on the American political system.

Throughout the earliest stages of the twentieth century, state and local party organizations dominated congressional elections: they recruited many of the candidates, funded their campaigns, and turned out the votes. This was no longer the case in the 1970s. Already weakened by civil service reforms and the institution of direct primaries, state and local parties lost what hold they still had on congressional elections with the adoption of campaign finance reforms and a sizable erosion in the electorate's attachment to parties. While national party organizations eventually adapted to some of these changes by providing financial support and technical assistance in congressional elections, the parties of the 1970s atrophied, leaving a void that congressional candidates filled themselves. Many of these candidates were self-selected, created their own political organizations, raised their own money, and conducted their own campaigns.[71] They now made their political career not as "party men" but as "largely freewheeling political entrepreneurs."[72] Ultimately, just as those at the helm of the different congressional parties were being forced by reforms to bargain with an increasingly large number of lawmakers in processing legislative proposals, they were less able to depend on party affiliation to build coalitions to support their initiatives. As rank-and-file members gained greater leverage in the legislative process through congressional reforms, those same members, elected in campaigns they and their own organizations had in good part designed and executed, gained greater independence from their party and were less and less willing to surrender it.[73]

This decline of political parties and increase in the permeability of Congress from outside forces coincided with an explosion in the number of Washington-based interest groups. John Tierney and Kay Schlozman reported that of the organizations that had lobbying offices in DC in 1982, "40 percent have been founded since 1960, and 25 percent since 1970."[74] At the same time, the variety of groups who entered the political fray also increased.[75] One significant development was the noticeable proliferation of groups that coalesced around a set of ideas, such as the environment or consumer safety, or a single issue, such as abortion or gun control, as opposed to some material benefit to be provided by the government.[76] Another important change was "fragmentation" of interests in particular "policy domains." Whereas in the 1940s and early1950s one or two influential though broad-based organizations exercised hegemony over a specific policy domain, like agriculture or health care, by the 1970s and 1980s that "quasi-monopoly power" had in good part been displaced with the emergence of more narrowly focused pressure groups.[77]

This vibrant and growing constellation of interests assumed some of the responsibilities political parties normally fulfilled. Interest groups have the wherewithal to provide money, information, volunteers, and other support directly to candidates and lawmakers who share their legislative goals and who need resources to put together their own campaigns. These groups also serve as communications links between their members and legislators in Congress, informing the former about the actions that representatives and senators took on their behalf, and reminding the latter about the group's potential to help, or hurt, their careers.[78]

Yet, unlike traditional American parties, these groups typically represent a relatively small percentage of citizens. They also take positions on but a few policy issues, and on some of these they are intractable—especially those committed to a set of ideas or a single issue. Parties, by contrast, usually want to grow their coalitions in ways that will enable them to gain control of both ends of Pennsylvania Avenue. Their desire to win elections and shape policy outcomes gives them incentives to compromise and mute their internal differences. The result is that they exert a centripetal influence on the American political system.

Without the integrative impulse provided by parties, the political arena becomes fragmented and fractious. This is to a certain extent what happened as more narrowly focused interest groups multiplied and started to make directly available to congressional candidates and office holders the kinds of support parties formerly provided. Instead of having their demands mediated through parties, many interested citizens began advancing their preferences directly through interest groups in different policy sectors, with each group using its resources to pressure members of

Congress they had supported to hold fast to their demands. This further undercut the old order's commitment to ideological moderation and policy compromise. The result at the end of the 1970s was a "new Congress" of "buzzing confusion," as Roger Davidson noted. "In place of party labels there are," he wrote, "individual politicians in business for themselves, and a series of shifting coalitions around specific issues. It is as if we are witnessing a reincarnation, on an enlarged scale, of the one-party factionalism that the late V. O. Key, Jr., identified in the southern states of an earlier day: 'multifaceted, discontinuous, kaleidoscopic, fluid, transient.'"[79]

The evolution of Congress over the 1970s and the weakened state of parties brought new challenges for incumbents. Some found that the turbulence unleashed by the changes on Capitol Hill made service in the institution less rewarding, prompting many of them to retire.[80] While old age, electoral insecurity, and ambition for other political offices certainly account for some of this era's retirements, variables traditionally associated with voluntary departures from the postwar House were not strongly correlated with the sudden upsurge in numbers. After all, 1970-era retirees were on average younger, from safer districts, and less likely to pursue a political career than were retirees from the 1950s and 1960s. Nor is this rise in retirements explained by pointing to the frustrations and limitations that inhere in being a minority member in a majority-run legislature. Democrats, not Republicans, dominated retirees in the 1970s. Ostensibly, some midcareer legislators who came to Congress before the reforms and who had success in that older institution simply decided to leave public life altogether rather than continue to serve in the new political community in which they found themselves.[81]

In addition to, and in part because of these departures, an unusually large number of freshmen (House N=92; Senate N=10) were elected in the aftermath of Watergate. This made the Congress a more junior institution than it had been in quite some time.[82] These newer members, in turn, demonstrated success in this more fragmented, individualistic political system. They came to Washington by winning elections in campaigns with, comparatively speaking, less party support than their predecessors, and having arrived on the Hill due largely to their own efforts, they expected to continue to chart their own way once they began to serve.

Many of these more "entrepreneurial" members first elected in the 1970s also had great skill in using electronic media like television.[83] In fact, the extent to which they used media in their campaigns and in-house television and radio recording studios once in office actually set them apart from their more senior colleagues who entered the Congress in the preceding two decades.[84] They thus appreciated the value of media politics, and they knew how to elicit favorable coverage. "If you say something pithy or clever," explained Rep. Thomas Downey (D-NY), who came in with the class of 1974, "you can find yourself on the national news in a matter of hours.... News management by members through the electronic media is a more viable option than it ever was."[85]

The bottom line is that, in many respects, members first elected during this era constituted a significantly different type, one that was far removed from the old order's "responsible" member.[86] They were less dependent on party, more outwardly ambitious, and generally more comfortable using media to realize their objectives. Speaker Tip O'Neill (D-MA) captured these differences when he contrasted those who comprised the old guard, which included people like himself, with the bloc of members who first arrived in Congress in the wake of the reforms:

> The old guys worked their way up through the chairs.... They're very hierarchical. They kept their friendships. They keep their alliances. They dance with the girl they came with. They stick together. The new-breed guys play one night-stands. They're always forming new coalitions. They're always worrying about their image and how to position themselves. They decide what image they want to project, and they position themselves to project that image.[87]

The rising influence of interest groups in Congress at this time combined with the internal dispersion of institutional power to splinter the legislative process, thus diminishing the ability of a relatively small number of House and Senate leaders to deliver floor majorities through personal one-on-one negotiations and compromises. As private, face-to-face conversations among congressional elites became an increasingly ineffective way to shape and move the policy agenda, members, many of whom had been elected to Congress in the 1970s by skillfully running media-focused campaigns, began to employ public relations activities in carrying out their responsibilities, thus applying what they had found successful on the campaign trail to carrying out their responsibilities on the Hill.[88] For many of them and their successors, seeking publicity became an expeditious way to realize the principal goals—reelection, policy, and power—motivating those who embark on congressional careers.[89] As a former House member first elected in 1974 explained to Burdett Loomis, "you get publicity around here for three reasons: First, to get re-elected.... Second, on behalf of a cause;... other members pay attention, especially if you're down on the lower half of the order. Third, there's political advancement."[90]

The way of thinking represented by this member's comments distinguished the Congress of this era from its baronial predecessor. While members of a preceding generation certainly envisaged public relations strategies as important in getting reelected, most of them, given the prevailing normative structure of the institution in which they served, would have balked at using such overt approaches to advance their lawmaking and career objectives. These more modern, entrepreneurial actors, however, found that in the sort of Congress in which they worked, publicity could serve both their electoral and their programmatic and career objectives. Through carefully orchestrated public relations strategies, they could bring their pet projects and programs to the attention of others. Reliance on media became a more efficient and effective way for congressional members working within this less structured, egalitarian environment to stake out positions on particular issues, advance their agenda, communicate with their attentive publics and financial backers, signal their intentions to other institutional policymakers, and mobilize popular support needed to achieve their aims.[91]

The internal pressures working against an outside strategy thus eventually gave way. By 1977, the House of Representatives, which since the 1950s had tenaciously resisted allowing television into its chambers, dropped this prohibition and allowed its activities to be broadcast. The Senate followed suit in 1986.[92] Capitol Hill culture had changed enough that by the end of the 1980s there was evidence to suggest that "media exposure," at least in the Senate, was actually "more likely to attract respect than to repel it."[93] Having been "turned upside down," the Congress had, when it came to members' strategies, now also been turned inside out.

As the President Goes, So Goes the Congress

Just as forces were coalescing to produce a fragmented, decentralized Congress, and as the institution was becoming more "outward looking," Ronald Reagan was elected president. His strategic use of media and public appeals to galvanize support for his legislative agenda and foreign policy objectives came to define a new style of leadership: "going public."[94] While he was certainly not the first to use the media to help him meet his responsibilities, nor, as the case of President John F. Kennedy makes clear, the first to exploit the power of television, Reagan, perhaps more than any other modern president, "personifies the prominence of public relations symbols as a tool of presidential governing."[95] He frequently spoke with and to reporters in ways that gave the executive branch favorable media coverage. At times he also engaged public attention to mobilize citizens to pressure members of Congress to support his initiatives, to raise money for Republican officeholders, and to shape the polity's perception of the major issues of the day. Reagan's media-centered strategy of taking his case directly to the public was so successful in the opening months of his administration that, for a short time, the House Democrats, who held the majority, actually lost control of floor procedures and congressional legislation was effectively drafted by the White House.[96]

Reagan's successors have, to different degrees and with different levels of success, continued this presidential practice of "going public." Like Congress, presidents in the contemporary era inhabit a political system inhospitable to building and sustaining broad-based coalitions based on face-to-face conversations among political elites. In an earlier time, presidents and their staff could influence congressional decisions by working directly with the congressional oligarchs. Senator Alben Barkley (D-KY) captured this when he recounted FDR's bargaining relations with the Hill on his New Deal agenda:

> When President Roosevelt came into power in 1933, he inaugurated such a variety of legislative proposals that it was essential he keep in close touch with Congress through the leadership of the two branches. In the matter of the Economy Bill, the new Banking Law and many others, he consulted with the leaders of the two houses and the chairmen of committees, with respect to the measures before they were introduced.[97]

Once the leaders, relevant chairs, and on occasion, even ranking members had been brought on board, they would use their formidable institutional leverage to uphold their end of the deal and deliver coalitions for the president. While presidents like Roosevelt and some of his immediate successors certainly made concessions as they negotiated their way to agreements, they found that their success as leaders ultimately hinged on their skills in bargaining behind the scenes with a few strategically placed actors.[98] Yet by the late 1970s congressional reforms and an increasingly fragmented political arena had altered the political landscape in ways that made it too difficult for the president to conduct business with Congress the way someone like FDR had managed his responsibilities. Hamilton Jordan, a key White House advisor to President Jimmy Carter, pointed to this fundamental shift:

> Twenty years ago a President [could go] to Lyndon Johnson and Sam Rayburn and George Meany…and together they would write a tax bill and the leadership would get it approved. Now you can have the President, the leadership, the committee chairmen, and the subcommittee chairmen all in favor of something, like hospital cost control, and a group of young Turks in the subcommittee can run over you. It means you have to deal with scores and sometimes hundreds of people to pass a bill.[99]

Unlike FDR and his immediate successors, presidents like Carter had to work with "nervous and unstable coalitions" and a legislative body where "deals and accommodations devised at one stage" could be subsequently "reopened" and modified.[100] Legislative leaders of the president's own party, even in the majority, found they occasionally could not muster the necessary support for the White House in such an unpredictable environment. The problem, simply put, was that they no longer controlled "the significant blocs of votes" that they had relied on in the past.[101] Eventually, presidents like Reagan responded to the dilemma of building majorities within this increasingly "atomized" environment, as Kernell recounted, by enlisting a more public strategy as a sort of "cost effective" way to attain their partisan and programmatic aims.[102]

Frequently, the Reagan White House fashioned a political message and then aimed to elicit the sort of media attention that amplified its position so as to connect with the numerous and diverse elements of this increasingly fragmented political order. With skill and discipline, his administration tried to use publicity strategically to highlight problems, shape the agenda, communicate with attentive elites, mold public opinion, and mobilize grassroots efforts to pressure other political actors to support the president's program. While Reagan's ability to shape popular sentiment and move Congress on many issues is certainly subject to debate, he was able to create, in the minds of many who inhabited Capitol Hill, the perception that a president who followed a carefully orchestrated public strategy could bring the legislative branch around on policies that mattered to him. Near the close of the Reagan years, even scholars started to spill a lot of ink on the "plebiscitary president" that had displaced the bargaining president of pluralistic lore.[103]

Several years ago Sen. Daniel Patrick Moynihan (D-NY) formulated his well-known "iron law of emulation." It stipulates that "whenever a branch of government acquires a new technique which enhances its power in relation to other branches, that technique will soon be adopted by the other branches."[104] Moynihan's "iron law" perhaps captures some of what happened on the Hill in response to President Reagan's policy successes gained through a public strategy.[105] Following the president's lead, members of Congress turned to their leaders to map out and direct a more proactive public relations approach to governing.

The character of congressional membership in the 1980s set the stage for the parties to answer the president's public relations savvy with communication strategies of their own. First, many representatives and senators were already experienced with using media in their own careers, both to get elected and to shape policy outcomes. They consequently grasped from firsthand experience the strategic value of publicity. One prominent member of this new generation of congressional politicians, Rep. Richard Gephart (D-MO), later recounted: "We all came knowing the power of television, knowing the power of having messaging on television and believing that our leaders had to carry a message."[106]

Second, changes within the congressional parties created conditions that made it possible for them to try, as organizations, to emulate the president's strategy of going public. Because of retirements, the creation of majority–minority districts, and southern partisan realignment, congressional parties, as we noted earlier, grew increasingly ideologically homogenous. This change, already in motion, accelerated at about the same time that Reagan started using a more aggressive public relations strategy to help him set the legislative agenda and advance his programmatic goals. As the chambers' caucuses/conferences grew more cohesive, parties also moved further away from each other on the ideological spectrum. The ideological division between the two congressional parties was, in turn, further solidified as the "sorting out" of the electorate around more contentious cultural issues continued over the course of subsequent decades.[107] Thus, beginning in the mid-1980s and extending on to present day Washington politics, party unity scores climbed. And, as we discussed in chapter 2, in this more partisan and polarized setting members of the Congress, especially those in the House, found that this greater internal homogeneity of preferences within their own parties decreased the "costs" of ceding their leaders more power. In return, members expected and put pressure on those leaders to use their institutional powers and visibility to advance their party's collective goals.[108] They thus anticipated that those at the helm would combine an aggressive use of the powers of their offices with an active role in using the news to explain, promote, and defend their programmatic and partisan objectives.[109]

Initially, this was clearest in the case of House Democrats. They were after all the ones getting rolled by a Republican president, Ronald Reagan. Thus, first Speaker O'Neill and then his successors pressed to wield greater institutional and persuasive power to counter the president and advance their agenda.[110] House Republicans followed suit shortly thereafter. As a more activist, conservative wing gained greater leverage within their party conference, they pushed for stronger leaders who would protect congressional prerogatives and help them make their case in confrontations with a Republican White House that, in their eyes, had grown too comfortable working with a Democratic majority.[111]

Because of the culture of the institution and the prerogatives of its members, parties of the more individualistic Senate were not as amenable to the types of centralized leadership structures that appeared in the House.[112] Still, by the early 1980s even senators realized that their leaders needed to plan and conduct more aggressive publicity campaigns to advance their partisan goals and claim credit for their political achievements. Coordinating a communications strategy and serving as spokesperson for the party therefore came to be understood as "integral" to the floor leader's job.[113]

The increased polarization of interest groups and the growing and changing roles played by think tanks in the policy process also had an impact on leaders' responsibilities. As the 1980s unfolded and as parties became more ideological and opposed, many pressure groups found they could no longer "play both sides of the political fence." This produced a sorting out of groups and parties, thus giving parties stable allies who could help them wage their fight in their public relations battles.[114] Think tanks also proliferated on the national political landscape as interests were allying themselves with parties. Many of the think tanks that emerged during this era, like the Heritage Foundation, the Cato Institute, and the Progressive Policy Institute, assumed more partisan stances than their predecessors, and from their earliest beginnings they took on a rather substantial role in shaping and fueling the nation's policy debates. This, in turn, made them valuable partners for parties trying to marshal public support for their policy initiatives.[115] Combined, these developments further heightened the role of leadership in public relations activities. They now assumed some of the responsibility for coordinating pressure groups' and think tanks' messages on policies with those of their members.[116]

Devising and implementing a successful public communications strategy consequently became an inescapable requirement for congressional leaders in the more contemporary Washington community. While the oligarchs in the older Congress did not totally shun the press, their interactions with reporters, apart from those that took place behind closed doors, tended in many instances to be brief and perfunctory; it was, most certainly, never an integral part of their overall governing style. Their main focus, appropriate for the postwar congressional context, was on the internal workings of the House and Senate, since the ability to move those chambers consisted of controlling committee assignments, legislative calendars, and other internal institutional resources. Near the end of the 1980s and the start of the 1990s, however, congressional leaders found that their portfolios had expanded to include the responsibilities of both regularly and routinely interacting with the media and plotting out and coordinating their members' and allies' communications strategies to present coherent messages that clarified and supported their parties' brands.[117] Former House Speaker Newt Gingrich (R-GA) captured this point shortly after he assumed the speakership in 1995: "The most accurate statement of how I see the speakership [is] somebody who could somehow combine grassroots organizations, mass media and legislative detail into one synergistic pattern."[118]

Thus, by the time dramatic changes in the media environment started to unfold and accelerate, forces on the political landscape and in Congress itself had already pretty much turned the institution inside out. Transformations in the media that produced the variegated, fast-paced news world in which we now find ourselves only reinforced that development. At the same time, those changes in how news or information is disseminated and accessed have created new opportunities and posed significant challenges as congressional parties routinely take their cases public.

Conclusion

In the older, post-World War II Congress, members oftentimes had to make a "basic decision" about the kind of career that they wanted to pursue: they could either obtain influence inside the Congress by working quietly and cooperatively with their colleagues, or they could exchange institutional influence for the pursuit of a national reputation by using the news to address actors outside of the Congress. As the careers and rather paltry accomplishments of media-oriented mavericks like Sen. Kefauver intimate, gaining publicity and building up name recognition did not result in a distinguished legislative career crowned by major policy achievements or advancement up the congressional rungs of power; in many instances, it actually hindered effectiveness and made it impossible to secure the plum assignments necessary to exercise leverage over Hill activities. Those members who wanted to realize their ambitions by making a meaningful mark on policy and the institution instead had, as Norman Ornstein once put it, to "ride up the power structures inside the House or Senate. But the elevators were not self-run; rather, the operators were the senior party leaders and committee chairmen. These people pushed the internal button for numerous internal reasons."[119]

Things could not be more different in the contemporary Congress; it is a place where this "basic decision" has been turned on its head. For both leaders and many members and their parties, success and influence on today's Hill often hinge on their ability to mold popular sentiment and communicate through the media with executive branch personnel, organized interests, key constituency groups, and attentive citizens all over the country. The old strategy of obtaining and wielding legislative power by appeasing, and quietly negotiating with, a few influential actors, while not wholly obsolete, is generally less useful today. Changes that swept across the American political landscape prompted congressional leaders and members to concentrate ample amounts of time and attention on shaping the messages that carry outside their institutions if they want to amass influence, promote their agendas, shape policy, and improve their electoral fortunes. While some members still shy away from the public spotlight, many of today's representatives and senators, much like presidents, bureaucrats, interest groups, think tanks, and politically active citizens, routinely engage in public relations campaigns. This applies to the more junior backbenchers as well as congressional leaders and the more institutionally influential legislators. Just how these members and leaders supply, organize, and structure their operations to mount their public relations efforts in ways that enable them and their parties to realize their objectives are the topics of our next two chapters.

4 Congressional Responses to Changes

Members Adapt to "Going Outside"

Congress is a "robust human institution."[1] The key to its survival, like that of any other complex organization, is its ability to manage internal and external pressures in ways that enable its members to realize their "discrete goals."[2] Upended by internal changes and reforms and buffeted by forces sweeping across the political landscape, Congress adjusted as it transformed itself from a relatively closed, "baronial" body to the more partisan, increasingly publicity-oriented assembly it is today. That ability to accommodate change is also very much in evidence as members find themselves negotiating, for themselves and their parties, a media environment that is undergoing rapid changes in how information is gathered, evaluated, amalgamated, transmitted, and received.

Individual members have adapted to a more externally oriented approach to governing within a highly unpredictable news world that prizes instantaneous communications and incorporates multiple media platforms, by beefing up their public relations resources, both in terms of personnel and communications technologies. They have thus enhanced their abilities to widen the breadth, heighten the intensity, target the direction, control the content, and synchronize the timing of political messages they seek to communicate outside their chambers' walls.

Staffing to Play the Game

One sign of Congress's accommodations to its transition from an inward- to an outward-looking organization is the institutionalization of the position of congressional press secretary or communications director on Hill staffs. The chores and even job titles assigned to such aides, of course, vary considerably, for much depends on the member's personality, office management style, comfort with the press, and ultimate goals. As our interviews with communications personnel suggest, some lawmakers place a heavy premium on proactive public relations operations.[3] They expect their press staffers to monitor their coverage and aggressively promote their presence and interests in a wide band of social networks and local, regional, and national media outlets. Still, even today there are those who prefer that their press aides run a more low-key publicity shop.[4] They are satisfied if their communications people draft and send out press releases, pitch personal interest stories to the local weekly papers, book interviews on small-town radio shows, tinker with their websites, write an occasional tweet, oversee incoming e-mail correspondence, and keep track of their news clippings.

Notwithstanding these differences from office to office, the institutionalization of publicity operations on various Hill staffs is nonetheless significant, since formally designating someone to handle communications systematizes members' exchanges with the media, thus providing the press corps with an identifiable person in a congressional office or on a committee's or a party leader's staff that they can contact directly while giving a member of Congress or a committee head or chamber leader someone who can concentrate on media relations.[5] This specialization has multiple benefits. Press officers can help representatives and senators craft and fine-tune their messages, design and oversee strategies for getting those out, and help legislators understand how news organizations gather information, craft narratives, and time stories. They can also devote considerable chunks of their workloads to cultivating relationships with the media and negotiating with them to market and even shape their bosses' messages. The bottom line here is that a press officer both helps lower members' transactional costs in media exchanges and improves their chances for success as they take their cases outside their chambers. Thus, having such a person on board reflects, at least in part, the importance both members and their parties assign to media and publicity in conducting business on the Hill.

The Old Regime

Both office and committee staffs were considerably smaller and less developed before reforms transformed Capitol Hill power structures and increased rank-and-file members' institutional resources. The total number of staffers assigned to House and Senate offices in the mid-1950s was about a third of what it was by the time the reforms had run their course in the late 1970s. For congressional committees, the picture was roughly the same. The total number of aides assigned to committee staffs in the mid-1950s was about one-fifth of the House's and one-third of the Senate's totals in the late 1970s.[6] Congressional staffs were also not very complex back then, since many of them lacked even the beginnings of the functional specialization of institutionalized organizations.[7] Donald Matthews, for instance, found that while some senators' offices in the late 1950s had assumed "bureaucratic" traits, many others reflected a "division of labor [that] is relatively amorphous."[8] Charles Clapp likewise discovered that in the early 1960s House members "were sorely pressed for staff assistance" and lacked even the resources necessary to hire a "qualified legislative assistant."[9]

To be sure, even on these smaller, inchoate staffs, senators and representatives employed folks who handled relations with various external constituencies, including the press corps. After all, communications with home-state journalists for the purpose of keeping constituents apprised as to what those on the Hill were doing to help them out served members' reelection goal, something even the oligarchs encouraged. But lawmakers' concern for press coverage rarely went beyond that. Many lawmakers therefore delegated press responsibilities to an administrative assistant or personal secretary who had to juggle public relations work with sundry office chores.

Overall, this resulted in a relatively meager Capitol Hill press secretariat. Even in the twilight years of the baronial Congress, when reformers gained some traction in the 87th Congress (1961–62) with the 1961 expansion of the House Rules Committee and Sen. Mike Mansfield's (D-MT) ascension to the post of Majority Leader, press personnel were scarcely found. The *Congressional Staff Directory* reveals that precious few House members of the 87th Congress employed someone formally charged with the task of dealing with the press, such as a press secretary, assistant press secretary, press assistant, communications director, news secretary, public relations secretary, or director of public relations. Listings show that slightly less than 4% had press aides.[10] None of those was a chair or ranking member of a House standing committee. Including only those who had full-time press aides, the total falls to about 3% of the entire House membership.

The relative absence of press secretaries on House members' staffs, however, is only part of the picture. Members of Congress also have committee and subcommittee staffers who help them carry out their chores and promote their fortunes, which include activities that involve some sort of publicity.[11] These staffers, for instance, can assist members or congressional parties in plotting out communications strategies. They can also manage transactions with the press to shape news coverage on pending legislation, congressional hearings, upcoming votes, legislative conferences, and negotiations with other political actors, including the president. A better perspective on communications personnel can therefore be ascertained by examining committee staffs, since they provide members with additional resources that can be tapped. These resources would not have been equitably distributed in the prereform Congress but would have instead primarily benefited the Democratic oligarchs, since they were the ones who controlled committee staff.[12] It may be the case that some House committee staffers informally handled communications responsibilities, but as befitted a more "inward-looking" House, *Directory* listings indicate none of the chamber's standing committees had on board someone assigned a public relations role.[13]

Press secretaries were more common in Senate offices. This can be attributed perhaps to important differences between the two chambers, and it extends beyond senators' historical advantage in having more resources to hire office personnel.[14] For most senators, the larger size and greater diversity of their constituencies, coupled with the greater number and complexity of local media they have to deal with as a result, likely gave them, as it does today, more incentives to employ someone to manage their press relations.[15] Conceivably, this was compounded, as is the case today, by the media's predilection to gravitate to the Senate.[16] Even then, on those Hill events they did cover, news organizations most often found Senate activities made for better story lines, including as they did the verbal jousting of its floor debates and the spectacle surrounding the occasional filibuster mounted to thwart some highly contentious piece of legislation,. As Donald Matthews recounted, most of the era's reporters considered the Senate a "'cockpit of drama.'"[17] Many journalists, in contrast, perceived the larger, more byzantine House of Representatives, too complex and mundane to supply the elements necessary to construct the compelling narratives they so prized. *New York Times* congressional correspondent, William S. White, frankly confessed as much. "Though it has not always been so, the press for many years," he admitted, "has been enchanted with the Senate and largely bored with the House. It is a matter of which I personally have rueful knowledge; as a Congressional correspondent in younger days I was unable to bring myself to go to the House when anything at all was doing in the Senate."[18]

It is also conceivable that some senators recognized the value of having full-time press aides after they discovered a certain level of notoriety outside the chamber could be used to mount campaigns for the White House. Take the case of a maverick like Senator Estes Kefauver (D-TN), who led a special panel's 1951 congressional investigation into the activities of organized crime syndicates. Under his direction, this committee took the unusual step of televising its hearings, which he exploited to draw attention to himself. Public reaction to the broadcasts was, by most accounts, "phenomenal."[19] Kefauver's antics and overt display of ambition put off many senators, and as we noted earlier, diminished his stature inside the chamber, but he emerged from these investigative hearings as one of the "most widely known" members of the Senate. This left him well positioned to mount two credible, though unsuccessful, contests for his party's nomination for the presidency in 1952 and 1956.[20]

Others with interest in higher office, like Senator John F. Kennedy (D-MA), soon followed Kefauver's lead. Kennedy's elevation to the presidency confirmed the value of playing to the media and that "was not lost on his colleagues."[21] It was also about this time that the informal pressures discouraging the use of publicity in conducting Senate business, while not vanishing, started to wane as Mansfield assumed the helm of the majority party and gave individual members greater leverage and leeway within the chamber. The overall result was that for a number of politicians interested in the office at the other end of Pennsylvania Avenue the Senate gradually became, as Nelson Polsby wrote, a "publicity springboard from which they could launch themselves."[22]

Still, even in the Senate press secretaries were hardly ubiquitous.[23] Fifty-nine Senate offices during the 87th Congress had no formally designated press secretary, and of the remaining forty-one offices that had such a post, three had a part-time press secretary, thirty-seven had one full-time press person, and one office had two full-time press staffers. Even this modest level of press personnel in members' offices was not reflected in committee staffing arrangements. There the Senate clearly resembled the House. Although slightly more than half (N=8) of the fifteen chairs did have full-time press secretaries assigned to their personal offices, not one single Senate standing committee employed someone officially assigned responsibilities for dealing with the press.[24]

Congressional party leaders of this era, of course, usually followed a behind-the-scenes, personalized bargaining approach that meshed with their legislative order's normative and power structures. Sen. Lyndon Johnson (D-TX) and Rep. Sam Rayburn (D-TX) epitomized this style of leadership, achieving legendary status for the way they handled their respective chambers. Their leadership savvy was manifested in the impervious settings of Congress, based on their mastery of complex procedures and their skill in discerning and crafting legislative compromises that maintained calm within the party while promoting the preferences of the powerful barons who controlled the committees.[25]

Johnson clearly understood the salience of favorable news coverage, and he knew how to manipulate the press in ways that worked to his own advantage. He also maintained close ties with an array of influential Capitol Hill reporters and columnists.[26] But he preferred "one-to-one relations" with reporters to the more transparent, extemporaneous forums like weekend television shows and open press conferences. In the more familiar, opaque settings of the Hill's offices and corridors or the isolated confines of his Texas ranch, he could cajole, flatter, manipulate, and physically dominate the press instead of having to respond, perfunctorily, to questions over which he had little control.[27] His successor as Democratic floor leader, Sen. Mansfield, was no more amenable to the talk-show circuit. By all accounts, he disliked publicity and employed no press secretary. He even was referred to by the media as the "fastest gun in the West" for his rapid-fire "monosyllabic replies"— "Yep," "Nope," "Can't Say," "Don't know"—to journalists' queries. Mansfield was so taciturn in exchanges with the media that he oftentimes left television panelists to "run out of questions."[28]

Speaker Rayburn likewise did not see publicity as integral to congressional leaders' responsibilities. Believing the roles of show horse and workhorse to be mutually exclusive, he steered clear of the spotlight. Like Johnson, he had little interest in being booked on Sunday morning television interview shows. They were, as he put it, a "chore" he "never relished." He did not, of course, completely ignore the national press, but his dealings with them were usually restricted to informal sessions with small groups of DC reporters he knew and trusted and brief news conferences attended by "regulars from the gallery." The Speaker's general aversion to media attention was for the most part emulated by his immediate successors, Rep. John McCormack (D-MA) and Rep. Carl Albert (D-OK), both of whom concentrated their efforts on the inside game.[29]

There was, however, a noteworthy exception to this pattern. While Democratic congressional leaders pursued strategies of persuasion and bargaining shut away from the press, some of their GOP counterparts came to recognize the partisan value of courting news coverage. Important for bringing this about was the change in the political context that occurred after Kennedy assumed the presidency in 1961. With Kennedy at the other end of Pennsylvania Avenue, Democrats in Congress had front and center a compelling figure who had good relations with the press and who was very much at ease using television to woo the public. GOP congressional leaders soon recognized that Kennedy's media prowess put them at a strategic disadvantage. They responded by making direct public appeals to the American people. House Republican leader, Rep. Charles Halleck (R-IN), and later his successor, Rep. Gerald Ford (R-MI), teamed up with Senate minority leader, Sen. Everett Dirksen (R-IL), to conduct a series of press conferences that outlined Republican policy responses to presidential initiatives. These media events played out for several years and enabled the GOP minority to solicit news coverage and disseminate its message to a burgeoning television audience.[30] Though Republican leaders never came close to garnering the amount of media attention accorded the president, their "initiative" was nonetheless significant, for it represented the "first calculated maneuver" by anyone in the ranks of the congressional leadership to employ an outside media strategy.[31]

Patterns of press staffing for those in the upper echelons of the congressional parties resembled those found elsewhere in the 87th Congress. This included even the minority Republican leaders who enlisted television to take their message beyond the beltway. Not a single member in the House leadership's top tier—speaker, majority and minority leaders, and majority and minority whips—had a formally designated press aide, even on their personal staffs. This pattern was pretty much replicated in the Senate, where only Majority Whip Sen. Hubert H. Humphrey (D-MN), had a press secretary on his personal staff.[32]

Given the overall dearth of congressional press aides, it should come as no surprise that there was little palpable evidence that such staffers constituted a distinct, identifiable profession on the Hill. The first professional association of congressional press secretaries did not appear until 1961. It was then that Senate press aides coalesced on a bipartisan basis to form the Senate Association of Press Secretaries. And it would be another fifteen years before press staffers in the House of Representatives followed suit and organized themselves along partisan lines.[33]

The Contemporary Congress: Hiring Help to Get Out the Message

Congressional staffing has changed to accommodate today's more "outward-looking" legislative body. Press secretaries or communications directors are now found in almost all members' offices as well as on many committee staffs, and they comprise major communications operations within the administrative offices of congressional party leaders. Figure 4.1, which presents information on press staffing at selected intervals, shows that press secretaries or communications directors specifically tasked to members are now the norm.[34] Using data from the 87th Congress as a baseline for comparison, Figure 4.1 covers the 98th Congress (1982–83) that convened shortly after the reforms had taken root and the institution as a whole had become more aware of the salience of public relations activities, and the more contemporary 109th Congress (2005–2006).

The percentage of members' offices employing press secretaries was substantially greater in the 98th Congress than what appears roughly two decades earlier, when the institution was still a predominantly inward looking body. Roughly 95% of Senate offices and 66% of the House's had someone formally charged with press responsibilities. That represents a twofold increase in the Senate and an approximately nineteenfold increase in the House from the 87th Congress. Most of these aides, moreover, were full-time; indeed, part-time press officers were almost nonexistent in the Senate, and the number of House members who had staffers balancing press responsibilities with other chores was only a fraction of the number who had full-time press officers.

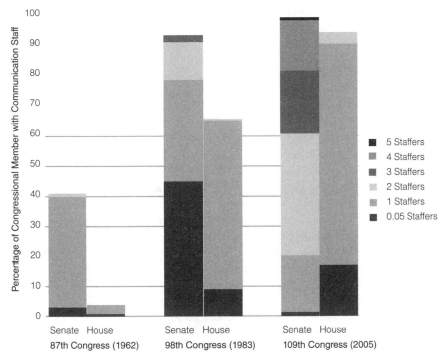

Calculated by authors from the *Congressional Staff Directory* 1962, 1983, 2005

Figure 4.1 Senate and House Communications staffers.

Figure 4.1 also shows an increase in the percentage of offices employing one or more such aides. This is most pronounced in the Senate, where almost half of the senators had more than one press person, with 15% employing three or more. Scholars document this growth in press officers, already seen in the 98th Congress, as coinciding with the dramatic increase in staffing resources made available to individual members offices during the 1970s just as the Congress was turning outward.[35] While such an explanation cannot be discounted when it comes to this initial increase, it adds little insofar as subsequent growth in press personnel is concerned. Indeed, in the years separating the 98th and 109th Congresses the total number of staffers allocated to members remained relatively constant. Occasionally, there were slight increases in numbers in those intervening years, yet even those were offset by a slight decline in totals in 1995, when Republicans assumed control of both houses of Congress and imposed modest funding cuts for staffing members' offices.[36] These marginal declines in budget allocations for office personnel, however, did little to dampen the upward trend in the institutionalization of press officers in members' staffing arrangements in either chamber, as Figure 4.1 shows.

Today, few senators and representatives are without someone designated to handle public relations responsibilities. Every Senate office and roughly 95% of the House offices of the 109th Congress had someone formally charged with press responsibilities. The number of aides with full-time press responsibilities also increased. This is most noticeable in the House. There the number of full-time press aides expanded by about a third. Although the percentage of individuals who balanced press responsibilities with other activities also increased in the House, that growth occurred as the number of offices without even a part-time press secretary sharply declined. Figure 4.1 also illustrates higher levels of density of press staffers within offices of the 109th Congress. This is, again, most pronounced in the Senate, though there has been a slight uptick in House numbers.

Most congressional committees also institutionalized the position of press secretary or communications director. But this did not come with the 1970s increases in Hill staffing. Dramatic growth in the overall number of staff personnel that appeared during the era of congressional reforms instead coincides with only a modest increase in communications staff assigned to House and Senate standing committees and subcommittees. *Directory* listings indicate that fewer than half the House's standing committees, and less than a third of the Senate's permanent committees had, at either the committee or subcommittee levels, on board someone specifically designated with a title—press secretary, communications director, and director of public affairs/public relations/public information—that clearly indicated some sort of public relations responsibilities. Of all of these, only the Senate Budget Committee showed signs of a more complex or institutionalized communications operation. *Directory* listings show it was the only standing committee in either chamber to have more than one formally designated press officer, and it was also the only such committee to have one or more staffers on both sides of the aisle. All of the remaining standing committees that had a press officer had only one such person on staff, and of those less than half were identified as serving either the majority or minority party.[37] The bottom line here is that even in the 98th Congress, a time when press aides had become very much a part of many members' staffs, only a very few committees had institutionalized public relations staffing to serve more overtly partisan ends.

By the 109th Congress, however, that had changed. Press operations were more pervasive, complex, and partisan on committee staffs. This was true for both chambers and both parties, though such aides were more often tied to House committees, and in both chambers, more frequently associated with the majority party. Listings for the 109th Congress show roughly 80% of the Senate's sixteen standing committee staffs and 95% of the House's twenty committee staffs had press officers, all of whom were attached to one party or the other. Republicans, who controlled both chambers, had press officers on 69% of standing committee staffs in the Senate and 95% of those in the House, while minority Democrats had at least one press officer on nearly two-thirds of the Senate's and three-fourths of the House's standing committees' staffs. The *Directory* shows the GOP as having two or more press staffers on more than a third of the Senate's panels and three-fourths of those in the House.

Interestingly, this increased presence and density of committee press personnel coincides with a lower total number of staffers allotted to congressional committees. Because Republicans slashed the size of committee staffs when they assumed control of Capitol Hill in 1995, the overall number of staffers working for committees in the 109th Congress was about a third smaller than what it had been in the 98th Congress, which actually had fewer press aides working for committees.[38] The critical point here is that even though committees have had to make do with fewer staff members overall, chairs and ranking members have in the face of these cutbacks increased the number of staff positions tasked with communications responsibilities, thus institutionalizing public relations in staffing arrangements and expanding the number of bases from which members and parties can carry out messaging activities.[39]

Communications personnel are now also an important part of contemporary congressional leaders' offices. Earlier we noted that tending to public relations became very much a part of leadership activities, especially as parties became more ideologically opposed and as presidents like Reagan routinely adopted proactive public strategies of leadership. This was, perhaps, best exemplified by Speaker Tip O'Neill, a consummate old style politician tutored by Rayburn. When Republicans captured the presidency and Senate in the 1980 election, O'Neill, as the head of the House Democratic majority, found himself cast as the opposition's spokesperson. Speaker O'Neill responded by enlisting the services of a former speechwriter from the Carter administration, Chris Matthews, to help him mount a more polished public response to the president's programmatic initiatives.[40]

But O'Neill was not the only one in the ranks of the leadership who had come to rely on the assistance of communications personnel. By 1983, most of the leaders in both chambers had one or two or, in one instance, three press aides assigned to either their leadership offices or personal staffs or both.[41] This stands in marked contrast to the relative absence of press aides associated with chamber and party leaders of the 87th Congress. Still, the press operations presided over by congressional leaders as little as twenty years ago generally pales in comparison to current leaders' robust communications staffing arrangements. Most likely much of this change can be attributed to the very visible position those at the helm of Congress now assume both as carriers of their parties' messages and as architects and coordinators of their parties' communications strategies.

Press staffing in the speaker's office grew from O'Neill's single aide, Matthews, to a whole communications division. In the 109th Congress, Speaker Dennis Hastert's (R-IL) office included a director of communications, a press secretary, a deputy press secretary, an assistant to the speaker for communications and outreach, and a press assistant. In addition, the speaker employed a press secretary on his personal office staff in Illinois. This substantial presence of press personnel is found elsewhere in the ranks of the House majority party leadership. Both Majority Leader Tom Delay (R-TX) and Majority Whip Roy Blunt (R-MO) had three communications people in their leadership offices, and Blunt also had one on his personal district staff.[42]

Similar patterns exist in leaders' offices on the other side of the aisle. Rep. Nancy Pelosi (D-CA), who was minority leader in the 109th Congress, had close to fifteen people listed as holding responsibilities related to communications activities. As we will discuss in greater detail in our next chapter, House Democrats tend to concentrate responsibility in their top leader, and the size and complexity of Pelosi's communications operations certainly attests to this. Rep. Steny Hoyer (D-MD), the minority whip, also employed a press staff slightly larger than that of his majority party counterpart.[43]

In the early twenty-first century, Senate leaders have also beefed up press staffing arrangements. On the Republican side in the 109th Congress, Majority Leader Bill Frist (R-TN) superintended a large, complex communications structure. In addition to having two press secretaries on his personal staff, Frist had a bevy of disparate communications specialists working for him out of the majority leader's office: communications director, deputy communications director, press secretary, and speechwriters.[44] His counterpart on the other side of the aisle, then Democratic Minority Leader and Conference Chair Harry Reid (D-NV), launched the Senate Democratic Communications Center shortly after he took over as his party's floor leader. This "aggressive operation" to "ensure that all Americans—from… [Reid's] rural hometown of Searchlight to the nation's big cities—know the values and principles for which Democrats stand" included roughly fifteen different staffers. During the 109th Congress, Reid's staff included a general staff director, several communications directors, a press secretary for Nevada, communications specialists assigned to working with Latino media outlets and the Internet, as well as additional support personnel.[45]

Changes in the press staffing arrangements of the two Senate whips are more modest. During the 109th Congress, GOP Majority Whip Sen. Mitch McConnell (R-KY) had only one press aide assigned to his office. His counterpart on the other side of the aisle, Sen. Richard Durbin (D-IL), had three press officers on board. These numbers were pretty much in line with the whips' press staffing operations in the 98th Congress.[46]

The CyberCongress

Institutionalization of Capitol Hill press secretaries or communications directors has also coincided with the emergence of online congressional offices. These venues are made possible and even amplified by many of the new information technologies—electronic mail, the Internet, and social media—transforming human interactions and fundamentally reshaping many of our social organizations' structures and processes. As a result, a creative synergy has taken place as this Congress, which was turned inside out nearly four decades ago, continues to adapt to outside forces.

Getting on the Information Highway

To say that the institution is adjusting to a new media age is not to suggest that lawmakers have proceeded to the information highway at breakneck speed. After all, members of Congress are cautious in the face of uncertainly, as suggested by even the safest incumbent's desire to build up big campaign war chests as he or she heads into an upcoming election. They recognize that change of any kind has the potential of altering the institution, upending careers, and reshaping the current distribution of power. Presented with departures from existing practices, even in matters of technology, members must first calculate the benefits and costs and ponder the possibility of unanticipated consequences. This situation perhaps explains many representatives' and senators' initial tardiness in adapting information technology to their daily routines and moving some of their operations online.[47]

In 1993, both chambers took their first steps into the information age and world of real-time communications when seven House members tested an e-mail program and Sen. Charles Robb (D-VA) established the first public e-mail address. Sen. Edward M. Kennedy (D-MA) joined these pioneers the following year when his office activated the first website for a member of Congress. Momentum picked up shortly after Republicans assumed control on the Hill in 1995. The institution moved beyond these incremental changes and turned to establishing the infrastructure and operating standards necessary to transform a predominantly "'paper based' institution" into one founded on real-time, electronic communications. The House of Representatives took an additional, highly visible step down that path the same year when it launched THOMAS, a web portal that promised to provide the public with immediate and easily accessible online access to congressional information and documents.[48]

Still, many members of Congress were skeptical about taking themselves and the institution on the information superhighway. Some neither grasped nor appreciated how the Internet could be profitably integrated in Hill activities. A few were even obtuse on the most basic matters of technology. Senator Patrick Leahy (D-VT), who earned the sobriquet "Cybersenator" for his technological acumen and efforts to nudge Capitol Hill into the information age, alluded to that problem when he joked that some of his colleagues still thought of a computer as "a not working television that won't give you CNN."[49] A survey of Congress in 2000 confirmed this perception; it reported that roughly one-fourth of the fifty lawmakers it had interviewed had never once been on the Web.[50]

Other lawmakers' initial reluctance to venture into cyberspace stemmed from different reasons. Some feared these new tools would lead to exponential increases in public correspondence, swamping their staffs, and overloading their circuits and equipment. "Somebody mad at us, somebody who thinks our vote depends on how many e-mails we get, they could bury our machines," Rep. Scott McInnis (R-CO) warned as Congress slogged through the process of setting up electronic mail service.[51] Even those eager to incorporate information systems in their legislative work recognized these technologies could impair deliberation. Rep. David Dreier (R-CA), who spearheaded the drive to take the House into cyberspace, later alluded to the reasons underpinning this uneasiness when he pondered the possibility of a "virtual Congress." "Technology," he acknowledged, "has been wonderfully applied to enhance the sharing of information and can even be used at a basic level to allow for argument and persuasion." Yet, he cautioned, "for all its possibilities, no technology exists that can fully reproduce the engagement and emotion that occurs during the face-to-face, interpersonal bargaining and sharing of ideas and passions that is at the core of the deliberative process in Congress," ultimately concluding that "its impact on the deliberative nature of the legislative process may in fact be detrimental."[52]

Some lawmakers who favored taking Congress online addressed some of these misgivings in 1996 when they established the Internet Caucus, a bipartisan group of tech-savvy members organized to familiarize colleagues with new information systems and the policy issues engendered by their growing presence in society. Shortly after its inception, the Internet Caucus tried to allay the fears of their less computer literate, dilatory colleagues and jump-start the process of bringing the institution into the new communications age. To that end, the caucus introduced a resolution exhorting Congress to "educate itself about the Internet and use the technology in personal, committee and leadership offices."[53]

But even with prodding from more cyberfriendly members, technological innovation did not come to the Hill overnight. A year after the Internet Caucus was formed, *Congressional Quarterly Weekly* reported lawmakers were still only "gingerly" moving "into the information age." [54] It took five years from the founding of the Internet Caucus before all senators had their own websites up and running. That same year, 2001, Congress reached another milestone when all members' offices were finally linked to an electronic mail delivery system. By the following year, roughly eight years after Sen. Kennedy launched the first site and six years after the Internet Caucus's founding, all personal, committee, and leadership offices had web pages.[55]

The Cyberoffice and Political Communications

Congress has come a long way since it first lumbered onto the information highway. Today's members, by all measures, are more comfortable with online communications activities. Many now routinely envisage their web page, as Rep. Xavier Becerra (D-CA) once described it, as an "extension" of their regular office.[56] At the same time, while today's members are probably more technologically deft and aware of how cybercommunications serve their interests, something that is reflected in the growth of the Internet Caucus, even today's Capitol Hill online office remains very much a work in progress. As is the case with the structure of members', committee chairs', and party leaders' regular office staffs, these virtual district offices vary considerably, both in content and technological sophistication.[57] We can only speculate as to why these differences exist. Some of these variations, especially for committees and congressional party officers, have been linked to differences between the parties as well as the prevailing distribution of power on Capitol Hill.[58] Others, perhaps, are more clearly rooted in the chambers themselves. Separate committees—the Senate Rules and Administration Committee and the House Administration Committee—oversee the implementation of informational technology systems within offices of their respective bodies, and the two chambers have had divergent rules governing what can appear on office websites.[59] Senators also have more office resources—

staff and money—to support and maintain online sites than their counterparts in the House, several of whom have had to contract out to private, third-party providers to design and maintain their web pages.[60] At the same time, some of these differences are a function of more than party ties, or being in the majority or the minority or even the effects of bicameralism. A few early studies, for instance, point to a relationship between electoral competitiveness of members' districts and the type of content they emphasize on their sites.[61] Anecdotal evidence also suggests that more recently elected members and members who represent more "wired" constituencies have more sophisticated sites.[62]

Yet what is probably most important for variations in virtual district offices are individual legislators' proclivities and goals. Dennis Johnson, the "principal investigator" for the Congress Online Project, a major research study carried out under the auspices of the Congressional Management Foundation (CMF), thus concluded: "Some offices are at the leading edge of online communications; others are barely aware of the possibilities and opportunities missed. Much depends on the attitude of Members of the Senate or House, filtered down to their senior communications staff."[63]

Although virtual district offices vary, congressional web pages are especially important for public relations activities, both for members and their parties.[64] Rep. David Dreier (R-CA) pointed to their public relations potential in an essay covering the House's transition to the information age. On the one hand, an operational, up-to-date Capitol Hill web page, he wrote, is an "around-the-clock *brochure*"; it highlights members and their "service." On the other, it

> plays an important part *promoting* the member's legislative activities and policy agenda. At this level, the member Web pages serve not only as a basic informational resource, but as a tool *advocating,* in the member's own words, their work. As the Internet continues to grow in usage, this unfiltered and member-controlled source of information will continue to grow in value as constituents, the press, and other people and organizations come to rely on it, and as members continue to come to terms with and appreciate its benefits and possibilities.[65]

As Dreier suggests, an obvious benefit of an online presence is the unmediated communications link it provides. It enables members to trumpet district service and legislative accomplishments, stake out policy positions, and build their image without having to depend on a more critical intermediary who determines *how* and *when* they will be covered. Thus, it provides lawmakers with greater control over focusing the attention of other actors and setting the premises from which those other actors reason, while giving members greater opportunities to manage the narratives they would like to construct about themselves and their careers.

The extent to which members use their online offices to shape how they present themselves and communicate directly and instantaneously with different publics, which include constituents, pressure groups, partisan activists, and even members of the press corps, is conveyed by the CMF in its occasional studies and published findings—*Gold Mouse Report*—on the state of congressional websites.[66] Its 2006 and 2007 reports suggest congressional web pages were strategically deployed to help lawmakers bolster their images and disseminate their partisan and programmatic messages. These analyses show that press releases were among the most common features posted on lawmakers' web pages. They were included on nearly 100% of congressional sites. The only other items appearing that often were biographical information postings and member photos. The 2007 *Report* also reveals that approximately three-fourths of all online offices posted material pertaining to legislation the member sponsored or cosponsored. This represented an increase of about one-third over the preceding year. The CMF also found that close to 40% of representatives' sites and slightly less than two-thirds of senators' web pages presented content specifically pertaining to state and local issues. Interestingly, the 2007 report shows that nearly all members in both chambers used online offices to discuss or take stances on national issues, a proportion almost double what it had been the year before. It also indicates that members commonly post speeches, statements, editorials, and news stories. The 2007 analysis found lawmakers' floor statements on roughly 69% of the House's, and 87% of the Senate's web pages. At the same time, CMF data show that the percentage of online offices with press releases eclipses, by rather healthy margins, the proportion of sites including more constituency-oriented features. In its 2007 analysis, for instance, CMF found that only 32% of the House's and 43% of the Senate's office web pages included specific information guiding constituents as to how they could communicate with their lawmakers. Somewhat higher proportions of sites contained material directing constituents on how to initiate action for casework (House 58%; Senate 60%) and forms requesting tours of Congress (House 51%; Senate 52%), though both fall well below the percentage of sites with news releases.[67]

Our own analysis of the 112th Congress's websites also suggests a substantial majority of lawmakers direct the timing of information made available to interested and relevant constituencies. We found, for instance, that 86% of individual House members' online sites, and 66% of the Senate's, include the option to subscribe to lawmakers' electronic newsletters or e-news releases. What is especially important in disseminating information to other media, interested constituencies, and other attentive elites, is the capacity to deliver that information (i.e., press releases, statements, editorials, and television and radio appearances) directly in real time. Here our analysis shows that roughly 80% of the House's and 60% of the Senate's individual web pages included links to a news feed service that provides subscribers with continually updated information.[68]

Stepping Up the Operation

While still very much a work in progress, online offices have become more robust and complex, and members have expanded avenues of communication, as many on the Hill have linked them with other new communications technologies. Especially noticeable here is the growing use of the "new new media"—blogs, YouTube, Facebook, Flikr, MySpace, Twitter, and podcasts—that appeared on the scene but a few short years ago.[69] Yet here again, representatives and senators have proceeded with caution. Nowhere is this clearer than when it comes to their use of web-based communications platforms to engage in the more impromptu, less-scripted forms of political communications, especially blogs or microblogs. Though weblogs have proliferated and taken on increased importance over the last several years, most on the Hill, as one reporter put it, have been "slow to catch on to [the] blogging phenomenon."[70] This is confirmed by the CMF studies, which reported that as late as 2007 only 10% of member sites featured any kind of regular political blog.[71]

Perhaps some of the early hesitancy to cross that technological divide can be attributed to lawmakers' lack of familiarity with these edgier forms of interactive communications and their concern about any sort of possible fallout they might engender. After all, the rather free-flowing writing and spontaneous exchange of ideas about events and issues just as they are unfolding, which are the hallmarks of the interactive forms of communications that constitute things like true blogs and microblogs, pose many risks that members, who are almost preternaturally averse to uncertainty, would prefer not to chance. "If you get ahead of the curve and jump on the issue and take a position before the issue has been defined, you might want to change it down the line," noted Rep. Verne Ehlers (R-MI). "And that's hard when you've been blogging about it."[72] At the same time, few on the Hill have the time to attend to blogs and other social media, and most are pressed to find personnel and resources necessary to monitor and maintain highly interactive, real-time forms of correspondence. It is very labor intensive to keep communications timely and meaningful and ensure that citizens' postings remain civil, and many lawmakers preside over office staffs that already feel pinched by having to deal with the high volume of e-mails that routinely swamp their offices.[73]

Still, many lawmakers recognize that their chances of realizing their collective and individual goals rest on exploiting opportunities to deliver a message and showcase their credentials. Rep. George Radanovich (R-CA) intimated as much shortly after his initial foray into the blogosphere. "We're always," he frankly admitted, "looking for ways to communicate with people."[74] And congressional use of these new communications technologies points in this direction. A growing number of today's lawmakers, for instance, now post their thoughts on an issue on their own web pages or on blog sites sponsored by outlets like *The Hill's Congress Blog*, the *Huffington Post*, *National Review Online*, *Real Clear Politics,* and a plethora of others spreading across the web. This goes beyond a "self-described 'Internet Geek'" like Rep. Mike Pence (R-IN) to include more seasoned, old guard legislators like Rep. John Conyers (D-MI) and Rep. Paul Gilmor (R-OH).[75] For some, blogs have, as a spokesperson for Speaker Dennis Hastert (R-IL) once noted, emerged as a sort of "new talk radio" of our times.[76] Indeed, Antoinette Pole has found that the number of members of Congress who blog, while still relatively small, often use this venue to "engage in position taking."[77] Some members, meanwhile, enlist blogs as venues of real-time communications to solicit information from their constituents as they go about the business of legislating. Senate Majority Whip Richard Durbin (D-IL), for example, has experimented with interactive blogs to gather information from concerned citizens and attentive interests in drafting bills for congressional consideration.[78]

Other signs that members are trying to ratchet up their use of new social communications platforms also abound. The House GOP, for example, established a New Media Caucus in 2008. The following year, with then House Minority Leader John Boehner (R-OH) declaring that "social media platforms like YouTube, Facebook and Twitter have become an indispensable component of House Republicans' efforts to communicate our better solutions to the American people," the New Media Caucus activated its own website.[79] In May 2010, House Democrats followed suit and created their own New Media Working Group, giving both House party caucuses charged with responsibilities for introducing representatives to, and establishing "best practices" for, applying social media in their work.[80] Some anecdotal evidence also suggests a growing presence of social media in lawmakers' offices. House Republicans, for instance, considered their party's use of social media important enough to warrant issuing a press release from the minority leader's office boasting of studies that showed their "unmatched ability to connect with the American people" through the use of new social media like Twitter and YouTube.[81] They have even held contests and awarded prizes to those Conference members who secured the largest increases in the number of "social media fans"[82] By the same token, popular accounts highlight Congress's "new love affair with Twitter," while DC communications professionals allude to what they see as congressional offices' growing interest in hiring staffers specifically skilled in many of the newer digital technologies.[83]

Yet perhaps the most telling confirmation that representatives and senators no longer conceive of Twitter, Facebook, and YouTube as exotic forums is the healthy and ever-expanding number of Hill offices employing them. Just in the last few years, two hubs, "TweetCongress" and "Congress on Facebook," were created to provide direct access to, and information on, members who deploy these two social networking media. At the same time, Congress eased restrictions on linking to third party websites, thus paving the way for members to post videos on YouTube.[84]

The Congressional Research Service (CRS) found that near the end of the first year of the 111th Congress close to 40% of the combined membership had joined the ranks of those who tweet. CRS data also showed that in a two month time frame (August 1–September 30, 2009) they posted over seven thousand tweets.[85] Our own analysis of congressional websites conducted in the first year of the 112th Congress points to growing interest in this social networking platform. We found that roughly 65% of the lawmakers made it possible through their online offices to sign up to follow them on Twitter.

Facebook is even more of a staple in lawmakers' communications repertoire. Facebook officials, for instance, found that well over half of all members of the 111th Congress had their own Facebook pages.[86] And, as is the case with Twitter, the number of lawmakers who use this medium continues to climb, as our analysis of representatives' and senators' websites of the 112th Congress suggests. We found that more than three-fourths of the lawmakers have links to their own Facebook page through their online offices.

Just as Twitter and Facebook have become more pervasive in lawmakers' communications activities, so has YouTube. In the first days of the 111th Congress, both the House and Senate launched new ventures with YouTube to post gateway web pages—Househub and Senatehub—that make it possible for every member to set up his or her own video channel, creating a sort of "miniature C-SPAN studio inside of their office."[87] By the middle of the second year of that Congress, close to 80% of Hill offices had set up their own YouTube pages that could be accessed through the Senate and House YouTube hubs.[88] Less than a year later in the 112th Congress, we found that the percentage of congressional offices with YouTube pages had climbed to over 93%.

The full impact of the Hill's use of these new technologies, of course, remains to be seen, but there are reasons to believe that they will only assume greater importance in lawmakers' communications operations. Social media, after all, are becoming increasingly popular. Current Pew data indicate that 75% of American adults use the Internet, and of those close to half (47%) use a social networking site like Facebook and nearly one-fifth (19%) use Twitter or some other instant messaging service.[89] These expanding audiences will continue to provide incentives for members of Congress to enlist these new forums. Meanwhile, a number of high-profile politicians have already shown that these social media can be profitably applied to communicate with folks and raise funds as they campaign for office, something President Barack Obama demonstrated in his successful 2008 campaign for the White House.[90] Just as the previous generation of senators and representatives incorporated television into their professional lives, contemporary lawmakers are likely to expand their use of social media as they become more familiar with them and as they watch the president profitably engage these venues. Majority Leader Sen. Harry Reid (D-NV), for instance, marked the 75th anniversary of FDR's first fireside chat by saturating the country with a podcast blasting the GOP on its economic policy while House Minority Leader John Boehner (R-OH) used his own channel on YouTube to make his party's case against President Barack Obama's stimulus package that was winding its way through the House in the first weeks of the 111th Congress in 2009.[91]

Stepping Up the Operation

While important in itself, what makes the virtual district office and accompanying social media especially powerful communications instruments in today's Congress are the leverage they afford members in integrating publicity on Hill activities. Although the online office, for example, provides lawmakers with a direct, "unfiltered" channel of instantaneous communication, the "Internet audience" is, as Stephen Franzitch reminds us, "more *intentional*" than what we find with other media. Individuals looking for information on the web, after all, usually have something fairly specific in mind, beginning from the moment they plug the terms of their query into a search engine.[92] The number of citizens or even representatives of key pressure groups who consciously friend members of Congress, peruse their web pages, or who sign up to receive the occasional e-mail, electronic newsletter, or tweet from their representative or senator, while certainly growing, is still small. And in many instances their interests are also relatively narrow.[93]

Members interested in shaping policy outcomes and moving up the ranks of power within their chamber or even in going on to higher office must therefore couple unmediated public appeals with a pitch that reaches a larger, more variegated audience. They need to attract the attention of colleagues, other government actors, and the increasingly complex and expanding array of interests found in today's Washington policy communities. Occasionally, they must gin up support among partisan activists or even national constituencies on behalf of their proposals. This, in turn, requires the attention of audiences made available by the legacy media— radio, television, and newsprint outlets.[94] These more mainstream vehicles, in both traditional formats and corresponding web pages, cast a wider net. Their audiences are also perhaps more "inadvertent" or less "intentional" than those searching the Internet, putting them in a position "to be enticed by clever presentation and grabber headlines."[95]

Getting the attention of more established news organizations, and even completely online digital news outlets and blogs, not only extends the scope of lawmakers' communications, but it also enhances the credibility of their public appeals. Daniel Lipinski and Gregory Neddenriep argue that the putative independence of more established media forums provides members with an opportunity to impart a kind of "legitimacy" to congressional publicity that they "cannot achieve through unmediated self-promotion." What this means is that even in a new media age members cannot ignore the older media. It is here, Lipinski and Neddenriep suggest, that online offices and new social media technologies come in handy. By constructing "media friendly" websites, members can actually develop platforms from which they "court" the more established media's attention.[96] Then, to complete the circle, they can post coverage received from the legacy media on these newer platforms.

Today's news world invites lawmakers to use their sites and linked social media networks to leverage greater, and possibly more favorable attention from the traditional venues like newspapers, radio and television, and the news and political sites proliferating on the Internet. Staffing cutbacks in news divisions and the increasing demands of a hurried, breaking-news cycle have prompted folks employed in more established media to incorporate the Internet in their work.[97] Many of them now use the Internet for communications and for carrying out their investigations. Pressures to cross over into the world of "hybrid journalism," which have grown more intense as news organizations have evolved toward blending different platforms in their move to "real-time journalism," have reinforced this turn to the Internet. Many reporters working for the legacy media contribute to their news organizations' websites. There they stream video clips, deliver podcasts, and respond to the continuous news cycle by intermittently updating stories as they unfold over the course of the day. A growing number even blog, posting less formal, instantaneous comments on breaking news stories and dissecting important political developments.[98]

The general upshot is that the Internet has become an integral part of journalists' work, something that recent large-scale surveys of newsprint reporters confirm. One recent study showed that close to 90% of the journalists surveyed acknowledged they regularly use the Internet for research or reference.[99] Another showed a slightly lower, though still substantially large proportion of reporters at small weekly and daily papers in rural communities routinely use it in their work.[100]

Other findings highlight congressional websites' value to news organizations. A 2003 CMF survey of national and local political reporters located in or near the District found that almost all of the respondents (N=31) visited lawmakers' websites in covering Hill activities, with many indicating that they used online offices on a regular basis.[101] This does not mean that journalists are ignoring more traditional ways of practicing their craft. Indeed, reporters interviewed by CMF researchers indicated that they supplemented information taken from websites with other material, including one-on-one interviews with senators and representatives and their communications staffers. Still, these sites do provide real-time snapshots of members, including information on their backgrounds, constituencies, district service, committee work, legislative interests, stances on issues and policies, and appearances in the news, and for reporters working under constraints imposed by shrinking resources and a rapidly changing 24/7 news cycle, these are valuable and readily accessible bits of data they can quickly access to flesh out their narratives.[102]

Thus, for many members of Congress the online office is a "good medium" to attract attention and quite possibly even shape how they are covered by other news media.[103] And perhaps equally important, members can concomitantly use their presence in older, more mainstream forums to enrich what they post in their online office and disseminate through accompanying social media. After all, the old and "new new media," Paul Levinson writes, are in a "symbiotic or mutually catalytic relationship."[104] Newer media can be used to gain older, more established providers' interest, and the results of that attention, which include things like write-ups and editorials in newspapers and magazines and interviews on radio, cable television, or network shows, can in turn be included in online office press releases or blogs, tweeted to followers, posted on Facebook, or linked to YouTube sites in ways that enable members to enhance their stature and project and amplify their messages.[105]

Rep. Todd Tiahrt (R-KS) provides a textbook example of how members of Congress have employed their virtual office in conjunction with other media to gain public attention and shape coverage on a policy directly important to constituents. This happened as he endeavored to scuttle an Air Force deal that awarded a $40 billion, fifteen-year contract to build its line of aerial refueling tankers to Northrop-Grumman and the European Aeronautic Defence and Space Co. (EADS) instead of Boeing. Tiahrt, along with two Kansas senators, Sam Brownback (R-KS) and Pat Roberts (R-KS), and several members of the Washington state congressional delegation, mounted a vigorous public relations offensive to call into question the Air Force's decision to rebuff Boeing's bid. They argued that it promised to be a major windfall for a foreign defense contractor, one that would undermine U.S. security interests and cost several thousand American workers their jobs, many of which were in Kansas. Tiahrt used his virtual office to carry video clips that showed him denouncing the deal on the House floor and in other media outlets. He also posted a *Tankers blog* to stir up opposition to the administration's decision and to attract attention to his cause. He even engaged in a bit of a publicity stunt by including an online petition opposing the deal on his site, inviting those who visited his virtual office to register their concerns on outsourcing this military contract.[106] Local media took notice of Tiahrt's frenzied public activity and gimmickry. So did Lou Dobbs, the brash, self-proclaimed populist defender of the American middle class, whose harangues on U.S. immigration and trade policies and corporate practices had earned him sizable media market shares for his radio broadcasts and cable television show. Dobbs directed his audiences to Tiahrt's petition. He also encouraged them to visit Tiahrt's website to learn more about the deal.[107] Within but a few days Tiahrt's site had an astounding 250,000 hits. Dobbs subsequently invited Tiahrt to appear on his popular cable television show *Lou Dobbs Tonight* on CNN. He once again directed his viewers to Tiahrt's virtual office to read about the deal and sign the petition, and he posted a link to Tiahrt's congressional Internet site on his show's web page. Tiahrt followed up his appearance on *Lou Dobbs Tonight* with an interview on the tanker decision on the high-profile talk radio show hosted by Michael Savage. Tiahrt subsequently posted through Facebook and YouTube links to the video clips of these more high profile media appearances in which he lashed out at the deal, as he continued his public relations crusade.[108]

While the direct effects of Tiahrt's actions are not fully clear, the public relations campaign that he and members from other affected regions mounted did increase the visibility of the issue. Such actions also most likely helped build pressure within Congress to broach the idea of getting the Pentagon to split the contract between Boeing and its competitor, the Northrop-Grumman and EADS alliance.[109]

Conclusion

Members and their parties have adjusted resources as their incentives to use media to get out their messages have increased, and the congressional press secretariat has swelled as a result. Today, most representatives have at least one communications person on board, and a growing number of senators employ two, three, or even more press aides. By the same token, communications specialists on committee staffs, once quite hard to come by, are now more routinely found on both sides of the aisle, while offices of party leaders on both sides of the aisle and in both chambers have expanded to include rather formidable communications divisions.

At the same time, online offices are now ubiquitous on the Hill, and an increasing number of lawmakers have linked these with newer and edgier social communications technologies to advance their publicity aims. And given what we have seen regarding the Internet's role in other facets of life, including political campaigns and elections, we can only surmise that congressional sites and web-based social media will take on increasing importance in members' and parties' communication activities.

These changes, combined with the rise of a more fragmented, dynamic media and around-the-clock news coverage, have augmented members' abilities to take their cases beyond Capitol Hill chamber walls. One commentator summed it up this way: "Forget C-SPAN gasbaggery or starchy pronouncements in *The New York Times*. Today's savvy Hill denizens…are using tools like Twitter, YouTube, Facebook, the celeb obsessed TMZ.com, and 'The Colbert Report' to give America a peek at what its elected officials are really like. At the rate things are going, even the staunchest fans of transparency in government might soon have had enough."[110] While that perhaps overstates the case, there is no question that these developments, which have given more individuals more access and more opportunities to wage their own public relations battles through the media, have most certainly magnified the collective action problem of parties interested in getting out coherent messages that clarify and shore up their "brands."

Congressional parties, however, have not stood pat. They have tried to rein in members and harness the forces of that new media environment in ways that enable them to disseminate more consistent and calibrated messages. Just as they have maneuvered around other collective action problems, the parties have adapted by devising structures, pursuing strategies, and deploying resources to help them mount public relations offensives that advance their policy agendas and improve the marketability of their brands.

5 The Parties' Public Relations Response
Marketing the "Brand"

Republicans found little to rejoice about as final tallies of the special run-off election for the open seat in Mississippi's first congressional district came in during the evening of May 13, 2008. Returns indicated that Travis Childers (D-MS), the Democratic candidate, had handily vanquished his GOP opponent, Greg Davis, a highly respected, well-financed contender. The outcome left many Republicans "shellshocked."[1] They had dominated that district since the popular conservative Democrat, Rep. Jamie Whitten (D-MS), retired in 1995. Perhaps even more disturbing, this decisive rejection at the polls represented the third straight loss dealt to a House GOP candidate in a special election in less than a year. This series of defeats included the turnover of a safe seat in Louisiana and an especially stinging loss of the seat once held by the former Speaker of the House of Representatives, Rep. Dennis Hastert (R-IL).[2]

In the days following Childers's victory, influential figures within GOP congressional delegations vented their frustrations and expressed their concerns about their party's grim prospects in the upcoming 2008 election. Some blamed their leaders for ignoring problems that had already appeared on the horizon when they lost control of Congress in the 2006 midterm election. Others groused that too many high-profile GOP scandals had undermined public confidence in their party. Quite a few also complained that they were tied to an unpopular war, and some even openly grumbled that they were yoked to a feckless president whose favorable ratings in the polls barely registered above 30%, among the lowest ever recorded for a sitting president. Many acknowledged they had tarnished their own public image, confessing they had sloughed off fiscal responsibility by pursuing power rather than reform. Here they pointed to instances in which they exacerbated government waste and bloat by proliferating earmarks and enacting costly welfare state programs such as the one that provided senior citizens with prescription drug coverage.[3]

Rep. Thomas Davis (R-VA) diagnosed the GOP's dismal condition in a memorandum to party leaders and warned them to expect the kind of calamitous results not witnessed since the election of 1974, when a tidal wave of discontent with the GOP touched off by the Watergate scandal engulfed the country and added to their opponents' solid control of the Hill by sweeping forty-nine additional Democrats into the House and three into the Senate. The reason for his unalloyed pessimism, Davis frankly explained, is that "the Republican brand is in the trash can.... If we were a dog food, they would take us off the shelf."[4] Others in the GOP concurred.[5]

Prescriptions for this "election anxiety disorder" varied.[6] Some Republicans counseled colleagues facing especially tough races to localize their elections. A growing number, however, concluded that the GOP needed to recuperate its national "brand." They argued that as a party Republicans needed first, to clarify what they stood for, and then make good on, and claim credit for, what they promised to deliver.[7] Speaking to reporters in the wake of the Mississippi election, National Republican Congressional Committee (NRCC) Chair Rep. Tom Cole (R-OK) voiced this sentiment: "What we've got right now is a deficiency in our message and a loss of confidence by the American people to do what we say we're going to do.... When you lost three of these in a row, you have to get beyond campaign tactics and take a long hard look: Is there something wrong with your product?"[8]

GOP rumblings about honing and delivering an updated and more appealing message had been percolating about the Beltway since the party lost the Hill.[9] More than a handful of Republican lawmakers recognized that the White House could not resuscitate public confidence in their party. Bush was well along into lame duck status, and to many he was the source of their difficulties. Some even harbored suspicions that when it came to messaging he would bungle the job. "When Bush tries to articulate a vision," Rep. Davis confessed, "he will butcher the Gettysburg Address."[10] Many members argued instead that they needed to take up the call and aggressively make the public case for a proactive agenda that resonated with a disenchanted American citizenry. As Sen. Lamar Alexander (R-TN), chair of the Senate Republican Conference, explained, "[w]e have to remind voters of who we are, what we're going to do about real problems like gas prices and health care and why what our opponents want to do is wrong. We stay on offense."[11]

Republican introspection that followed this series of special election setbacks underscores the extent to which parties are concerned with maintaining the quality of their brands. Partisan trademarks constitute an important part of electoral politicking in this more partisan and polarized era; they provide salient information or signposts to attentive interests, campaign contributors and a politically active electorate. A string of losses in places where a party once held a comfortable electoral cushion signifies that a brand, once popular, has become shopworn. Revivifying a political brand name, however, demands more than coming up with catchy slogans and phrases and identifying themes that knot together a batch of policies or governmental programs. "Branding" instead requires what *New York Times* columnist David Brooks described as the "location and arousal of affection."[12] Seen from the perspective of politicians, benefits must be promised, goods need to be delivered, and credit has to be claimed. Successful political branding operations therefore demand that lawmakers market their partisan and programmatic wares to concerned constituencies and a politically interested public and then link those brands, in the minds of their followers and potential supporters, to successful policy consequences.[13] Thus, to have their desired effects, political brands need to be popularized.

Contemporary representatives and senators certainly have the wherewithal to help drive the sort of public relations campaigns required to shore up and popularize their parties' trademarks. But that is only part of the more complex tale of Congress's "outward" turn. More ideologically coherent and polarized congressional parties and the rise of a more diverse, competitive, considerably more dynamic, and arguably more partisan news world have also shaped public relations activities on the Hill. Because of these contextual developments, congressional parties have greater incentives to choreograph publicity activities. The parties can clarify for the different consumers of political information what it is that they are offering by disseminating consistent messages through a multitude of diverse news forums, and they can use a coordinated message operation to prompt their followers and other concerned actors to mobilize on their behalf during critical stages of the legislative process. Moreover, by claiming credit for their accomplishments and by countering their opponents' assertions, they are able to refurbish their public image, reinforce brand loyalties, and improve rank-and-file members' chances of securing their preferences and realizing their political ambitions.

The need to provide consistent, unambiguous, and strategically timed messages across an ever-expanding number of forums, however, presents a monumental collective action problem.[14] Congressional parties, as we have noted earlier, must get members to go out in the public realm to carry their messages to relevant audiences, and they must tie those campaigns to discrete legislative actions like a key vote, committee hearing, or filibuster, all the while choreographing their public responses with actions taken by other branches of government as well as events unfolding on the electoral calendar. Finally, they must keep members reading from the same script when it comes to their collective policy preferences and goals, something that becomes more difficult as individual lawmakers gain more resources and opportunities to make their cases in public.

Today's congressional parties have ways of handling collective action challenges. They have improved their chances for programmatic and electoral success by developing institutional and leadership strategies that promote greater coordination, predictability, and control in the legislative process.[15] In recent years, they have likewise tried to negotiate the collective action problem of getting out consistent, forceful messages, adapting structures and resources in ways that help them synchronize communications operations and push their partisan messages with greater unity and clarity.[16]

Challenges of Getting Out the Party Message

Presidential public relations strategies are prototypical of the public tactics employed by others in today's political arena.[17] Still, although those at the other end of Pennsylvania Avenue have followed the president's lead and pursued a more public and media-driven approach, important differences distinguish the two sides. Those differences, in turn, throw into bold relief challenges congressional parties confront and must negotiate as they try to popularize their brands.

The Presidential Advantage

While presidents no longer command the kind of public presence they did only a few decades ago, they are still unrivaled in their ability to attract news providers' attention.[18] News organizations' routines and preferred narratives direct the media to the chief executive for many reasons, which most certainly include the growth of the administrative state, the continued accretion of executive power, an expanded White House apparatus, and the special roles assigned to the president in foreign affairs, national defense, and as head of state. "In drama, magnitude and finality," as Supreme Court Justice Robert Jackson once wrote, "his [the president's] decisions so far overshadow any others that, almost alone, he fills the public eye and ear."[19] Also implicated in the greater news visibility of presidents are the personalization of the office and the tendency of the media to develop story lines that accentuate conflict, personalities, and high drama, which the presidency easily supplies.[20] Hence, "instead of having to seek out news opportunities, presidents have the news come to them."[21] Though clearly an advantage, this can also be a mixed blessing, for more expansive coverage oftentimes brings with it greater public attention to political machinations, personal and policy conflicts, and administration scandals.[22]

Presidents also have greater institutional capacities for getting out coherent messages. That is not to say that presidents do not have to deal with an airing of dissonant views, since even in the most disciplined administration some high placed executive branch official or political surrogate will periodically wander off message and muddle the White House's public position. Indeed, just as President George W. Bush was making the rounds arguing for fiscal restraint in the months leading up to the invasion of Iraq, White House economic advisor Lawrence Lindsey left the reservation and upstaged the administration by publicly highlighting the huge costs that such a war would entail.[23] Nonetheless, contemporary presidents have considerable leverage as they wage their public relations campaigns. First, they have on tap a burgeoning bureaucracy to help them manage news-making activities. Central to this structure is the White House Office of Communications. Created during the first year of the Nixon presidency (1969), it plots the administration's communications strategy and choreographs its messages. This White House communications bureaucracy enables the administration to gain some measure of control over news-making efforts in relevant departments or offices so as to increase the chances that everyone speaking for the White House is reading, with almost monotonous regularity, from the same script at the right time and in the appropriate venues.[24] The promise inherent in such communications support systems has certainly not been lost on recent presidents. President George W. Bush used these institutional levers to tighten his grip over executive branch communications. As George Edwards recounted, the Bush White House brought discipline to its message operations by screening departments' selections for publicity officers and by exercising strict control over their press releases.[25]

Presidents can also fire high-placed political officials who go off message, a fate eventually dealt to Lindsey for his ill-timed, unsanctioned comments on the anticipated costs of the Iraq war and one shared on the same day by Secretary of Treasury Paul O'Neill, a somewhat disgruntled figure who had earned the administration's distrust for contradicting some of its most cherished themes on behalf of tax cuts.[26] Through a strategic use of this unilateral authority presidents can therefore discourage others from wandering too far from preferred story lines.

The Congressional Challenge

Congressional parties have a steeper hill to climb. Today's more homogenous and polarized congressional parties encourage their leaders to mount public campaigns on behalf of collective partisan goals, and leaders have responded by working the press corps and appearing on the talk show circuit.[27] Still, they attract only a fraction of the breadth and volume of news attention accorded the White House, those rare instances when someone like Speaker Newt Gingrich (R-GA) comes along and manages to rival the president notwithstanding.[28] So partisans on the Hill have adapted; they have compensated for their leaders' smaller public presence by evolving strategies to get more of them reading from the same script at the same time in the public realm. "We're relying on the philosophy of strength in numbers," as a Democratic spokesperson put it. "We have a better chance of being heard when we do these things together."[29] And evidence gathered so far suggests that there is more than a kernel of truth in that sentiment. Patrick Sellers, for instance, found a clear and consistent message carried by a "large number of legislators" does increase the volume of media attention.[30]

Besides piquing the interest of the media, getting out a coherent message through the ranks yields other benefits. First, it enables a party to distinguish itself from its opposition. Second, it reassures and activates the party's base of supporters. Finally, it provides, as Rep. Nancy Pelosi (D-CA) put it, "the inspiration" to those who fill the party coffers.[31] Yet cohesion in disseminating a party message or publicly promoting the brand is frequently hard to come by, especially when you have five-hundred and thirty-five politically ambitious members supported by their own communications operations encountering an ever-growing number of around-the-clock venues through which they can disseminate their views.

Bicameralism and separation of powers further complicate matters. First, partisans in one body of Congress must link their communications efforts with those of their counterparts in the other. Failure to orchestrate their political communications leads to incoherent messages and sends mixed signals to the public and concerned interests; it also produces results where the party in one chamber steps on its counterpart's message. Senate Majority Leader Bill Frist (R-TN), for instance, publicly endorsed expanding the stem cell research program just as the House GOP launched its public relations blitz on behalf of its transportation and energy policies. Frist's statement made a big news splash, but it effectively buried the House GOP's preferred story line.[32] Members on the Hill whose party controls the White House must at the same time finesse the difficulties of harmonizing their publicity efforts with the ones followed at the other end of Pennsylvania Avenue. One challenge they must address is timing; they need to avoid being blindsided by the president, who both garners considerable media attention and bears a good chunk of the responsibility for communicating the party's message. When a party controls both the White House and the Congress it must also surmount interbranch differences in the content of messages if it is to send clear, reinforcing signals to its constituents and the electorate, with respect to both its partisan message and its overall record of achievements.[33]

A significant dilemma arises for congressional parties on both sides of the aisle when it is necessary to get out consistent partisan statements within a context where power is divided between different institutions of government and where many of the principals involved have the interest, means, and opportunity to take their case to the public. Tim Groeling and Samuel Kernell describe this collective action problem as the "potential Achilles' heel of party action." Given the limits of party control of "political talk" and the expanding opportunities for lawmakers to speak with the press, the "temptation for members to defect" from the party's message, they note, is just "too great."[34] Yet apart from being able to withhold a few perquisites, parties have little wherewithal to contain deviations in message. They certainly cannot bounce members who sound discordant voices; nor can they jettison those who prefer to stay clear of the public spotlight. Instead, they try to negotiate their collective action dilemma by evolving institutions and operations that direct members' activities in the public realm and limit dissonance in their public communications. Many of the strategies they pursue are primarily designed to make it easier for lawmakers to participate in communications activities and appeal to rank-and-file members' interests in being involved and empowered.[35]

Congressional Message Operation: Finding Ways to Hook Up

Parties in both chambers have created "communications enterprises" to help them plan, coordinate, and manage their public relations efforts.[36] These disparate communications enterprises have similar incentives and goals and follow many of the same strategies, but they also bear the marks of their respective political and institutional contexts and the historical events that shaped them. The structures and workings of these enterprises and the interest in maintaining them are especially affected by the distribution of power. In particular, it is quite common for those without any institutional hold on power to be the most preoccupied with building up their congressional communications machinery.

Directing House Communications: The Nerve Centers of Partisan Message Operations

Today's party leaders are the core of congressional communications enterprises. They shoulder many of the responsibilities for developing, coordinating, and even delivering their party's messages.[37] As the Hill's communications operations have grown more important and complex, requiring more time and attention because of proliferating media venues and a 24/7 news world, House GOP and Democratic parties have concentrated authority over publicity activities. For both congressional parties, this adaptation came into focus as they found themselves in the minority struggling to shape outcomes in one of the few ways available to them in the majority rule institution that they inhabit, that is, by mounting outside appeals to attract supporters to their side.

It is true, of course, that all House GOP leaders are to one degree or another involved in designing and managing their party's public relations activities. After they lost the House in the 2006 election, then Minority Leader John Boehner (R-OH), for instance, brought together a "core group of members" and folks from a few issue groups to rebrand the party and come up with a strategy for getting that across to the American public.[38] The House Republican Policy Committee likewise serves as a forum through which leaders work with members to enunciate programmatic initiatives and policy statements.[39] By the same token, the National Republican Congressional Campaign Committee (NRCCC) frequently touches upon public relations activities in trying to advance the electoral fortunes of the party, as it did when, in the months leading up to the 2010 midterm elections, it joined with its counterpart in the Senate to mount a publicity campaign gauged to turn popular sentiment against the major health reform package signed into law by President Barack Obama in March, 2010.[40] Still, while many in the upper echelons of the party are at various stages involved in developing and sharpening messages, plotting strategies, and actually promoting the brand, the party's Conference is the core of House Republicans' communications enterprise.

The Conference's emergence as an institutional support and control center of the House Republicans' public relations operations is, at least in part, traceable to the party's electoral failures in the post-World War II era. Having lost every election since 1952, the House GOP had by the 1980s become the "permanent minority" on the Hill.[41] House GOP frustration that grew out of this protracted minority status was further exacerbated, beginning in the mid-1980s, as the parties started becoming more ideologically monolithic and polarized. This left House Republicans more united in their opposition; it also put Democratic leaders under increasing pressure from their party members to employ a more partisan, heavy-handed use of rules and procedures to shut down Republican opponents. As House GOP disenchantment and anger mounted, a large contingent within the rank-and-file pushed their Conference to take up activities that would help them win a majority. This tipped the balance of the Conference toward an orientation that was more "external" than its counterpart across the aisle, the Democratic Caucus.[42]

The Conference's outward focus became clear when Rep. Richard Armey (R-TX) took the reins as Conference chair in December of 1992. He quickly established a "rapid response truth squad" to mount a vigorous public counteroffensive to legislative initiatives introduced by President Bill Clinton during the first two years of his administration.[43] After the GOP seized full control of the Congress in 1995, the Conference chair assumed primary responsibility for superintending

House Republicans' public relations efforts.[44] Current roles include serving as "the spokesman for the Republicans in the House," being "in charge of coordinating media strategy," and making sure that members have the resources necessary to communicate with "their constituents."[45] Today, these responsibilities figure into House GOP members' calculations as to who is best equipped to fill the slot as their Conference chair. Indeed, one of the principal reasons Rep. Mike Pence (R-IN) was selected in late 2008 to succeed Rep. Adam Putnam (R-FL) was that in the judgment of many of his colleagues he was especially well-prepared for the task of directing the party's communications campaigns.[46] Similar reasons were at work in enabling Rep. Jeb Hensarling (R-TX) to beat back a challenge from the more flamboyant Rep. Michelle Bachmann (R-MN) to snare the Conference chair slot when Pence decided, shortly before the start of the 112th Congress, not to seek another term as chair. Hensarling built up support early on because, as one GOP aide put it, he could be effective in getting out the party message "without setting his hair on fire."[47]

The Conference's press staffing operations grew in size and complexity as it assumed an outward tilt. In the early 1980s, shortly after the reforms had run their course, and just as Congress commenced turning outward, the Conference chair of the 98th Congress, Rep. Jack Kemp (R-NY), employed but a single press aide. And that aide was on his personal, not the Conference staff.[48] The Conference's bureaucracy has since swelled. By the start of the 109th Congress, its staff of slightly more than twenty people included, among others, five communications directors or press aides, a speech writer, a managing editor for the conference web page, and a floor debate coordinator. The number of folks officially designated as communications directors or press secretaries was on a par with the number employed for communications by then Speaker Hastert.[49] The size of the staff declined slightly at the start of the 110th Congress, when Republicans once again assumed minority status. Since then, the Conference staff's overall size, and the number of aides directly involved in communications activities, have decreased somewhat and stabilized, though Pence subsequently added staffers tasked to deal with new media and minority outreach.[50]

House Democrats in recent years have tied control over communications more closely with rank in the congressional party hierarchy. When Rep. Richard Gephardt (D-MO) stepped in as Minority Leader in 1995 after Democrats lost control of the House for the first time in forty years, he moved to concentrate power in his office. This included assuming greater responsibilities for coordinating the party's message operation and controlling its communications resources.[51] Since then, the party has continued to vest most authority for superintending public relations activities in the top leader, who is the speaker if they are in the majority and the minority leader if they are not. This assignment of duties helps explain, in part, the sizable press staffing operation that has served Rep. Nancy Pelosi (D-CA) during her tenure as both Minority Leader and Speaker. During Pelosi's tenure as Speaker in the 110th and 111th Congresses, for instance, slightly more than a fifth of the over fifty different part-time and full-time positions in her office carried titles showing responsibilities for dealing with media and message operations, including providing media assistance and public relations guidance to members.[52]

Pelosi certainly expanded her office's communications authority, but she also delegated some tasks associated with messaging to others in the House Democratic hierarchy. At the start of the 110th Congress, for instance, then Speaker Pelosi assigned responsibilities for agenda building to Rep. George Miller (D-CA), who took over as one of the cochairs of the Democratic Policy Committee, which falls under the Democratic Steering and Policy Committee that is chaired by Pelosi. She also ceded some public relations turf to Rep. Rahm Emanuel (D-IL) during his stint as chair of the Democratic Caucus in the 110th Congress. This came as part of a deal she cut to dissuade Emanuel from mounting what could have been a bruising challenge to derail Rep. James Clyburn's (D-SC) bid to become majority whip after the previous occupant of the office, Rep. Steny Hoyer (D-MD), was elected majority leader.[53] In addition, she elevated Rep. Chris Van Hollen (D-MD), chair of the Democratic Congressional Campaign Committee (DCCC), to a position as assistant to the Speaker at the beginning of the 111th Congress. Because the DCCC, like its counterpart across the aisle, the NRCC, frequently lends a hand in support of partisan communications, this move at the time forged a stronger institutional connection between message operations undertaken on behalf of policy with those pursued to make electoral gains.[54]

While both parties vest someone with the charge of working out, coordinating, and directing administrative support to their communications activities, in practice those lines of authority are not always upheld. Most in the ranks of the congressional leadership, after all, are from time to time expected to take the lead in advancing their parties' brands, either by developing messages and strategies or by directly getting out themselves. Much that goes on in political communications must, as we have already noted, be linked with what happens in committees or on the floor. These are spheres of activities that more or less fall within the purview of different members of the party hierarchy as well as committee chairs, who also play important roles in news-making activities that center on what happens in their panels' jurisdictions. Finally, party officials' responsibilities are hardly set in stone because individuals frequently shape the offices they occupy. As Rep. Artur Davis (D-AL) explained after Emanuel was selected as chair of the Caucus: "[That position] is always dependent on the personality of the person in the job…[it] is always more ambiguously defined."[55]

Historically, this sharing of responsibilities and blurring of roles has prompted some to try to expand their portfolios, leading to problems and occasionally rather sharp conflicts over the direction of a congressional party's public relations activities. When Rep. John Boehner (R-OH) was Conference chair, for example, he frequently saw his communications strategies upstaged or complicated by Rep. Newt Gingrich (R-GA), whose "speakership was built on talk" and who, especially in his early days at the helm of the House, "would not shut up."[56] In the late 1990s, the GOP Conference Chair Rep. J. C. Watts (R-OK) clashed repeatedly with Minority Leader Tom Delay (R-TX) when Delay tried to exert more muscle over party communications by issuing talking points and other public relations directives to

Conference members.[57] Republican confusion and collisions over public relations roles got so out of hand at the time that one frustrated member pondered whether or not it would be better to have "someone in the Conference who is just dedicated to communication—not to coalition building, not to whip strategy—just communication."[58]

Confusion and intramural struggles over communications have certainly not abated. House Republican Policy Committee Chair Thaddeus McCotter (R-MI) caused some consternation in the ranks in 2007 when he publicly distanced the work of his Policy Committee, which he construed as "ideation," from Minority Leader Boehner's and GOP Conference Chair Putnam's rebranding effort, which he identified as "communications."[59] Democrats, while they have more clearly tied control over communications to authority, have also had their problems. Relations between Minority Leader Nancy Pelosi (D-CA) and then Democratic Caucus Chair Robert Menendez (D-NJ), for example, grew contentious when Menendez's office commenced a press booking operation, "Democrats on the Record," to increase members' visibility in radio and television outlets, a task generally considered part of Pelosi's portfolio.[60] As House Speaker in the 110th Congress, Pelosi also tangled with Emanuel, the Caucus chair, and on more than one occasion had to check his efforts as he tried to broaden his role in party communications.[61]

House Parties' Message Activities: Creating the "Drumbeat across America"

House parties work through communications enterprises to minimize departures from their messages and maximize public visibility for their policy positions. Their objective is to create, as Representative Pelosi once put it, a "drumbeat across America."[62] Toward that end, they organize and script rank-and-file messengers during key points of the legislative session and create structures that prompt and even subtly pressure members to plan, target, synchronize, and execute partisan publicity operations. Both parties also help members negotiate the media environment so as to get more of them into the news cycle speaking with a calibrated and unified voice.[63]

Working through their communications structures, the two House parties convene frequent meetings with members' press secretaries to coordinate newsmaking activities and communications strategies. Through their Conference and Caucus the parties offer guidance on how to communicate to both lawmakers and their press aides, frequently supplying them with carefully calibrated poll-tested language and themes that they can invoke when presented with opportunities to sell their party's messages to the American public.[64] They also give members briefings on policies and political developments and provide them with talking points, that is, highly scripted and strategically formulated bits of information intended to concentrate and synchronize members' publicity efforts on specific messages in ways that create that steady public drumbeat and shape the news narrative in support of their political and programmatic goals. Both parties expect members to enlist these points to press their interests at town hall meetings with constituents and through news releases and personal exchanges with the local, regional, and even national media.[65] The House GOP conference, for instance, armed members with talking points and data pertaining to the surge in Iraq so that when they went home on their 2007 summer recess they could respond to local media's questions and constituents' growing uneasiness about U.S. military commitments in the Middle East.[66] Meanwhile, for the congressional interregnum during the winter of 2007, Democrats furnished members with a script specifically written to steer the public's attention away from their failure to bring down the number of U.S. troops in Iraq. To try to move the narrative to more favorable terms, they sent members home with a publicity playbook that stressed domestic policy achievements like the minimum wage increase they had shepherded through Congress.[67]

While talking points are used to guide and time members' discussion in news outlets and in their constituencies, there are certainly limits as to how effective they are in practice.[68] Members coming from those districts that are still somewhat competitive or are less supportive of the incumbent's party must tailor their messages to their constituents' preferences, as opposed to conveying hard-edged, partisan positions drafted for standard political talking points. Some communications staffers working for members in these kinds of districts indicated in interviews that some of the more ideological preferences on cultural and economic issues advanced by their parties did not always resonate with their bosses' more moderate constituents. Several, in fact, admitted that their bosses did not faithfully employ these scripted messages because they wanted to avoid drawing public or media attention to an unpopular party message that might turn off the folks back home.

House Republicans and Democrats also hive off groups of members to help them orchestrate and promote their public relations aims. These include both more institutionalized entities like the GOP Theme Team and the Democratic Message Group and a host of more fluid, ad hoc organizations created to mount an intense and targeted public relations strategy to advance a party's stance on a specific problem, policy, or set of issues.

The GOP Theme Team is a direct descendent of the Conservative Opportunity Society (COS) organized in the early 1980s. Born out of members' growing frustration as a perennial minority party, the COS brought together a number of partisan, confrontational lawmakers. Initially, members of this faction gained notoriety and earned the enmity of their opponents by using C-SPAN broadcasts of "special order" addresses and floor debates to advance their agenda and draw the media's, and ultimately the public's attention to what they perceived to be the flagrant abuses and corrupt practices of a hegemonic Democratic party.[69]

Today's Theme Team, which consists of anywhere from fifty to ninety members, is a more structured, mainstream body within the House GOP that follows much the same path charted by the COS. With Conference staff assistance, it organizes members to give prepared daily "one-minute" floor speeches and "special order" addresses around a political issue or policy matter selected by the leadership. These refrains on the floor are intentionally designed to focus discussion and attract publicity so as to help the party drive its preferred narrative.[70] The Theme Team, however, has in recent years broadened its range of communication activities beyond floor speeches. It has, for instance, been used for "grooming relations" with the media. To overcome members' resistance to dealing with a media perceived as antagonistic to GOP interests, the Team has sponsored occasional roundtable discussions between House Republicans and selected representatives from the press.[71] It has also spearheaded efforts to teach members about the public relations potential of new media, in particular, the blogosphere. Thus it has held cybercommunications workshops for members and their staffs. These have been convened to facilitate discussions with bloggers from influential conservative sites and to alert party members and their press officers to the ways that these new venues can be enlisted to supercharge their public communications operations.[72] Finally, the Team holds regular sessions, "salons," with small groups—a "rolling congregation"—of representatives and their aides. Here the Team brings in celebrity experts of the day, such as pollster Scott Rasmussen, Vice President Richard Cheney, Supreme Court Justice Antonin Scalia, television commentators like Dick Morris and former White House press secretary Dana Perino, and even noted Democratic opponents such as Rahm Emanuel to educate members and provide them with fresh, outsider perspectives on politics and selected issues.[73] While Rep. Vernon Ehlers (R-MI) acknowledged that some of his colleagues just attended these sessions to gather ammunition for their floor speeches, others found these "just a good thing to…talk about what's going on with our constituents and how we can best make our position known to the public."[74]

The Republican Conference has also experimented with flexible, ad hoc communications organizations. When Rep. Deborah Pryce (R-OH) was Conference chair, for instance, she created eight groups of representatives organized around different policy issues to work with party staffers on publicity strategies centering on GOP initiatives in each of the selected policy domains.[75] House Republicans also established under her direction a Message Action Team, a collection of about thirty members, who, "because they are good on camera and good on their feet," were singled out to help develop and present the party message to the media.[76] When Putnam (R-FL) assumed the mantle of Conference chair, he reinstated rapid response teams and even dedicated Conference staff resources to assisting them in executing their communications responsibilities, something that was continued by his immediate successor, Rep. Pence.[77] Occasionally, the Conference follows practices commonly associated with political campaigns and White House communications activities and sets up "war rooms." Most often these involve fairly senior lawmakers and press staffers who monitor news coverage and mount coordinated, highly focused, strategically timed public relations offensives on specific hot button issues, such as immigration or the war in Iraq—or on behalf of one of their legislative maneuvers or pieces of legislation directly pending in Congress.[78]

House Democrats employ similar public relations arrangements. Their counterpart to the GOP Theme Team is the Message Group. Like the Team, it focuses on disseminating the party's position by attracting and concentrating news attention through "one minute" floor addresses by members. Yet it is not quite as institutionalized nor has it taken on as many roles as its Republican counterpart. Its members, for instance, have traditionally not relied on press aides to prepare the content of their "one minute" addresses. The Message Group has also been less inclined to hold court with representatives from the media.[79] Party leadership resources and staff, however, are used to organize or line up the different participants' floor speeches.[80]

Like their opponents, Democrats have also from time to time employed a medley of ad hoc public relations groups to get their message out. In the early years of George W. Bush's administration, for example, they set up rapid response units similar to those established by their partisan opponents. These consisted of legislators with policy expertise in different areas who were assigned the responsibility of saturating the media with timely partisan responses to White House initiatives and public announcements.[81] They also experimented with slightly more structured Message Teams, small groups of lawmakers organized around five key Democratic issues—Social Security, the environment, pension reform, education, and prescription drugs. The party charged these teams with the task of carrying out at least one publicity event per week—town hall meeting, newspaper editorial, press conference, and talk radio or television program—that highlighted key Democratic initiatives in their assigned policy areas. Leaders also assigned them to work with advocacy groups and their counterparts in the Senate to get out the message on the party's programmatic goals in their five designated domains.[82]

Besides providing information to guide members' public activities and developing structures to focus and carry out their publicity campaigns, the parties also provide help to members interested in expanding their own media visibility. This is especially important for members of the House, which, as we have already noted, is frequently overshadowed in the news by the Senate. It is here that leverage from the party can come into play, though it cannot always overcome the media's proclivity for senators. As noted earlier, both House parties employ rather sizable communications bureaucracies. These include staffers who provide technical assistance and media advice to help members make their party's case.[83] House parties also assist members by running press-booking operations through their principal communications structures. Here staffers work with and periodically pressure television and radio show producers to get their party's views or positions represented on the different media outlets. Although important, these efforts to get representatives into the news also have limits. As some assisting the leadership have occasionally complained, "a lot of the TV bookers don't want the House Members. They're obsessed with Senators."[84] There are, at the same time, some representatives who do not need the Conference's press-bookers' assistance to get a spot on a television or radio show. A number of the House press secretaries we interviewed indicated that they negotiated directly with television and radio bookers or producers to schedule appearances for their bosses, several of whom had shown great acuity with the news and had already developed a reputation on a certain policy or legislative issue. Our interviewees also revealed that even in today's more outward-looking Congress some representatives prefer lower public profiles. Even today there are enough of those around for *Roll Call's* correspondents to publish an occasional piece on what it refers to as the "obscure caucus," those members who "resist the limelight" to labor behind the scenes on behalf of their constituents.[85]

Finally, House Republicans and Democrats have in recent years deployed their communications support systems or staff to launch websites that highlight their policy preferences and provide information to the press critiquing their opponents' stances and highlighting the soundness of their own initiatives. These Internet forums, which are still very much works in progress, also post clips and news accounts that showcase members' appearances in disparate media venues as they wage public relations battles on behalf of matters of interest to their parties. The House GOP site (GOP.gov), which falls under the auspices of the Conference, hosts a blog to disseminate a real-time partisan perspective on pressing issues, with links to other media stories. It also provides Republican policy proposals and features talking points on party initiatives. GOP.gov makes it possible to sign up for news feeds and even includes links to social media platforms like YouTube, Facebook, and Twitter.[86] Democrats' use of their Caucus website (dems.gov) in many respects parallels that of their counterparts.[87] The bottom line here is that these sites serve manifold ends. They promote the messages of the parties and get them out directly to the media and other interested constituencies and actors, including members and their own communications' staffs. By posting pictures, video and audio clips, and published commentaries, and by highlighting selected individuals and what they are doing, writing, or saying, these sites also serve to draw news organizations' attention and coverage to those members who have demonstrated their talents in advancing the parties' collective goals and messages on a specific issue or policy domain.

The Senate: Who Directs the "Independent Rascals'" Choirs?

Traditionally, coordinated message operations in the Senate have been more limited and arguably less efficacious than those found in the House of Representatives. Much of this is likely rooted in differences between the chambers. Senators, after all, usually represent more heterogeneous constituencies than representatives and that occasionally creates competing pressures to which they must respond in their public relations activities.[88] The cultures of the two institutions also have some bearing on the matter. Senators clearly have more latitude than what the more structured House permits its members. This permissiveness, as we noted earlier, dates back to when Sen. Mike Mansfield (D-MT) took the helm as majority leader and assumed a laissez-faire approach to guiding his troops. Rules and procedures that afford senators substantial leverage over the legislative process compound their more individualistic tendencies. The chamber's structures of leadership, as a result, are less centralized, and they are vested with less authority and influence than those found in the House. Senate leaders therefore confront challenges considerably more vexing than those faced by their House counterparts. Even in these partisan, polarized times, senators are less predisposed to follow leaders' cues. "The job of leading the Senate," as Steven Smith noted, "has been likened to herding cats. If only it were so easy."[89]

Media preferences as well as greater staff support for public relations activities also give individual senators a leg up in attracting news organizations' attention.

They are therefore less dependent on the congressional party's help with the media than their House colleagues and usually have more opportunities to make news on their own. Perhaps this further diminishes senators' responsiveness to more centrally directed news-making activities. Sen. Trent Lott (R-MS) put his finger on the Senate leadership's overall challenge in getting out a coherent message when he quipped: "Senators are kind of independent rascals."[90] The general upshot of all of this is that it is oftentimes harder for Senate parties to keep their members—those "independent rascals"—on the team "speaking with one voice."

But that does not mean that Senate parties have stopped trying to get their members to strike the same chord in public. Like their House counterparts, they certainly understand the value of coordinating their messages. Sen. John Kyl (R-AZ) once acknowledged as much, observing that "our [Republican] policies are best communicated when we're working as a team."[91] It is therefore unsurprising to find that in recent years both Senate parties have concentrated on building up rather sizable, complex communications structures.

The two Senate parties diverge in how they actually organize and conduct their communications enterprises. These variations flow from subtle differences in their respective leadership structures as well as the personalities and political ambitions of the occupants of those structures. Such divergences are also shaped by existing configurations of power on the political landscape. Frequently this includes circumstances like whether or not their side is in the majority or the minority on the Hill and whether or not it controls the other end of Pennsylvania Avenue. These differences notwithstanding, both Democrats and Republicans have in recent years made notable moves to bring greater coherence to their Senate message operations.

Today's Senate Democratic communications enterprise bears the imprint of the party leadership's formal structure. For years, the Democratic floor leader chaired both the party's organizing body, the Conference, and its agenda setting panel, the Democratic Policy Committee (DPC). The charges of the Policy Committee are twofold. First, it works on Senate Democrats' agenda and highlights how their initiatives differ from the ones put on the table by their opponents. Second, it gathers information and publicizes issues by conducting hearings. For all practical purposes, the Policy Committee's staff was until recent years deployed as the floor leader's "instrument."[92] When Sen. George Mitchell (D-ME) was elected majority leader in 1989 he named Sen. Thomas Daschle (D-SD) as cochair of the DPC, and he assigned him the task of enlisting the committee's resources and considerable staff to serve the party's communications needs.[93] Daschle adhered to this arrangement when he succeeded Mitchell in 1995, though he subsequently relinquished control of the DPC in 1999, when Sen. Byron Dorgan (D-ND) was named as the single chair of that party committee.

Senate Democrats redefined the DPC's mission in Sen. Harry Reid's first years as floor leader.[94] With a Republican president in the White House and the GOP in control of both congressional chambers, the committee concentrated on convening hearings on executive initiatives and supporting congressional oversight activities. In doing that, the DPC initially set its sights on turning up the heat on the administration by directing public attention to the Bush administration's lapses in domestic and foreign policy. When the Democrats returned to power on Capitol Hill in the 110th Congress, the policy committee devoted more time to developing the Conference's position papers and policy alternatives, what in effect are the ideas that drive the party's message.[95]

Under Reid's direction, the responsibility for overseeing the day-to-day workings of Senate Democrats' publicity machine shifted to the floor leader's office. Shortly after he assumed that post in the wake of Daschle's 2004 defeat at the polls, Reid aggressively moved to make his party's public relations activities more competitive in an environment in which the GOP controlled both ends of Pennsylvania Avenue. He stepped up his own involvement in delivering the message and verbally sparring with his opponents, and to supplement his own exchanges with the media he established within the floor leader's office a Democratic Communications Center to drive the party's message and get more of his colleagues into the news cycle. In doing this, he aimed to provide immediate and pointed responses to initiatives and statements that emanated from a Republican president and GOP controlled Congress.[96]

Reid's early public relations moves set him apart from Daschle, who many believe had let their party's press operation in the Senate languish. True, Daschle did have a respectable enough track record in getting his party to speak with greater unity.[97] Still, there were rumblings that in the waning days of his tenure his "press shop," as one spokesperson noted, assumed an outlook that "was too narrow. They just didn't do enough for other members. The message always just seemed to be Daschle's—as opposed to the message of the party."[98] Reid, by contrast, grabbed the reins and created an apparatus designed to bring coherence to Senate Democrats' national messages and to push those views through different media outlets. The floor leader's public relations bureaucracy swelled and grew more complex as a result.

There are close to thirty people currently working in the Senate Democratic Communications Center, which has been dubbed the "war room." The center is even substantially larger now than when it was created during Reid's initial year as minority leader back in 2005.[99] Its mission is to provide assistance in hammering out a message and coordinating members' public relations activities so as to create the desired drumbeat across the country. Thus, the Communications Center isolates and develops themes and messages, and it provides members with information by making available to them briefing materials and talking points. It also helps get Democratic senators onto national, regional, and local news forums and furnishes them with technical and administrative support. Finally, it engages in media outreach, in particular, working to help party members tap underutilized venues like talk radio and local news outlets and newer media platforms like the Internet as they promote the party brand.[100]

At the start of the 112th Congress, Reid somewhat decentralized his communications operations by delegating certain responsibilities to Sen. Charles Schumer (D-NY).[101] Reid merged the DPC's work and staff with that of his Communications Center to create a Democratic Policy and Communications Center (DPCC), and he charged its chair, Schumer, with overseeing much of its communications work. Reid initially made this move to integrate policy development and legislative activities with those of messaging and to build yet again a more effective communications operation. Still, within months of having made this change there were already signs of tension and infighting between the staffs of the two principals, Reid and Schumer.[102]

For contemporary Senate Republicans, authority for public relations operations has been less concentrated than that found on the other side of the aisle during much of Reid's tenure as Democratic floor leader. Overall, the division of labor on the Senate Republicans' communications front in part reflects or parallels a Senate GOP organizational structure that separates the position of Conference chair from that of floor leader.

Beginning in the early 1980s, when the GOP was in the majority in the Senate and held the presidency under Reagan, the Conference turned its attention outward. It was then that the chair, Sen. James McClure (R-ID), transformed it "into a sophisticated public relations operation." The Conference under his direction took on the responsibility for providing members and their press officers with advice and technical support in getting out their messages. This new twist in organizational roles "represented a striking enlargement of the conference's activities."[103] It immediately led to a pronounced growth and specialization in staff positions, most of which were dedicated specifically to communicating with external constituencies.

Today, the party conference envisages itself as "the communications arm" of the GOP leadership.[104] Its stated "mission" is to act as "a means of informing the media of the opinions and activities of Senate Republicans," and with that in mind it promises its members a "full range of communications services including Graphics, Radio, Television, and Internet."[105] The senator who chairs the Republican Conference oversees an organizational staff of close to twenty members, including specialists dedicated to radio, television, the Internet, Latino media, as well as general press officers and media support staff.[106] Thus the Conference chair is institutionally well-positioned to play an important role in getting members to disseminate coherent partisan messages and helping them obtain the technical support necessary to meet that challenge.

Senator Reid's success in using the communications center to push his party's message contributed to Senate Republicans' anxiety about their public relations activities. "We have been on the short end of the stick when it comes to defining ourselves to the American public," Sen. John Cornyn (R-TX) noted as he observed the ostensible successes of his Senate Democratic opponents' communications campaign during the Bush years.[107] Sentiments such as these prompted their leaders to act. Senate Majority Leader Bill Frist (R-TN) had attempted to respond earlier to these very same concerns by setting up a more structured communications operation, the "peace room," to counter Democrats' public thrusts and coordinate members' news-making activities.[108] But from the perspective of many in the ranks, this communications initiative fell short of the mark. Some members blamed Frist for their party's feeble public response, with a few speculating that the whole operation had been derailed by his rather thinly veiled interest in seeking the presidency. "I thought it [communications strategy] left something to be desired," observed Cornyn. "You can't serve two masters. When you have divided allegiances, something has to suffer."[109] Electoral politics figured in another way as well. Sen. Rick Santorum (R-PA), the head of the Senate GOP Conference at the time, had gotten tangled in a tough reelection battle, which diverted his attention away from exercising his responsibilities over the GOP communications operation.[110]

After losing control of the Senate in 2006, the Senate GOP resurrected efforts to bring greater coherence to its messages. As the 110th Congress commenced, Minority Leader Sen. Mitch McConnell (R-KY) set about rectifying his party's public relations lapses. McConnell's overhaul of the party's public relations program, which included increasing the staff, has initially produced a publicity structure, the Senate Republican Communications Center, that is still smaller, less established, and somewhat less centralized than the one on the other side of the aisle. Communications responsibilities for Senate Republicans are parceled out to members of the party hierarchy as well as several other key figures of their conference. The chair of the Conference continues to oversee the message operations, though McConnell has encouraged bringing more attention to policy in carrying out that role. He has also aimed to get the chair of the Policy Committee and other members of the leadership more involved in communicating the party message. And he has singled out certain members to lead key communications initiatives.[111]

Senate Message Operations: Getting Those "Independent Rascals" Singing in Harmony

Senate parties' strategies to get out coherent messages are similar to those followed in the House. Both Senate parties have centralized online offices or web pages sponsored by their Caucus (Democrats.Senate.Gov)/Conference (src.senate. gov) and Policy Committees. They use these sites to publish information on their leaders, highlight their parties' agendas, offer critiques of their opponents, provide details on policy and legislative issues, and post news releases. Both Senate parties' sites also provide a substantial menu of multimedia features that showcase members. These include links that stream video of members' press appearances or news conferences, and in the case of the GOP, radio clips and graphics as well as a number of real-time feeds and podcasts.[112] Policy Committee sites (rpc.senate.gov and democrats.senate.gov/dpc) highlight issue or position papers, which can be downloaded.[113] The DPC site also includes reports on its oversight activities that can be accessed, and both parties' policy committee sites offer links to social media like Twitter and YouTube. Overall, these sites enable the parties to directly transmit their stances on issues, highlight the work of their members, and focus the attention of journalists and political commentators, thus affording them opportunities to shape political story lines and strategically drive those narratives in ways that work to their parties' advantage.

Senate parties, like those in the House, provide technical resources, services, and advice to get members into the public realm and help them with their exchanges with the news world. Although news gathering routines and greater resources in staff give individual senators a leg up in gaining publicity, many still benefit from their parties' technical assistance and support, especially when it comes to dealing with less familiar terrain like blogs, soft news programs, talk radio, and specialized cable shows. The parties profit from this as well, for such operations can help them identify and promote Senators best equipped to drive the message. As Sen. Jim DeMint (R-SC) explained: "The media tends to go to a few high-profile members and want to hear from them, but I think it's important to get members with particular expertise and push them out front."[114] Finally, by engaging in an aggressive outreach program that extends to less traditional media, parties can expand for all members the forums through which they can convey their messages. Thus, both Senate parties have in recent years worked to get their members and their messages in many of the new media platforms, including the growing number of sites popping up in the blogosphere.[115]

Senate parties also mirror their House counterparts by periodically deploying rapid response teams who can go to the floor or to the media to rebut their legislative opponents or the administration. In the early years of the Bush presidency, for instance, a group of Senate Republicans informally known as the "GOP Frontline" organized to follow floor debates and provide "emergency" responses to Democratic attacks on their party initiatives, both on the floor and in the press galleries.[116] Frequently, these efforts are targeted to delivering floor addresses crafted to focus attention and attract publicity on a selected political issue or legislative initiative. As the Senate parties were skirmishing over Democrats' use of the filibuster to block floor votes on some of President Bush's more controversial judicial nominees, then Majority Leader Bill Frist (R-TN) set up a public relations gambit known as "Advise and Consent." It enlisted a group of senators who recruited colleagues to take to the floor to address contentious issues surrounding judicial selection.[117] Another textbook example of using orchestrated floor debate to gin up publicity can be seen in Senate Democrats' response to the sharp partisan conflict that erupted as Congress considered the Bush administration's requests for additional funding for the Iraq war. The party's communication operation e-mailed members' offices with requests to take to the floor and drive their message of opposition: "they could be five-minute riffs, 10-minute outlines, 30 minute rants.... Anything that gets your boss to the floor.... The effort begins now."[118] Not to be outdone, the Senate GOP in the 110th Congress assembled a group of media-savvy members to monitor chamber activities, check for upcoming developments, hold weekly meetings, and develop media friendly messages for members to take to the floor.[119]

Both parties even use new technologies to follow debates, keep track of who is speaking, and calculate the amount of time they rack up on the floor compared to that amassed by their opponents. This information can then be shared to prompt members to take up the cudgel and go to the floor on behalf of the party and its publicity efforts. Sen. Cornyn, who once led this initiative for the Republican Conference, observed that "now I've been able to—I wouldn't say shame the senators, but at least show them how their performance measures up with their colleagues' and how Republicans measure up to the Democrats." This, he suggested, can provide just the right kind of subtle pressure to get the job done: "We're a competitive lot, so when you tell Republican senators that we're being out-spoken by Democrats, it gets 'em going. It provides the additional nudge to get them on the floor."[120]

The Senate parties have also established working groups of senators to publicize important policy initiatives or issues. Shortly before the midterm election, Democrats, for instance, set up groups to publicize their initiatives on key issues—education, the environment, prescription drug coverage, pension reform, and saving Social Security—and to join forces with their colleagues in the House. By coordinating senators' efforts and by linking them with their counterparts in the House, the congressional party's message operation aimed to tamp down discordant voices within their party across the chambers while magnifying and shaping news visibility of its programmatic agenda.[121] Similarly, as part of the GOP response to some of President Obama's initial legislative initiatives, Minority Leader McConnell and Conference Chair Sen. Alexander, established a number of issue-based task forces to study selected policy issues, develop alternative legislative proposals, and educate members so as to prepare them for upcoming public skirmishes with the administration and their opponents on the Hill, as many of them were also expected to take to the airwaves to advance their party's take on the policy issues to which they had been assigned, such as health care, energy, Social Security, and housing.[122]

The parties also supply members with "message points" that they can raise when they go back to their states and speak to their constituents and the media. The Senate GOP Conference, for instance, drafted for its members a script that provided, week by week, themes to be addressed during the 2005 summer recess.[123] Along similar lines, in the months leading up to the 2006 election Reid's communications center put in motion the "Six for '06" regimen of talking points for Democrats. It encouraged senators to stick to discussing six policy issues from a prescribed list. Thus, it gave them a set of talking points to guide them in their exchanges, and even included examples of the kind of language they could use to evoke the specific affective sentiment they hoped to arouse.[124]

Of course, as is the case with the House, these partisan scripts are of limited value to those representing constituencies where the message does not resonate. This is more often the case for senators, since states are generally more ideologically diverse than all but a few of the 435 House districts. The Senate's normative order also establishes important parameters that determine the acceptability and thus the efficacy of a strategy based on talking points. Senators, after all, pride themselves on their independence and egalitarianism. As a result, they are much less predisposed to follow top-down communications instructions than are their cohorts in the House, where even the message of the day oftentimes comes down "from the Oracle of Apollo [the Speaker]."[125] The leadership strategy of "inclusion," which involves bringing in as many members as possible into decision-making processes, therefore seems as much a necessity for Senate party chiefs here as it is for them when they try to guide and coax their partisan colleagues through the twists and turns of the legislative process.[126] Indeed, one of the Senate GOP colleagues' and staffers' major criticisms of McConnell's predecessor as floor leader, Sen. Frist, was that he was much too "hierarchical" in how he handled the party's message operations. Many felt he concentrated too much on distributing talking points and not enough on listening to what members were actually working on and what they themselves wanted to communicate to the public about their activities and programs. With that in mind, McConnell commenced his communications overhaul by setting out to create a more broad-based operation, one that both solicited greater input about communications from members and aimed to get more of them onto the message team and into the news-making realm.[127]

Conclusion

Today's members and their congressional aides have greater incentives to use media to get their messages out, and they have responded by developing resources and structures to suit a more publicity oriented institution. They have beefed up their own communications operations. Thus, press officers, a rarity on the Hill when the oligarchs wielded power, are commonplace. Their numbers continue to grow at rates that match those in the years immediately following the reforms that decentralized power and expanded individual members' resources. The emergence and proliferation of online offices and social media made possible by new communications technologies have accompanied the institutionalization of press secretaries. Today's members use these cyberoffices and new communications technologies in ways that are most certainly gauged to serve their publicity aims. And given what we have seen regarding the roles of the Internet and web based media in other facets of life, including political campaigns and elections, we can only surmise that congressional use of these new technologies will continue to expand and take on increasing importance in members' and parties' communication activities.

We have also seen that these changes, combined with the rise of a more fragmented, dynamic media environment, have increased both the opportunities and means for individual members to take their case beyond the walls of their Capitol Hill chambers. Such developments most certainly compound the collective action problem of parties interested in getting out coherent messages that shore up their brand names. Yet Congress continues to manifest resiliency. As members expanded their capacities and opportunities to chart their own courses in news-making activities, congressional parties did not stand pat. They responded by creating communications enterprises to direct members' public relations efforts in ways that were specifically geared to exploiting the possibilities engendered by a new media environment. Thus, parties on both sides of the aisle, and in both chambers, possess and use structures, strategies, and resources to help them realize their collective interest in getting out clear and consistent messages to their disparate publics. We now look at how these different enterprises work to get out their collective messages.

6 Running Public Relations Operations on the Hill

Strategies, Successes, and Failures in Message Marketing

Having examined the communications enterprises that congressional parties use to help them finesse the collective action challenges they confront in disseminating their messages, we turn to exploring the strategies they employ in carrying out their public relations activities. Here we focus on three different cases in which congressional parties' publicity activities played an important role: prescription drug coverage and Medicare reform, expanded funding of the state children's health insurance program (SCHIP), and immigration reform. While these do not encompass all of the conditions that impact congressional communications campaigns, they do provide a cross-section of recent, highly salient policy initiatives undertaken in different contextual settings. The first case, on prescription drug benefits, involves a period of unified government. Expanded funding for SCHIP, meanwhile, is taken from a context of divided government. Our last example, on immigration reform, covers instances of unified as well as divided government. All three cases also represent policies on which there were different degrees of cohesion within the parties. As a result, we believe that, combined, these cases furnish valuable insight into the options, strategies, and difficulties encountered by congressional parties in pressing their arguments outside the walls of their chambers.

Prescription Drug Coverage and Medicare Reform

A survey released shortly before President George W. Bush took office in 2001 showed 73% of those polled considered Medicare beneficiaries' escalating prescription drug costs a "top" concern. Further, when asked who had "the best" ideas for resolving the problem, respondents preferred Democrats to Republicans by a healthy 19 point margin.[1] Bush's election gave Republicans an opening to neutralize this advantage. Campaigning as a "compassionate conservative," he promised to fix the problem. His party also controlled both ends of Pennsylvania Avenue, creating both opportunities and incentives for it to act.

The Foundation for Discussion: The Bush "Framework"

Bush elevated the issue at the outset, but quickly drove it to the sidelines by pushing tax cuts and education reform. Later, Sen. James Jeffords (R-VT) complicated the president's agenda setting strategies when he bolted his GOP Conference and handed control of the Senate back to Democrats. Bush's domestic initiatives were then sidetracked as national security concerns crowded out nearly everything else after September 11. Still, cognizant of the political importance of dealing with the problem, especially after his party had reclaimed total control of the Hill in the 2002 election, President Bush turned the spotlight back on the issue in his 2003 State of the Union Address. He followed with a proposal to use a prescription drug benefit as an incentive to move seniors from more costly fee-for-service plans to managed care alternatives. Responses to this trial balloon, though, were hardly reassuring, prompting the White House to modify its initial offering.[2]

The president's emended plan outlined three options for delivering drug coverage to senior citizens and reforming Medicare. The first provided Medicare beneficiaries who remained in existing fee-for-service programs with a discount card that enabled them to purchase prescription drugs at a reduced rate. The second option underwrote most of participants' prescription drug costs if they switched to some sort of managed care. The third choice allowed beneficiaries to select the lowest priced health care provider, including one without any Rx benefits.[3] Senate Finance and House Ways and Means and Energy and Commerce committees assumed responsibility for fleshing out the plan, with their members agreeing to report proposals for full committee action by early June. GOP leaders, eager to resolve the issue before the election season commenced, endorsed this schedule.[4]

A Bipartisan Senate Agreement: The Center Sets the Discussion

The congressional public relations campaign surrounding the bill came into view at the June deadline. Senator Tom Harkin (D-IA), Senator Debbie Stabenow (D-MI), and Senator Jay Rockefeller (D-WV) launched a preemptive strike at a June 5, 2003 press conference, where they framed Bush's gambit as a Trojan horse maneuver to privatize Medicare.[5] Later, a group of senators announced a bipartisan agreement to offer seniors governmentally regulated private insurance plans. The deal stipulated that, after paying a $275 deductible, beneficiaries would have close to half of the first $3,450 spent annually for prescription drugs covered by the government. They would then be responsible for the next $1,850 in expenditures. Once they spent $5,300 for the year, they would have 90% of remaining costs covered. The accord promised participants in fee-for-service plans benefits similar to those of preferred providers.[6]

Sen. Charles Grassley (R-IA), chair of the Finance Committee and one of the agreement's authors, took to the airwaves to frame the accord. He portrayed it as guaranteeing "maximum choice" for senior citizens and predicted it would accomplish the president's objective of moving more people into managed care. Grassley defended the measure's viability, contending that insurance companies' competitive bidding would hold down costs.[7]

Other leading legislators, including Sen. Edward Kennedy (D-MA), fixed their imprimaturs and provided public cover for the deal; but not all endorsed it. A few Republicans pushed for more incentives to entice beneficiaries into managed care, while some Democrats remonstrated that the proposal fell short in expenditures and coverage.[8]

On June 9, the administration signed on to the bipartisan accord, dropping its demand that levels of benefits be linked with types of health plans selected.[9] The Senate Finance Committee approved the bill (S1) by a 16 to 5 vote three days later, and House leaders added to the building momentum when they announced they were sending a similar plan to the House Ways and Means and Energy and Commerce panels.[10]

With the administration on board and the House marking up its plan, senators took up debate. Many combined this with a public strategy to shape popular sentiment at this critical stage and to signal other interested publics. The Finance Committee's vote portended pockets of resistance. Opponents included a faction of Republicans, who considered the bill long on costs and short on reform, and a group of Democrats, who found the legislation inadequate and impracticable.[11] These internal divisions strained the parties' abilities to mount centrally choreographed publicity operations in these early stages.

The bipartisan agreement's supporters tried to build public momentum. Senator Kennedy, for instance, turned to a cable news show to accentuate the urgency and magnitude of the problem, noting that "seniors will spend $1,800,000,000,000 over the next 10 years for prescription drugs." He also signaled colleagues and key constituencies when he declared that this was not a last step, but rather a "great opportunity to make a down payment [on which] we'll build."[12] Other proponents, Democrats like Sen. John Breaux (D-LA) and Republicans like Majority Leader Bill Frist (R-TN), publicly defended the package as an improvement over a status quo that provided seniors with little help with escalating Rx drug costs.[13]

Meanwhile, Senate opponents enlisted news-making opportunities to raise doubts about the plan. GOP dissidents like Sen. Don Nickles (R-OK) argued it was too costly and neglected Medicare's growing unfunded liability. These more conservative critics oftentimes went public to stump for initiatives with more choice and competition.[14] Recalcitrant Democrats used news appearances to portray the initiative as a Rube Goldberg-like solution that left noticeable gaps in coverage, with some like Sen. Jay Rockefeller (D-WV) and Minority Leader Tom Daschle (D-SD) emphasizing that $400 billion was not enough to get the job done.[15]

Kicking Off the Public Campaign: House Democrats Take It to Their Districts

On June 27, a bipartisan coalition of senators passed S1 on a 76 to 21 vote. An almost equal number of Republicans and Democrats opposed the legislation. The House approved its Medicare bill (HR1) later that day, 216 to 215, with only nine Democrats voting in favor of the legislation. Although Republican representatives supplied the bulk of support, nineteen resisted their leaders' entreaties and opposed the measure.[16]

Both measures offered similar benefits at a ten-year cost of $400 billion, but the more partisan House bill imposed a means test and included a "premium support" provision designed to bring more health care providers to the Medicare market and give participants greater choice. Through this provision the government would establish a benchmark amount to be spent on a health care plan, leaving participants who selected less costly options to retain 75% of the savings. Individuals who enrolled in plans that exceeded that predetermined amount would assume the additional costs. The House bill included this provision to attract recalcitrant GOP conservatives who wanted to use competition to reform Medicare's traditional fee-for-service delivery system. Democrats had grave concerns about this provision, for they feared it represented a first step toward dismantling Medicare.[17]

The bills' differences precluded quick resolution in conference. The measure needed to appease enough conservative GOP House members to get them to sign on while retaining enough of the more moderate provisions in the Senate bill to prevent a filibuster. Eager to realize a major domestic policy achievement before the election, Bush implored Congress to get him a bill he could sign.[18] Conferees, however, decided to hold off until after the summer recess.

For leaders of a fairly unified House Democratic party, the summer break provided a propitious opening to launch an organized public relations campaign to shape the context to their advantage. They also had several incentives to act because for one they faced a challenge on their own policy turf: a June 27 to 29 Gallup survey showed Republicans had gained traction on the issue. That same poll, however, signaled to Democrats inklings of strategic opportunities. In particular, most Americans had reservations about legislation currently before Congress, especially the provisions directing Medicare recipients into managed care. In addition, 80% of seniors, an important constituency, surmised that neither of the bills making their way through Congress would actually improve their situation.[19] Then again, as a minority party in a chamber where a highly disciplined partisan majority called the shots, marshaling public relations forces to elevate concerns about the House bill and turn popular sentiment against it was really one of the few ways Democrats could affect the legislation as it went to conference. Finally, unlike their Senate counterparts, many of whom joined with Republicans to pass a bill, House Democrats were generally united in their opposition, making it easier for them to agree on, and advance, a coherent message.

This mixture of opportunities, incentives, and conditions prompted Democratic leaders to write rank-and-file members a "Dear Colleague" letter, encouraging them to "take this debate directly to our seniors." They advised them that "the best way to do that is through the give-and-take of town hall meetings that individually generate favorable media coverage in your District and collectively generate a pro-active, positive message about House Democrats in the national media."[20] To gain maximum visibility for their party's position, leaders planned for the caucus to work with legislators to organize the forums on a single day, July 19. Democratic Caucus chair, Rep. Robert Menendez (D-N.J.) highlighted their party's goal: "This is clearly our effort to have echo chambers beyond Washington on a very critical issue."[21]

As party leaders ramped up their grassroots public relations campaign, the Democratic Congressional Campaign Committee (DCCC) ran complementary, hard-hitting advertisements against eight vulnerable House Republicans who supported the bill and whose districts included a hefty percentage of senior citizens. The spots criticized the GOP plan for having "no limits on premiums and a massive gap in coverage that will still cost many seniors thousands." Though the election was still more than a year away, the DCCC considered the issue ripe.[22] It concluded that the ads served Democrats first, in the immediate fight and second, in the struggle to take back the House. "Seniors need to know how bad the Republican prescription drug plan is, and these ads will help educate them," declared DCCC chair, Rep. Robert Matsui (D-CA). "House Republicans have passed a bad piece of legislation that does nothing to help seniors, and they are going to have to live with that come 2004."[23]

Slightly more than a week after House Democrats had announced their town hall initiative, *Roll Call* reported they had lined up legislators in twenty-seven states for the July 19 district meetings.[24] Caucus and leaders' websites publicized information pertaining to the meetings, and many of the participating lawmakers used the Internet to notify constituents about the nationwide event. Meantime, leaders worked with advocacy organizations to boost attendance at the sessions.[25] House Democratic leaders held a July 18, high-profile news-making rally on Capitol Hill to kick off the Democrats' National Day of Prescription Drug Town Hall Meetings. There they announced that over seventy members, more than a third of their entire caucus, would participate in the event.[26] The next day, as these centrally choreographed district forums played out, piquing seniors' interest, Democrats produced some of the beyond-the-Beltway echo chambers they were after. Local and regional outlets across the nation featured accounts of the pending drug bill and seniors' strident responses to it: *Akron Beacon Journal, Atlanta Journal-Constitution, Arkansas Democrat-Gazette, Denver Post, Hartford Courant, Seattle Times,* the *(Raleigh, NC) News and Observer,* and the *Register (Eugene, OR) Guard* among others. The meetings also spawned a story line on the CBS national evening news.[27] At the same time, the day's events and some of the stories that ensued made their way into electronic newsletters and news reports disseminated by policy and advocacy groups to constituencies interested in health care issues.[28]

Republicans did not cede the public relations battle, but they found their ability to plot and disseminate a clear message complicated by fissures both within the party and between the party and several significant allies, including elements of their political base.[29] A small yet vocal wing of conservative activists, especially in the House, even publicly challenged their leaders and the president as they tried to drum up opposition to adding a new entitlement benefit. Republican holdout Rep. Jeff Flake (R-AZ), for instance, used an opinion piece in *The Hill* to argue that the benefit promised by HR1 "is wholly unsustainable" and at odds with core Republican precepts of "limited government, economic freedom and individual responsibility."[30] Perhaps more importantly, several significant actors who frequently abetted the GOP's communications operation echoed Flake's views. These included conservative policy think tanks like the American Enterprise Institute (AEI), the Cato Institute, and the Heritage Foundation; high-profile talk radio hosts like Sean Hannity and Rush Limbaugh; and the editorial page of the *Wall Street Journal*.[31]

Negotiations resumed after the recess and continued through much of the fall, going well beyond the conferees' mid-October deadline. The issue bedeviling their work was HR1's "premium support" provision.[32] Many lawmakers addressed this contentious issue as they took their case to the media. Rep. Bill Thomas (R-CA), one of the lead negotiators on the bill and chair of the House Ways and Means committee, presented one of the early cases for "premium support."[33] He tried, in a weekend talk show that aired as conference negotiations accelerated and became more complex, to reframe the problem by portraying the real challenge as one of shoring up Medicare, which was in an ominous "death spiral" and required a timely injection of "private competition" to put pressure on escalating costs.[34] Other Republicans used news-making opportunities to express variations on this theme as well as to underscore the proposed benefit's importance.[35]

Democratic opponents cast GOP preferences in a different light. Minority Leader Tom Daschle (D-SD), for example, held a Capitol Hill press conference on October 23, where he was accompanied by several other senators, including Senator Kennedy, whose early, surprisingly stout support for the Senate's bipartisan accord had provided cover for those Democratic colleagues who wanted to pass a bill. They drew a line in the sand, announcing that forty-one senators, enough to mount a filibuster, had notified Bush that any bill resembling the House's would languish in the Senate. They also tried to reframe the issue to their advantage, charging House Republicans with using Rx benefits as a lure to privatize Medicare. That, according to Daschle, was a "show stopper" for Democrats.[36] The same, perhaps, could be said for the American people, for polls indicated only 29% of the population supported privatizing Medicare.[37] From this perspective, Democrats' portrayal of the Republican plan was a shrewd political move, since it exploited public skittishness about keeping guaranteed health care benefits intact.

Congressional Passage

GOP House and Senate leaders intervened to resolve the impasse on premium support by including it in the report but restricting its application. The AARP gave the legislation a critical boost on November 17 when it endorsed the deal. Four days later conferees filed their report.[38] It promised a means-tested prescription drug benefit linked with Medicare reform and included assistance to low-income participants, subsidies and tax expenditures to encourage businesses to maintain their retirees' health care coverage, and monetary incentives to entice purveyors of private plans to enter the Medicare market. The deal prohibited the national government from negotiating Rx drug prices, expedited the process of moving generic drugs to the market, imposed restrictions on drug importation, and increased funding levels for rural health care, physicians, and hospitals. It also mandated that the controversial premium support provision be tried for six years in six different metropolitan regions, starting in 2010.[39]

The public battle came into focus once the AARP signed on to the legislation. Democratic opponents exploited Americans' concerns. First, they charged that the plan did little to contain spiraling costs of medication that made the issue a top priority for nearly three-fourths of the population. Rep. Lynn Woolsey (D-CA), for instance, noted in a CNBC interview that the conference deal included a provision that prevented "the federal government from negotiating with pharmaceutical companies to lower the price of prescription drugs."[40] The bill also omitted expanded drug importation, something most Americans favored, prompting several House Democrats, and even a couple of Republicans, to hold a Capitol Hill press conference calling for the restoration of the importation provision initially supported by the House.[41]

Democrats also portrayed the program as not providing the security in benefits most wanted. Representative Harold Ford's (D-TN) televised exchange with Representative David Dreier (R-CA) provides a textbook example of this. Ford stressed that under the conference proposal "there's no guarantee that seniors will be afforded" access to "new and improved drugs" as they become available on the market.[42] Some Democrats, in fact, used these opportunities in the news to heighten citizens' fears that the program would actually make them worse off. Minority Leader Thomas Daschle (D-SD), for instance, noted in a CNN interview that "they estimate that two to three million retirees are going to lose their private drug coverage when this legislation passes."[43] In reframing the bill as providing little security for seniors, they oftentimes portrayed it as creating a steady windfall for insurance companies, HMOs, and the pharmaceutical industry.[44]

Democratic leaders and critics, especially in the House, eventually settled on what Rep. Ron Kind (D-WI) described as a "very simple message"; once again they raised the specter of privatization to shape the public's perceptions of their opponents and construct a narrative of what they were doing.[45] Frequently when Democrats went public they charged that what came out of conference did not, as most Americans preferred, build on the existing Medicare program but instead aimed to dismantle it. This, for instance, emerged as a recurring theme at a Congressional Black Caucus (CBC) press briefing, where members charged that the market based mechanisms allegedly included to reform Medicare really testified to Republican's "hope that it [Medicare] would die on the vines even now."[46] Others on their side of the aisle joined the refrain. Senator Kennedy, who opposed the conference report, observed in a CNN interview shortly before voting on the measure: "What we are considering is a rewrite of Medicare.... That [Medicare] is what is being undermined."[47] And in the context of their discussion they pointed to the inadequacy of the policy and again stoked the public's uncertainties surrounding it. As Rep. Cardin (D-MD) told Fox's Brenda Buttner, seniors are "going to have to pay more of their own health care.... It means it's going to be very difficult for them to find the type of health care insurance in the private sector that they really want."[48]

Democrats were not alone in public relations activities against the legislation, as Republicans struggled to keep some folks on message. A few economically conservative Republicans, squeamish about the size, scope, and direction of the program, had already mounted limited yet visible public relations battles against their party, and still not persuaded that the bill went far enough in reforming Medicare, they did so again. On the day before the scheduled pre-Thanksgiving recess House vote, Rep. Dan Burton (R-IN) appeared on *Your World With Neil Cavuto* and described the legislation as an "open-ended entitlement" that "we can't afford…. This is a turkey."[49] Later that week Rep. Mike Pence (R-IN), wrote an opinion piece in *Human Events* criticizing the program as too costly and too thin on free market mechanisms.[50]

Proponents defended the conference report against charges that it was a risky, ideologically driven policy solution. Majority Leader Frist tried to reassure the public by reminding them that the bill had received substantial external validation: "[A] lot of people have looked at the text, have studied the bill, and over 60 organizations have endorsed the bill…. Look at it as a bipartisan bill."[51] Supporters also used language that perhaps resonated with an American public that wanted a program built on the existing system and that, as polls also showed, liked the idea of choice. As Speaker Hastert pointed out in a weekend talk show, the reforms will provide people with "options that bring choice into Medicare." They were only "ways to test what the old fee-for-service system is as opposed to what these new competitive systems are."[52] Needless to say, Republican supporters stressed that the program provided relief to a predicament that had risen to the top of the nation's domestic agenda. "Every senior listening to me right now," Frist observed in an interview, "does not have access to prescription drugs through Medicare…. So you start with nothing. We're putting $400 billion in that doesn't exist today to give that benefit."[53]

After months of partisan wrangling, the House on November 22, 2003, adopted the conference report in a 220-215 vote. In the longest tally recorded since the chamber turned to electronic voting, sixteen House Democrats crossed the aisle to vote in favor of the legislation while twenty-five Republicans broke ranks to oppose it. Three days later the Senate endorsed the conference report by a more comfortable 11 vote margin, thus handing President Bush a historic legislative victory. Eleven Democrats joined forty-two Republicans and one Independent to favor the measure; nine Republicans and thirty-five Democrats voted against it.[54] On December 8, in a meticulously orchestrated ceremony held "in one of the largest halls in Washington, filled with thousands of cheering supporters," the President, flanked by a group of primarily GOP lawmakers, and in full view of the television cameras, signed the Medicare Prescription Drug Improvement and Modernization Act of 2003 (PL108-173) while Democrats countered with their own public relations volley at a DC rally where they reiterated their charges against the program.[55]

This law linked a new entitlement in drug benefits with a limited introduction of the premium support market-based reforms that promised to expand the role of private providers in the Medicare system and curb the rate of growth in governmental health care expenditures. It also contained several sweeteners, including subsidies for private providers, more money for rural health care, important concessions to the pharmaceutical industry, and higher payments to physicians and hospitals. Finally, it created an Rx discount card that beneficiaries could sign up for and use to purchase medications at reduced rates before full benefits kicked in during 2006.[56]

Continuing the Battle or "They Just Won't Quit"

Significant public clashes continued to erupt well after the president signed the measure. In the months leading up to March 3, 2004, the first day that seniors could register for the prescription drug discount card as the benefit was phased into effect, congressional parties' publicity activities hit a crescendo as members on both sides of the aisle found reasons to try to shape interpretations of the new drug benefit and claim credit for their actions. Surveys taken shortly after the legislation had passed indicated public sentiment had not crystallized in support of the new entitlement. Seniors, especially, registered their skepticism, with 62% indicating that the benefit program did "not go far enough."[57] "Skeptical retirees" also provided palpable evidence of the passion underlying misgivings about the program, as a number of them turned up at lawmakers' town hall meetings to voice their concerns.[58] Besides this lack of popular support, and even complaints from beneficiaries themselves, resistance emanating from other politically salient quarters increased Republicans' incentives to market the measure. Rep. Butch Otter (R-ID), who initially opposed the legislation and only agreed to support it under pressure from the House leadership, observed: "It upsets our conservative base. If they look at the bill as a whole and what it could have been, our base will come back. It's our job to educate them."[59] Meanwhile, many Democrats believed the public's misapprehension or lack of understanding about the program was a potential public relations bonanza. "We are going to continue to talk about it," Rep. Rahm Emanuel (D-IL) declared. "Republicans thought they were going to get a big political bang. They've got a dud. Unless they turn perceptions around, they've got an anchor around their neck."[60]

Republicans were slow to define and claim credit for the Rx drug benefit. Right after passing the bill, Congress shut down for the Thanksgiving holiday, and the administration's principal spokesperson for the program, Health and Human Services (HHS) Secretary Tommy Thompson, left for Africa to promote the president's AIDS program.[61] Divisions within the party on the issue also hampered their efforts.[62] All of this resulted in an opening for others to frame the legislation. As Rep. Jack Kingston (R-GA) lamented, "If you're not talking about [Medicare], somebody else is."[63]

Democrats seized the opportunity. Several convened a series of town hall meetings as part of an effort to shape popular sentiment. "Trying to influence public opinion," Rep. Benjamin Cardin (D-MD) observed, "is certainly part of our aim." He acknowledged that Democrats hoped to get "the same type of public opinion to jell that brought about [the] congressional action" that once culminated in the repeal (November 1989) of a policy—catastrophic insurance for seniors—less than a year and a half after it had been enacted. According to news accounts, by the time lawmakers had returned to the Capitol in January to start the new session, House Democrats had already convened close to sixty such gatherings. Meantime, their counterparts in the Senate plotted their own town hall offensive to keep the heat on the GOP.[64]

As they mounted their public relations campaign in the months leading up to the discount card sign-up date, congressional Democrats coordinated their public relations endeavors with those of strategically placed allies. Barbara Kennelly, head of the National Committee to Preserve Social Security and Medicare and a former representative from Connecticut, joined Democrats in district meetings to help them argue their party's case. Other interested organizations lent public relations assistance to the campaign. Families USA, a health care advocacy group that had lobbied against the legislation, produced and distributed a film that raised concerns about the program, while the liberal activist group, MoveOn.org, sponsored political advertisements critical of the administration and the Medicare changes.[65]

Congressional Democrats also indicated that a reworking of the plan would be a central part of the upcoming year's agenda, which they announced in a high-profile, and somewhat rare joint address at the National Press Club given by Senate Minority Leader Daschle and House Minority Leader Pelosi on the eve of the president's State of the Union speech. House Democrats made plans to push their proposals through a multipronged media campaign that combined district events with an especially aggressive use of talk radio and cable television.[66] As part of a larger campaign to popularize their message, Pelosi asked veteran lawmakers Rep. Charles Rangel (D-NY) and Rep. John Dingell (D-MI) to attend district gatherings held across the country to highlight what Democrats took to be the flaws of the Rx benefit plan. The goal, as one of her communications staffers described it, was to "get local press coverage and local interest on the issue. It's about going beyond the Beltway, leapfrogging over the Beltway, to get Democrats on the road and on the record." Party leaders also instructed members to hold a second round of coordinated forums on the Medicare package in the middle of March, and even armed them with a video that they could air at the sessions.[67]

Democrats' unstinting public relations onslaught started to take its toll. A March 2004 Gallup public opinion poll showed support for the yet to be implemented legislation had dropped 11%, and a focus group study conducted for the Henry J. Kaiser Family Foundation in April revealed that a relatively high proportion of seniors seemed baffled and wary about prospective benefits.[68] "When we measure public opinion, what really stands out right now is that essentially the Democratic charge has taken hold," noted a policy director for the AARP, which had supported the measure.[69]

Perceptions that the Democratic assault was making inroads with the public touched off Republican recriminations. "It's the law of the land now," averred their Conference chair, Rep. Deborah Pryce (R-OH). "It's not a political fight any more—or shouldn't be."[70] Yet Republicans themselves belied their own complaint that it was no longer a "a political fight," for they responded with their own public relations campaign to clear up alleged misunderstandings about the policy and to frame it in a way that would move public sentiment in their direction and ease concerns expressed by core supporters. Part of that "campaign" involved a publicity tour by Secretary Thompson and high level HHS administrators, who joined GOP lawmakers at town hall forums to explain the program. The House Conference prepared members for these meetings, conducting public opinion polls to gather information so as to advise members as to how they should talk about the new benefit, and providing them with informational PowerPoint presentations and toolkits.[71] Within a few months, Republicans reported they had held over 150 district meetings devoted to the prospective changes.[72] To encourage members to gin up their publicity operations, the House GOP Conference introduced a "Theodore Roosevelt Award," an honor to be bestowed upon those "members who go beyond the ordinary steps to help win the debate on Medicare." It also established goals for members in publicity events like town hall forums, hospital visits, franked mail, editorial board visits, press conferences, and media interviews, "one minute speeches," and "special order" addresses. Members who racked up the most public relations appearances were singled out and praised at weekly conference meetings.[73] And in what was perhaps an unprecedented and thinly veiled partisan move, the conference also wrote scripts for members to read as they recorded public service announcements detailing the new Rx benefits and alerting seniors of the need to sign up to receive them.[74] This was in addition to a multimillion dollar HHS publicity campaign designed to get out the message on the new program that had already touched off charges from Democrats that their opponents were using public monies for partisan purposes.[75]

As they edged closer to when seniors could begin registering for their discount cards, both parties stepped up the public relations battle. Republicans, especially, understood this represented a choice opportunity. "We're still going to push hard on Medicare," observed Rep. Pryce. "That will be when seniors finally realize that there really are cost savings available."[76] Cognizant of what was at stake, lawmakers on both sides of the aisle continued to make their case directly with constituents at town hall meetings. The National Republican Congressional Committee also tried to prod public sentiment in their party's direction by booking media appearances for a number of their House members in selected districts so that they could discuss the cards and the benefits they would bring. Minority Leader Pelosi countered such GOP public relations moves by providing members' press secretaries with samples of a press release and an editorial as well as a number of fact sheets that could be used as caucus members publicly pressed the party's case.[77]

Parties' activities in this initial round of the public relations fight that followed the enactment of the legislation perhaps crested on March 3, 2004, the first day beneficiaries were eligible to register for the prescription discount card. Republican lawmakers staged demonstrations showing constituents how to obtain the card and also provided examples of the program's benefits. Democratic leaders and rank-and-file members meanwhile countered with their own constituent forums, where they cautioned seniors about the program and highlighted its shortcomings.[78] The next day, a host of national and regional electronic and print outlets carried accounts of the sessions and the program, many of which featured comments from members of Congress, the administration, and interested advocacy coalitions.[79] The two parties pressed this grassroots battle through the Memorial Day recess, with Republicans charging Democrats and liberal allies, the National

Committee to Preserve Social Security and Medicare, and Families USA, with using town hall meetings to disseminate misleading information about the new benefits.[80]

The passing of the discount card sign-up deadline, however, did not bring the battle to a close. The initial open enrollment period for beneficiaries (October 15, 2005 to May 15, 2006) once again galvanized the parties' public relations operations. GOP leaders directed members to use part of their summer recess to highlight their legislative achievements, chief among which were the full Medicare benefits scheduled to go into effect in the upcoming months.[81] The Senate Republican Conference, in particular, plotted a "very disciplined" public relations strategy for its members to follow during their summer break, even going so far as to instruct senators to discuss the Medicare benefit, and GOP contributions to bringing it to fruition, in the second week of the recess.[82] Meanwhile, the GOP House Conference worked with members to prepare another series of public service announcements on the Medicare drug benefit. This second round of PSAs, taped near the end of the summer recess as members also recorded announcements pertaining to governmental assistance for Katrina victims, informed Social Security beneficiaries about the enrollment deadlines for the new benefit.[83]

As the open enrollment deadline drew near, congressional parties armed members with talking points and other materials and encouraged them to hold town hall meetings and take to the airwaves and the Internet to advance their respective positions on the legislation. Near the end of February, Democratic lawmakers boasted about holding more than one hundred events, where they attacked the program as what then Minority Leader Sen. Harry Reid (D-NV) described as "an overly complex and poorly implemented giveaway to HMOs and drug companies."[84] Not to be outdone, the GOP mounted an aggressive PR response in the final weeks. In early April they promised a multifaceted public relations battle employing media interviews, public service announcements, blogs, e-mails, opinion pieces, and town hall meetings. The *Washington Times* reported that House Republicans, by themselves, had already set up two hundred events surrounding the program before the enrollment deadline.[85]

The intensity of the battle did not subside until after the open enrollment period lapsed. The parties made it a central part of their communications push during the summer recess, but as that came to a close the issue lost some luster. Other more pressing matters, like the war in Iraq, rising energy prices, and illegal immigration eventually displaced it.[86] Polls indicated that for most folks the problem had lost its salience. Survey data also showed that skepticism toward the benefit had declined and that seniors were remarkably content with the plan. While polls varied, anywhere from 75% to 80% of the elderly indicated they were satisfied with their new drug benefits.[87] Though Democrats continued to attack the program, their incentives to keep it front and center in their publicity campaigns became less compelling. Meanwhile, having eked out something of a victory in what turned out to be a protracted battle, Republicans appeared loath to trumpet their success for fear of alienating parts of their base and setting off a litany of public complaints from a restive faction of GOP lawmakers who never really warmed up to the program.[88]

SCHIP

A harsh dose of political reality hit congressional Democrats early in the first session of the 107th Congress. Despite having just reclaimed control of both chambers for the first time in twelve years, polls showed that, after a modest uptick following the election, public confidence in Congress had once again declined to alarmingly low levels. By May 2007, Congress's job approval rating had fallen below 30%. More than half of those polled had unfavorable perceptions of congressional Democrats. News for their leaders was especially brutal; only 30% approved of Speaker Pelosi's performance, while just 22% rendered a favorable judgment on Majority Leader Reid. More disconcerting were public opinion trend lines that appeared as subsequent polls were released. They showed that near the end of July approval of Congress's performance had fallen to a historic low of 18%. Just as surely unnerving was the finding that only 21% of those who identified themselves as Democrats gave Congress positive marks.[89] Surveys intimated that many in the base felt the president and Republicans were outwitting the party on critical issues like the war in Iraq and national security and important domestic initiatives on health care, the environment, and the economy. Activists and a few at the netroots were especially unhappy and at times even described Democrats as "panicked," "weak," and "spineless."[90]

Scouting an Offensive

Worried about their party's unpopularity, growing discontent in their political base, and the upcoming elections, some Democratic congressional leaders gathered to map out a plan to shore up their brand and deflect attention away from their failure to force the administration's hand on policies especially dear to their supporters. Part of the strategy they adopted involved redoubling efforts to reauthorize and expand the State Children's Health Insurance Program (SCHIP).[91] Recent scholarship suggests that in mounting strategic communications campaigns legislative parties focus on issues that favor their brand and on which they are united and their opponents are not.[92] From this perspective, SCHIP was an especially tempting public relations target.

SCHIP, which helps states cover health care costs incurred by low-income families with annual earnings too high to qualify for Medicaid, was highly popular. Over 80% of those recently polled favored expanding SCHIP to cover a greater proportion of the uninsured. Support for the program, moreover, was widely distributed; polls showed 79% of the Republicans and 88% of the Democrats supported reauthorization.[93] Its proponents even included a large chunk of the health care sector, whose business and advocacy groups lobbied to expand the program through a tax increase on tobacco, as well as most of the nation's governors.[94] Furthermore, though it came out of a 1997 bipartisan agreement during a period of divided government, most polls suggested the issue perhaps favored Democrats, for when it came to health care issues most people, when asked, generally responded that they trusted Democrats more than Republicans.[95]

At the same time, party members' preferences made SCHIP an especially apt policy from which to launch a public relations offensive. Democrats coalesced around it. Even many of the party's more economically conservative lawmakers supported refunding and growing the program, making it easier for the party as a whole to arrive at a coherent message they could disseminate to support their legislative efforts. Congressional Republicans, in contrast, were oftentimes at odds with one another on the program's future. A strong majority in the House Conference stoutly resisted expanding SCHIP, while a small group of dissenters, usually from less conservative or swing districts, preferred cutting a deal. Concerned with their own political viability, they wanted to take the issue away from their opponents in the next election. Republicans in the Senate were also at sixes and sevens: some wanted to cooperate with Democrats, others wanted to reauthorize the program without significantly expanding it, and still others wanted to use the issue to provoke a more expansive debate on health care.[96]

These divisions within the GOP's Capitol Hill ranks presented Democrats with an opening they could pry. Thus, SCHIP quickly emerged as the "wedge" the leadership had been trying to isolate to build their public image.[97] Pushing SCHIP expansion to the top of the legislative agenda created an opportunity for Democrats to cleave Republicans and even openly separate some of them from the president, and it also promised to provide Democrats with a good vantage point from which to shape perceptions of where they stood and what they were doing on a policy that met with such wide acclaim. The opponents' intramural divisions on the issue would make it hard for them to counter the Democrats' publicity offensive. One GOP staffer, after surveying the disparate perspectives emerging within the party on the policy, bluntly concluded: "Message-wise it's [SCHIP] tough."[98]

A final reason for settling on SCHIP was that it provided an issue tailor-made for framing in ways suitable to Democrats' interests. Republicans' political options were limited. They were more unpopular than Democrats and they found themselves lagging behind their opponents on their trademark issue of fiscal responsibility. Combined, expenditures for the war in Iraq, a waxing national security state, the creation of big-ticket programs like No Child Left Behind and prescription drug coverage for seniors, and a yawning deficit had taken their toll. A July 2007 *Wall Street Journal/NBC News* poll gave Democrats an astounding 25% lead on handling the deficit, a 15% edge on managing the economy, and a 9% margin on dealing with taxes. The *Journal* also reported that Republicans had been hemorrhaging losses among fiscal conservatives, suggesting a "historic shift" in the party's identity.[99] This steady erosion in the GOP's public standing brought members' concerns about their image to the fore. As Rep. Tom Feeney (R-FL) explained, "we can't win elections nationally if more Americans think Democrats are more fiscally responsible than Republicans."[100] Yet for Republicans to demonstrate the kind of restraint necessary to reestablish their brand they had to toe the line on spending on popular programs like SCHIP and frame their response as fiscally prudent, even though they had already supported other programs that brought increases in government and spiraling deficits. That presented a predicament. Symbolically, opposing aid for poor children would be enough of an uphill battle. Rep.

Ray LaHood (R-IL), a moderate Republican who supported brokering a deal with Democrats, identified this challenge when he admitted that "it's [SCHIP] very sensitive. It's about kids. Who's against kids' health care?"[101] But that would be only part of Republicans' problem, since any effort to reframe the issue by focusing on limiting spending and curbing governmental growth left them vulnerable to charges of hypocrisy.

The Early Skirmish

Congressional Democrats prepared the political terrain before moving ahead with SCHIP. Key lawmakers and staffers made overtures to health care and insurance groups, labor unions, and advocacy coalitions to obtain their backing for a publicity campaign to complement and support their legislative actions. As *Roll Call* reported, "it is a textbook, if rarely seen, example of Congressional operatives turning the tables on lobbyists—Democratic leaders pressuring downtown interests to provide them air cover for their plan."[102]

Lining up financial and organizational assistance to provide air cover, Democrats in both chambers forged ahead. Despite warnings and veto threats from President Bush, who was intent on restoring his party's brand by holding firm to reauthorizing the program with only a $5 billion increase in funding, House Democrats upped the ante. They pushed through, on a predominantly partisan 225 to 204 vote, a more expansive bill that promised to double the number of children covered. The legislation called for an additional $50 billion in expenditures, much of which they aimed to pay for by boosting taxes and reducing subsidies to private providers who had entered the Medicare market. Meanwhile, the Senate offered a more moderate proposal that passed with some Republican support. This plan also bumped up tobacco taxes but held down funding increases to about $35 billion.[103]

Public relations considerations came into play as both chambers considered and wrote their bills. Democrats, especially those in the House, moved and even timed their legislative activities with an eye toward advancing their SCHIP publicity campaign. Eager to post a first-round win before their summer recess, they shut down House Republicans' speeches and delaying tactics and passed their more partisan bill, putting them on schedule to iron out differences between the chambers and send a bill to the president in the early fall, well before program's funding lapsed on September 30, 2007.[104] That suited their messaging strategy. First, it kept them on track to realize their objective of forcing the president to make expanding health care for poor children the first bill of the session on which he would exercise his veto in defense of Republicans' efforts to recuperate their image on fiscal responsibility.[105] Democrats did not want to present Bush with an opportunity to veto another, less popular spending measure, since that would allow him to establish his party's credibility on fiscal austerity and make it easier for him and his Capitol Hill partners to get the upper hand in framing SCHIP around the issues of taxing and spending.[106]

The symbolism of that first veto promised Democrats a choice public relations opportunity, one where they could portray the president and their congressional opponents as standing with the tobacco companies, and only getting serious on curbing government and trimming deficits when it came to spending money to help poor, sick children. It also freed them to go back to their districts where they could use local venues to stump for a more encompassing and generous program.[107] Finally, it gave them an opportunity to launch attacks against Republicans who sided with the president just as those same Republican members were back home meeting with their constituents. In fact, the DCCC had already commenced its public campaign in selected GOP constituencies. And DCCC chair, Rep. Chris Van Hollen (D-MD), promised more to come during the recess: "This August we're going district by district to urge Republicans to stop obstructing progress. Republicans who continue to vote in lockstep with President Bush and against children and seniors in their districts will be held accountable." Several key advocacy groups working with Democrats, including the American Medical Association and the Robert Wood Johnson Foundation, gave the DCCC's effort an added boost by launching multimillion dollar publicity campaigns on behalf of SCHIP.[108]

The Second Round

After the summer recess, the House and Senate went to conference to settle their differences. The panel consummated a deal that jettisoned cuts in Medicare subsidies and increased spending by $35 billion, twice as much as the president requested but $15 billion less than what the House wanted. It also called for a steep increase in tobacco taxes to pay for funding growth. The report garnered support from most Democrats and even managed to win backing from more centrist Republican lawmakers.[109]

President Bush, however, held firm, reiterating his threat to veto any bill that exceeded his funding request, increased taxes, and dramatically expanded eligibility. Democrats, in turn, pushed for a direct confrontation. They believed they held the winning hand. "If the president signs the bill we present to him," declared Rep. Rahm Emanuel (D-IL) the chair of the Democratic Caucus, "it's a major accomplishment. If he vetoes the bill, it's a political victory for us."[110] And *Politico* reported that if, as expected, Bush vetoed the bill, Democrats planned to use that "political victory" to run ads attacking Republicans for "voting against poor children."[111] Meanwhile, some of the more moderate Republicans and GOP sympathizers advised the president to cut a deal and eschew getting pulled into what would most likely be a losing public relations volley.[112]

Democratic lawmakers cranked up their publicity campaign as they sent the conference report to the president. Senators Richard Durbin (D-IL) and Debbie Stabenow (D-MI), for instance, held a teleconference to announce they were introducing an online petition, to be delivered to the White House as the legislation made its way to the president's desk, on behalf of SCHIP.[113] A group of leaders subsequently appeared on Capitol Hill with Gemma Frost, a nine-year old from Baltimore, Maryland, who, along with her brother, Graeme, had suffered severe injuries in a car accident and had received medical assistance under the SCHIP program, to urge the president not to veto the bill. Majority Leader Reid and Speaker Pelosi then picked Gemma's brother, Graeme, to deliver the party's weekly radio address. Reading a speech drafted by Senate aides, he appealed to the president to sign the expanded program into law.[114]

The next week Speaker Pelosi and Majority Leader Reid presented SCHIP to the White House. Fearing distractions and wanting to keep the focus on their primary message on children's health care, Democratic leaders kept a heavy hand on the tiller inside their chambers as they carried on their public relations campaign. They scuttled a potentially headline grabbing proposal made by some senior House Democrats to impose a surtax to cover the costs of the Iraq war, and appearing at rallies and a series of press conferences, key Democrats continued to press the president to sign the bill.[115]

This scheme to raise the stakes through a series of orchestrated public appeals, even when combined with some pressure from moderates in his own party to agree to the bill, failed to dissuade the president from following through on his threat. He vetoed the legislation on the morning of October 3, 2007 and later explained his decision at a nationally televised forum. Speaking to a local Chamber of Commerce group, he contended that the SCHIP legislation delivered to him by the Democratic Congress was too costly and too generous. He also claimed that, by extending coverage to children outside lower income groups, it represented the first step down the road to federalization of the nation's health care system, a theme that some in the GOP had already tried to translate into sound bites when they accused Democrats of favoring "socialized medicine."[116]

Bringing It Back

Democratic lawmakers like Emanuel vowed to persist: "We're going to throw it [SCHIP] back at them time after time."[117] And once again they gauged legislative tactics in their public relations battle. Over a spate of protests from the House GOP, leaders delayed for two weeks taking up a measure to override the president's veto. Ostensibly, they intended to extend the period through which they could attack the president and his supporters and either create enough pressure to wear down the resistance of enough wavering lawmakers to succeed on the override or drive up their opponents' unpopularity and improve their own political fortunes. During that window of opportunity, Pelosi elevated her profile in the media to press the party's case.[118] The DCCC and allied interest groups meanwhile used that time to target Republicans backing the president with a series of hard hitting television and radio advertisements, phone calls, and e-mails.[119] And in a new twist, one important activist organization working with Democrats to pass the bill, Families USA, took its case to the Internet, posting its policy advocacy ads on a number of blogs as well as more traditional venues.[120]

These withering attacks left "some Republicans," as one GOP lawmaker put it, "bleeding like stuck pigs."[121] They also prompted Republicans to charge that Democrats were more interested in pulverizing their opponents and advancing their political fortunes than in getting medical assistance to poor children. "The idea that this is about health care," observed an aide to Minority Leader Mitch McConnell (R-KY), "is gone. It's about 30-second ads in congressional districts."[122]

House Democrats manipulated the chamber procedures to magnify their message in other ways. They strategically scheduled and used committee reports and legislation on fraud and profiteering and budget hearings to sharpen their framing of the public discussion. By bringing to the fore the costs and financial misdeeds associated with the Iraq war, they strategically counterposed what they took to be Republicans' willingness to tolerate profligacy, waste, and fraud in the war in Iraq with the GOP's tight-fisted abandonment of children among the working poor.[123] House Democrats also manipulated the legislative calendar to keep the spotlight on SCHIP, delaying votes on appropriations for defense, national security, and foreign affairs, since final consideration of those bills threatened to shift the public discussion away from their battle with the GOP on domestic priorities.[124] Indeed, *Roll Call* reported that the House Democrats intended to impose tight limits on the reauthorization of the Foreign Intelligence Surveillance Act (FISA), which came in the middle of the public battle over SCHIP. This is because it played to GOP strengths on national security and advanced Republicans' interests in deflecting attention away from the children's health program.[125]

Meantime, the Republicans' theme was less focused and clear. Many did make a forceful public case for holding the line on SCHIP. GOP leaders held press conferences, wrote editorials, and made the talk show circuit to defend the president's veto and their party's stance. Other members, especially those from the economically conservative RSC Caucus, lent their support with press releases, editorials in local papers, and postings on their office websites.[126] Still, as one GOP senator admitted, there was "no coordinated message to speak of," and internal divisions made it difficult for Republican lawmakers to develop one to counter Democrats' claims.[127] High profile Republicans like Sen. Orrin Hatch (R-UT) and Sen. Charles Grassley (R-IA) appeared with Democratic leaders to implore their colleagues to override the president's veto, while some rank-and-file Republicans, like Mark Kirk (R-IL), boasted on their online offices that they had broken with their party and voted to expand the program.[128]

The Republican message operation also had a steep hill to climb. The issue, as noted earlier, was especially hard to frame on Republican terms, given the party's previous support for programs that grew governmental spending. This stymied Republicans' efforts to get a handle on the issue and perhaps contributed to delays in finally arriving at a message, "covering the poor kids first," that would resonate with the American people.[129] Then again, as the minority party the GOP was unable to deploy control over legislative scheduling and procedures in ways that would leave them better positioned to advance their publicity campaign or to deflect the public's attention away from the issue by shifting to an issue that favored them.

The House sustained the president's veto on October 18, 2007. Immediately after the 273 to 156 vote, Speaker Pelosi announced that Democrats would send the president a "bill that insures coverage for 10 million children" within another two weeks. Later that day, the DCCC issued press releases in thirty-three Republican districts, whose representatives stood with the president in opposing the override.[130]

The House took less than a week to pass another bill. Although the legislation made adjustments to the original version, Republican opponents could not be budged. This revised proposal, in fact, garnered slightly less GOP support than what had passed in September. House Republicans were nonplussed. They accused the Democrats of failing to reach out and meet their objections in a meaningful way. On top of that, Democrats scheduled the vote as several members from the California delegation, Republicans as well as Democrats, were home visiting districts that had been ravaged by wildfires and declared disaster zones. Despite Republican entreaties to hold off on taking the vote, Democrats pushed ahead, prompting even some Republicans sympathetic to negotiating a deal to protest. "I used to think they [Democrats] cared about the policy," complained Rep. Ray LaHood (R-IL), who had been working behind the scenes to bring the opposing sides together. "Now I think they care more about the politics." Indeed, many Republicans believed Democrats had accelerated the schedule so that they could cut another round of political advertisements to advance their publicity goals.[131]

Congressional parties in both chambers, however, did try to move beyond the gridlock on SCHIP that settled on Capitol Hill. But positions taken by the bill's supporters, who were adamant on expanding the program, and its opponents, the president and a sizable core of House Republicans who firmly resisted any substantial increases in funding and coverage, could not be reconciled. With time running out, and feeling that they had made their case with the public, Democrats finally reached a deal to extend SCHIP through the early months of the next administration.[132] Still, feeling some pressure from their base for abandoning the fight, and wanting to set the stage for the upcoming election by clarifying what they stood for, Democrats resurrected the issue after the turn of the year and passed another expanded version of the program. Bush once again struck down the bill. Unable to muster the votes required to overcome a presidential veto, Democrats let the issue drop, though they hinted they would bring it back as the election season drew closer.[133] But as the campaign season got underway, SCHIP faded into the background as other issues came to the fore, and it did not emerge again as a central focus until Barack Obama was sworn in as president, giving Democrats control of both ends of Pennsylvania Avenue. In one of its first actions, the 111th Congress passed a bill expanding SCHIP, which President Obama promptly signed into law.[134]

Immigration Reform: What's Good For the Goose...

In 2006 and again in 2007 some of Washington's most powerful actors came together in an unusual bipartisan coalition to reform immigration. Their chances of success seemed promising. President Bush regularly cited this as a key goal, his party controlled the House and Senate in 2006, and Democratic leaders in 2007 indicated they would work with the president on the issue. He also had the support of the Senate's majority and minority leaders, and in 2007, the backing of Speaker

Nancy Pelosi (D-CA). In addition, a number of key senators, including Sen. Ted Kennedy (D-MA) and Sen. John McCain (R-AZ), joined the cause. Moreover this issue resonated with the Latino community, which Republicans had "spent years wooing" and whose allegiance the Republican National Committee (RNC) chair and most political strategists considered crucial for the party's future. Finally, throughout much of this period a majority of the people favored reform.[135]

Anatomy of a Failure

Despite these many advantages, Bush and his legislative allies were twice thwarted in their efforts to secure immigration reform. Several variables account for this: First, the congressional parties were, to different degrees, divided on this issue. Pushing hard for broad immigration reform stressed these internal fault lines and frequently prompted "vicious in-fighting."[136] Instead of gaining consensus on preferences, parties frequently got mired in "fractious backroom policy debates."[137] Any bipartisan coalition was thus always fragile; its members were regularly attacked and pressured by colleagues in their own parties.[138]

Immigration reform also excites powerful feelings across the country. As the spokesman for House Majority Leader John Boehner put it, "immigration [is] not a small-skirmish issue."[139] The politics of the initiative is entangled with larger cultural issues, such as the role that race and language play in the life of the country, and is frequently linked with the problem of terrorism and national security interests. One of the cosponsors of the bill, Senator Jon Kyl (R-AZ), captured the intensity of passions running up against sweeping reform when he admitted: "I have learned some new words from some of my constituents."[140]

Such emotional outbursts were not one-sided. Latino activists organized large nationwide marches on behalf of immigration reform. Some proreform advocates, meanwhile, explicitly made a policymaker's vote on this matter a test of whether they were prepared to accept Latino neighbors as full American citizens. For some, such votes were a "gauge [of] the level of respect a party or candidate has for this community."[141] And when Representative Tom Tancredo (R-CO), a prominent opponent of the bipartisan coalition, began to speak at Michigan State University, he was interrupted by protestors, who shouted that he was a racist, set off fire alarms, and generally so disrupted the gathering that he was unable to finish his talk.[142] Hence, not only were both congressional parties internally divided on immigration, but members also knew that this issue was "so sensitive and so explosive that it could easily blow up in [their] faces" if they agreed to follow their leaders' advice.[143]

President Bush, meanwhile, lacked the political capital to overcome divisions in the Congress and the public. He certainly supported the effort. He called legislators from the presidential airplane, assigned two prominent Cabinet officials to work with representatives and senators, and held a series of face-to-face meetings with members to keep the initiative alive. He also spoke to the nation from the Oval Office and engaged in several speaking tours around the country. Yet his waning job approval ratings, which had plummeted to 32% in June 2007, diminished his ability to provide momentum for any bill.[144] As early as 2006, a Republican with ties to the White House blamed the immigration reform coalition's troubles on "the total collapse of the president's numbers among conservatives."[145] And things only got worse as GOP polling organizations found Republicans' approval of the president's handling of the immigration issue fell from 61% to 45% as the legislative struggle unfolded.[146] The emerging presidential campaign compounded Bush's eroding support. Republicans vying to be the party's next presidential candidate did not even pretend to veil their criticism of Bush or his stance on immigration during early debates, where "the virulence of the criticisms stunned many in the audience, including those involved in the GOP nomination battle."[147] Bush had become so toxic that some prominent congressional Republican supporters of the coalition's measure actually told reporters they wished he would leave this issue alone. "With regards to the President on [immigration]," said Senator Trent Lott (R-MS), a key coalition leader and the Minority Whip, "I hope he concentrates on the G8."[148]

2006: The House Revolts

In 2005, the GOP House majority passed an immigration bill, putting them on a collision course with the president and many Senate Republicans. Responding to what many in their Conference perceived to be the casual flouting of immigration law and national security risks they associated with that lawlessness, their proposals focused on improving border security and punishing illegal immigrants and those who assist them. Their bill called for a mandatory employee verification system and a tamper-proof employee identification card. They also proposed having all illegal immigrants declared felons, building a border fence, creating a database of all lawful Social Security numbers that employers could access to verify workers' legal status, and increasing penalties for employers who hired or aided undocumented workers. The majority's goals, as an RNC talking points document later made clear, were to stop the flow of illegal immigrants at the border and to root out and deport those already in the country.[149]

The Senate took a different tack in early 2006. Majority Leader Bill Frist (R-TN) worked with a bipartisan group on a policy to beef up border security and create a process whereby illegal immigrants could normalize their status. Popularly referred to as the McCain-Kennedy bill, the legislation, like the House's, added resources to keep out illegal immigrants. Yet it also created a guest worker program for new immigrants, and a "path to citizenship" that allowed many undocumented immigrants to stay in the country if they paid a $2,000 fine and back taxes, underwent a background check, learned English, took civics lessons, and avoided legal trouble for six years.[150]

This initiative engendered fierce opposition from conservatives, who derided it as amnesty for criminals, and won only mild support from some liberal quarters. The Senate coalition thus needed a bill that could attract a chamber majority, stave off amendments designed to peel away wavering coalition members, and do it all by Memorial Day, for by then, as one Democratic aide said, "we're running up against election season," and in that "red-meat, vote-courting" atmosphere any bipartisan bill "will be on life support."[151]

By late April, this fragile alliance was in danger, prompting Bush to get more involved. He met with the coalition's leaders and traveled the country to speak on behalf of the Senate's moderate approach. While he avoided taking a position on any Senate proposals, he criticized the House bill, calling it "unrealistic."[152] He also tried to raise the stakes through a national, prime-time Oval Office speech, where he announced that while he had ordered more National Guard troops to the border, he favored allowing some undocumented workers to become citizens. Appealing to his Republican base and to the Latino community, he advocated a middle-ground position: "America can be a lawful society and a welcoming society at the same time."[153] On May 25, after six committee markup sessions and two weeks of debate, Majority Leader Frist stood alongside Minority Leader Reid to celebrate the bipartisan measure's 62-36 passage.

Summer Hearings: Let's Take This Outside

The Senate returned from Memorial Day recess eager to set a conference deadline, but House leaders dragged their feet. House Majority Leader Boehner, raising procedural objections, started talking about "*if* we go to conference."[154] On June 22, Boehner and Speaker Hastert held a news conference to highlight their plan to forgo a conference meeting and instead deploy committee chairs to hold a series of national public hearings through the summer. They aimed to frame the immigration debate as a law-and-order and a national security issue, and label the Senate's bill as a Democratic initiative, despite the high-profile support it enjoyed from the president and the 23 Republican senators who voted for it. To that end, they gave members recess communications packages referencing "the Reid-Kennedy Senate Democratic Immigration Bill" and said that "Americans should know what's in the Reid-Kennedy Bill.... We believe the Kennedy Bill does not go far enough to address illegal immigration or secure our border."[155]

House Republicans also organized a public relations "war room" to coordinate their communications efforts on their "enforcement-first" theme and to publicize their summer hearings. They divided the country into twelve different regions and designated press aides from individual members' personal offices to each one. Leaders had these aides monitor news in their assigned regions and report back. Based on these reports, leaders then asked members to write opinion pieces or do talk radio or television shows that explained and argued for the House Republicans' preferred position. Their goal was to put public pressure on the Senate and to frame that body's legislation as predominantly the work of Democrats. House Democrats meanwhile opted to keep their message focused on the GOP's failure to produce a bill.[156] Throughout July and August House Republicans appeared in a variety of media outlets and hammered home Hastert's and Boehner's message.[157]

The Senate's coalition leaders responded in kind, holding their own public hearings that centered on the need to find a way to accommodate the millions of undocumented people in the country and to highlight the important role they played in the economy. "We can use [our] hearings to show the importance of the provisions in our bill that are not in the House bill," said Sen. Arlen Specter (R-PA), and his ally Sen. Lindsay Graham (R-SC) warned that if the House waged a publicity campaign attacking the Senate bill that maneuver could "go both ways."[158]

The events of July 5 illustrate the nature of these dueling hearings that both sides organized in "a summer-long competition for public sentiment." The day began with a Senate hearing in Philadelphia that included New York Mayor Michael Bloomberg and other urban leaders testifying to the key contributions that undocumented immigrants make to the civic and economic life of their cities. It ended with a session, organized by Rep. Ed Royce (R-CA), which focused on national security risks posed by illegal immigrants.[159]

GOP House leaders convened an early September forum where committee chairs reported back from their summer public tours. There Speaker Hastert revealed intentions to pass a series of ten stand-alone, security-related immigration bills before the September recess. With leaders leaving more contentious, mandatory employee screening matters for another day, and planning to attach their security measures to the Homeland Security appropriations bill, the House passed the first item on that list—building a 700 mile fence along the U.S.–Mexican border. By cherry-picking the most popular parts of their earlier immigration bill and passing them as a series of discrete initiatives, the House's leadership undercut any bargaining power Senate leaders had hoped to wield in conference negotiations, and they applied enormous pressure on the Senate to approve at least some of their bills. When senators threatened to filibuster the House fence bill in a last-ditch effort to keep a more comprehensive reform measure alive, angry citizens flooded their office phones for a week and many sent members bricks, indicating support for the more restrictive House initiative. On September 28, the Senate ended debate and scheduled a floor vote the next day. Democrats announced they would no longer make opposition to the fence a test of party loyalty, and on the following day the measure passed by a whopping 80-19 vote. President Bush signed it into law just two weeks before the midterm elections. In what one GOP representative called an "eyeball-to-eyeball confrontation" with the Senate and the president, House Republicans clearly won the day.[160]

2007: The Center Cannot Hold

Midterm elections did little to change the underlying political challenges facing immigration reform. Coalition supporters took solace in the fact that the new leaders of the Democratic majorities in both chambers favored working with the president to resolve the issue. Additionally, a number of prominent critics of the Senate's effort lost their seats. Yet in those same elections several states approved ballot measures that were consistent with the "security first" position and sent to Congress several Democratic senators and representatives from Republican leaning constituencies.[161] What the elections did do, however, was to make the Senate the arena where immigration issues were to be decided, as House Democratic leaders made it clear that they were not going to ask the members of their new majority, including some from more competitive districts, to cast a politically risky vote only to see the Senate coalition fall apart.[162]

In mid-January, President Bush fired an early salvo in this round of the immigration battle by appointing Sen. Mel Martinez (R-FL) cochair of the RNC. Martinez was a prominent leader of the Senate's bipartisan coalition, and this unusual arrangement—only the third time in 36 years that the RNC had shared-leadership—clearly antagonized more conservative RNC members who protested the White House's "Politburo" tactics.[163] This early skirmish signaled both that the president was ready to keep fighting for a broader bill and that many Republicans were still prepared to resist him.

Some conservative GOP senators took the battle to their opponents. Sen. James DeMint (R-SC), for instance, used the Internet to gin up bloggers' and talk radio hosts' opposition to a moderate bipartisan bill. He fired off news releases that were picked up and posted on conservative news aggregation websites like the Drudge Report. And in early March he created a website (www.completethefencenow.com) to post a video about the need to build a fence and communicate with outside allies in an effort to scuttle any middle-ground reform initiative.[164] Still, the center of gravity for the coalition's principal opponents was a smaller and more united House Republican Conference. Its members now had to adapt to a different political terrain. In 2006, they controlled the chamber's internal mechanisms, and so coordinated their external public communications campaigns with their ability to schedule or postpone meetings and votes in ways that favored their position. This year they were left with the option of only a publicity campaign, which they commenced in late April when they joined thirty-nine talk radio show hosts from across the nation who set up shop at a hotel near the Capitol for a weeklong initiative called Hold Their Feet to the Fire. These morning-to-midnight broadcasts centered on the message that illegal immigrants cause "a cascade of problems in the [country] in public services, health care, public schools and law enforcement." Throughout the week interviewees included Republican members opposed to any effort to provide a mechanism for illegal immigrants to earn citizenship, and the event's media director alluded to the political power wielded by listeners who are informed and motivated by such events. "Immigration is one of those issues that light up the phones lines," a power that is especially important to congressional actors who cannot control the scheduling of committee meetings or floor votes.[165]

The bipartisan coalition's goals remained essentially the same. But in an effort to woo conservative opponents, their new proposal included "touchback" language that required some immigrants to return to their country of origin and start a process leading to reentry. This did little to appease conservative House Democrats dead set against "amnesty and it only stiffened the resolve of most House Republicans."[166]

The Senate coalition started to crack under the strain of unrelenting public criticism. President Bush, in an early May appeal to his opponents, said that he supported two new provisions that many of his Democratic allies opposed—a point system that favored highly skilled immigrants and disadvantaged low-wage ones, and limited "chain migration," which allows immigrants to sponsor family members. Latino groups and labor unions publicly pressured Democrats to resist these amendments and Majority Leader Reid scheduled debate to begin on May 16. Senator Kennedy, however, prevailed on Reid to give the coalition a few more days. He launched round-the-clock private talks between the coalition's bipartisan leaders and their staffers, and on the following day he emerged at a news conference, surrounded by nine senators—seven Republicans, two Democrats—and two members of the administration, to announce an agreement to bring a bill to the floor. The legislation survived its first few days, as the coalition fought off amendments that threatened to unravel their precarious majority. Supporters predicted victory was in the offing as they headed into the Memorial Day recess. [167]

Who Killed Immigration Reform?

Yet the relentless pressure that members received at home over the recess and on the day of the vote to oppose the bill enabled reform opponents to derail all of this careful work. Supporter Sen. Lindsay Graham (R-SC), for instance, was roundly booed at his state party convention over the recess, as was Sen. Johnny Isakson (R-GA), who had merely indicated that he might support the reform bill should it be brought to a vote.[168] Through its website, the predominantly Republican House Immigration Reform Caucus issued news alerts, media advisories, and interviews to publicize its opposition to the bill.[169] Interest groups opposed to the reform launched advertising campaigns to pressure Republicans to vote against any bill that provided citizenship. Some members of the House GOP minority openly assisted these efforts. Grassfire.org, for instance, worked with Republican reform opponents like Rep. Steve King (R-IA) to produce a "Where's the Fence?" series of cable television advertisements that depicted three elderly women on the Mexican border shouting, "Where's the fence?," as three actors portraying Mexicans "scurr[ied] across a road." At the same time, The Minuteman Civil Defense Corps funded radio ads that urged citizens opposed to the bill to contact their senators.[170] House Republican opponents gained support from key talk radio and cable news personalities in stoking the opposition. These figures elevated the issue to the top of the week's news cycle, and they echoed the GOP opponents' talking points on what they branded the "amnesty bill."[171] They also brooked little dissent within their ranks. On the day of the vote talk radio host Laura Ingraham "raked [fellow] conservative leader Grover Norquist over the coals" because he had called immigration opponents "a handful of loud people," who scared citizens away from Republicans.[172] Opponents in the blogosphere and more partisan media likewise lambasted Senator Lott shortly after he publicly complained about talk radio's influence on the debate.[173]

Supporters of the legislation were not strategically positioned to counter this growing opposition chorus; they were caught in a communications duel that pitted what Republican pollster Tony Fabrizio called "practical principle against practical reality."[174] House GOP opponents portrayed the bill as a "reward" for "lawbreakers," which resonated with an American public that supported border enforcement, not "amnesty" for criminals.[175] By contrast, the best that supporters could do is claim their bill, however imperfect, was still better than that offered by those "who want to do nothing."[176]

Republican opponents came back emboldened. The House GOP Conference passed by an overwhelming margin of 114 to 23 a resolution indicating its disapproval of the Senate bill.[177] Meanwhile, Senate opponents engaged in floor activity that "shocked" their leaders. Leaders from both sides of the aisle had agreed on a carefully crafted strategy for bringing certain amendments up for consideration, and they were stunned when four Republicans crossed party lines and voted with liberal Democrats to pass an amendment aimed at ending a guest worker program that they and the business community had long supported. When asked to explain their unusual vote, the four Republicans made it clear that they knew that weakening the guest worker program would shatter the fragile bipartisan coalition. Minority Whip Lott did not expect these four to defect from their heretofore united stand in support of the guest worker program and admitted that he was "embarrassed to say they were trying to kill the bill, and I'm ashamed of it."[178]

Democratic and Republican coalition members scrambled to resuscitate their bill, drawing up a host of amendments that might appease opponents, and with the president out of the country the White House sent Homeland Security Secretary Michael Chertoff and Commerce Secretary Carlos Gutierrez to the chamber to lobby fellow Republicans. Yet opponents rebuffed every effort, leading an exasperated Senator Lott to exclaim, "I've about had it. I will not be a part of a protracted filibuster. We are not going to let this bill die by endless amendments."[179]

But at the end of a long day, that is exactly what happened. Thirty-eight Republicans joined eleven Democrats and one Independent and voted against cloture. Opponents had employed a public communication strategy that helped stir up such a groundswell of opposition that the chamber's leaders surrendered control. Dejected coalition leaders shirked the spotlight. Senator McCain, for instance, "normally one to chat with reporters," brushed past reporters as he left the floor with a terse "I don't have anything to say."[180] Jubilant immigration reform opponents, however, were more than happy to talk. As one of them put it after the June 7 vote, "our neighborhoods across our country have spoken loud and clear, and the United States heard their concerns. This bill is dead."[181]

Bipartisan reformers made one last attempt to get a bill out of the Senate. President Bush moved his weekly radio address up a day and delivered it from Air Force One, asking Congress to revisit the issue. From Air Force One, he called senators and agreed to meet with Senate Republicans the following week.[182] On June 12, he went to the Capitol to meet with coalition leaders and Republican senators who opposed reform, and in a "frank but cordial" exchange he agreed to support an emergency spending bill to increase border security and the enforcement of immigration laws in advance of any immigration bill to assuage opponents who doubted his resolve to address their main concerns.[183] Given that commitment, Republican leaders were able to reach an agreement with their Democratic counterparts to revive the immigration bill, and coalition negotiators tried one more time to find a way to placate enough senators to bring a bill to the floor for an up-or-down vote.[184]

The morning of the June 28, 2007 vote began like the one three weeks earlier. Senators whose votes were crucial to passing the bill were targeted by "a deluge of phone calls from constituents, mostly clamoring for the measure's defeat." When after a series of votes the initiative stalled, proceedings broke down. Coalition leaders looked for Minority Leader Mitch McConnell (R-KY), who had supported President Bush's 11th-hour effort to revive the bill and had negotiated the parliamentary tactics under which it was being considered, to help them find a way past this obstacle, but he was nowhere to be found. Finally, he showed up to add his voice to the vote that helped kill the bill.[185]

What Have We Learned?

These three stories bring to the surface several important themes. First, they underscore the importance of coordinating or linking public relations campaigns with what happens inside the chambers. Congressional parties can strategically exploit agenda setting, the scheduling of debates and votes, and the timing of breaks in legislative business in ways that facilitate their message operation. House Democrats, for instance, deftly applied an inside-outside strategy in the public fracas that accompanied SCHIP. The issue they selected certainly met the conditions parties consider integral for publicity campaigns. Not only did it have strong public support, but it fit their own image or brand and it was a policy on which they were united in their preferences and their opponents were divided.[186] They pushed expansion of SCHIP to the top of the agenda, where it received high visibility, and then carefully calibrated their activities inside the chamber with those they pursued outside of it. Right from the beginning, concerns about their message and effectively getting it out weighed rather heavily on and in good part shaped when they considered the bill, what else they allowed on the legislative agenda, and even when they returned back to their constituencies.

While the House majority undoubtedly has the greatest leverage on the Hill in using control of procedures and scheduling to advance its message, the minority party, which is perhaps the most dependent on an outside strategy, can occasionally find significant openings in legislative business to mount publicity campaigns that support its interests. The House Democratic minority, for instance, successfully exploited breaks in the congressional calendar to mount publicity campaigns to try to define the meaning and import of the prescription drug policy. The House Republican minority likewise used the calendar to their advantage when they publicly elevated concerns about the immigration reform. Over the summer recess, they joined with others to keep their preferred course of action front and center and to call into question and ultimately derail the efforts of the fragile bipartisan coalition of senators working on the immigration bill. And in today's environment failure to exploit these opportunities when they are presented creates openings for opponents. Senate and House Republicans, for instance, found this to be the case when, immediately following enactment of the drug bill, they and the White

House neglected to follow through with a communications operation to explain, and take credit for, a policy that, from the public's perspective, was still open to interpretation.

Still, while procedures inside the chamber are often linked with an outside strategy, communications operations in today's political environment can extend well beyond the period in which a policy is conceived, advanced, debated, and passed. The case of the prescription drug bill shows that today's parties have incentives to engage in publicity campaigns not only to thwart or enact a policy but also to shape how it will be interpreted. On certain occasions, they even have the incentive and discipline to try to use a public strategy to bring about a reversal of course. Stages or milestones in the policy's implementation therefore present choice openings for congressional parties to mount efforts to shore up their "brand" and discredit their opponents' public standing. The prescription drug bill is by no means extraordinary on this count, as recurring public relations battles over other recently passed policies, the 2011 American Recovery and Reinvestment Action—the "stimulus"—and the Patient Protection and Affordable Care Act—"Obamacare"—attest.

Finally, all three of these cases serve to remind us once again just how difficult it is for congressional parties to shape and direct their members' messaging activities on behalf of their programmatic and partisan goals. Parties may certainly employ strategies and structures to rein in members' public communications, but internal party cohesion just as surely shapes and determines the efficacy of outside strategies as it does those pursued inside the Hill's chamber walls. Democrats, especially, were able to mount an effective public relations campaign on SCHIP not only because they opposed a Republican president but also because they coalesced behind the policy. This enabled them both to wield power effectively inside their chambers, especially in the House, and to keep their members together on the outside. This also made it easier for them to strike harmony across the chambers when it came to their partisan message. House Republicans, of course, managed to hang together on immigration, as the strong endorsement of their policy position by their Conference in 2007 signified. Still, their preferences and consequently their communications activities, which put them in line with some of their important constituencies and attentive publics, frequently set them at odds with many of their colleagues in the Senate and with the president, who preferred a more moderate stance on the issue. This, in turn, muddled the message disseminated by their party overall. Then again, on the other two issues, deviations from GOP party members inside the chambers occasionally erupted on the outside as well, thus undermining the "consistency" that is a defining attribute of a successful brand.[187] Thus, even in today's more polarized, partisan environment, congressional parties, while employing various strategies and structures to get out coherent messages, frequently strain to get their members speaking with the same voice to bring clarity to their public images and to advance their fortunes.

7 The President Meets Congress in a New Media World

The Public Relations Battle Over the Stimulus Package

Slightly more than a month after taking the oath of office in 2009, President Barack Obama signed into law the American Recovery and Reinvestment Act, legislation that promised to ameliorate the most severe economic downturn since the Great Depression. This historic stimulus established early perceptions of the Obama White House. "That accumulation of numbers on the TV screen night in and night out in those first six months I think deeply troubled people ...," as President Obama recounted. "They started feeling like ... here we've got these folks in Washington who just seem to be printing money and spending it like nobody's business. And it reinforced the narrative that the Republicans wanted to promote anyway, which was Obama is ... the same old tax-and-spend liberal Democrat."[1] Along with bailouts for the banks and the automobile industry, and a landmark health care reform bill that promised to extend medical coverage to the uninsured, the Recovery Act spurred antigovernment Tea Party protests that swept across the country in 2009 and 2010. As unemployment climbed, it also gave Republicans a potent issue they used in the 2010 midterm election to take back the House and make significant inroads in the Senate, a point even Speaker Nancy Pelosi (D-CA) admitted: "What made a difference in the election is the fact that they [Republicans] said we are spending money, and where are the jobs?"[2]

This sweeping $787 billion package of expenditures and tax cuts exacerbated partisan conflict and touched off public relations battles that recurred through the president's first two years in office and shadowed subsequent policy debates. Besides stirring public uneasiness, shaping election outcomes, and determining the public's first impressions of the Obama presidency, this political struggle, we believe, provides an important case from which we can glean insights into the organized public relations campaign strategies lawmakers follow as they join the president in a more dynamic, interconnected, around-the-clock news environment.

We begin by tracing the skills and innovations in communications President Obama brought to the White House and how he initially applied those in making the case for the stimulus. We then explore the communications campaigns that accompanied the bill as it made its way on the Hill and to the president. Here we highlight congressional parties' public relations initiatives and assess their efficacy. We then turn to the dueling publicity campaigns that followed the bill's passage and set the tone for the 2010 election and conclude by reflecting on what this case suggests.

The Presidency Enters a New Media Age: The "Bully Pulpit" 2.0

President Obama, by most measures, is well-suited to the bully pulpit. He has relied on and successfully honed his talent for public communications throughout his career, and he has already tapped many of the conventional tools and formidable advantages of the institution he inherited and followed other administrations' tactics in waging public campaigns to support his agenda.[3] At the same time, his White House has grafted new communications strategies to standard approaches to public relations, putting it more in sync with an age marked by the growing importance of web-based social media. This certainly fits with a general trend in which presidents bring their office closer to the American people and enlist campaign strategies as they try to govern.[4] Yet it has just as surely resulted in "qualitative breakthroughs" in the ways a White House executes its public relations operations.[5]

Obama's efforts to reconfigure public communications extend back through the transition to the early stages of the presidential campaign, where he successfully integrated social networking technologies with more traditional ways of campaigning. He brought to his run for the White House an "entrepreneurial" understanding of the web's political potential. Netscape founder, Marc Andreessen, recounted that Obama "was the first politician I dealt with who understood that the technology was a given and that it could be used in new ways."[6] Candidate Obama supported this entrepreneurial vision by hiring a number of technologically sophisticated aides who had pioneered use of the Internet on Howard Dean's 2004 campaign as well as folks from the high tech community, including one of Facebook's cofounders. Over the course of the campaign, they deftly employed the web and social networking venues to raise money, build a base of supporters, and directly communicate with the voters.[7]

Obama's vision of how social media can be deployed in politics, however, extended well beyond the election's immediate challenges. As he stumped for his change agenda, he made clear his belief that these same technologies could be applied to make government more transparent and accountable. He even pledged that he would tap the power of web-based media and use it to transform the White House, turning it into an interactive democratic forum for "21st century fireside chats."[8]

Obama started delivering on his promise shortly after the election by naming a director of new media to his incoming administration's Office of Communications and assigning him responsibility for taking the White House into the Internet age.[9] Drawing on campaign experiences, members of Obama's New Media shop set up the first ever online office, www.change.gov, for a president-elect. Besides providing information about Obama's agenda and transition, the site included a YouTube channel, a real-time blog, and several interactive features that enabled citizens to communicate their ideas, interests, and concerns directly to the incoming administration.[10]

Communications aides adapted many of the technological innovations of change.gov as they redesigned the White House web page during the transition. Literally within minutes after Obama took the oath of office, they had their online White House office up and running. In an announcement accompanying their site's launch, they invoked the vision of the more open, interactive presidency articulated by Obama on the campaign trail, promising greater "communication," "transparency," and "participation."[11]

This rolling out of new communications networks and technologies during the transition and the early weeks of the administration, combined with Obama's almost preternatural understanding of how to use social media to leverage political change, touched off early speculation about the president's communications operations. "It is," the *New York Times* reported, "now fashionable in Washington to talk about how Mr. Obama will transfer his technological tricks from the campaign trail to the White House."[12] Some who engaged in this "fashionable" discussion alluded to Obama's plans for rewiring the bully pulpit.[13] Others wrote about "Obama 2.0" and the advent of the YouTube presidency and speculated about how he might use social media to circumvent news organizations and speak directly to the American people.[14] Some journalists even postulated that the White House would take a page from the campaign and use social networks in lieu of party organizations and interest groups to mobilize supporters on behalf of its policies.[15]

The Obama White House's virtual office certainly has a different feel from previous administration's versions, one that perhaps reflects a "Web 2.0 philosophy."[16] His White House web page, www.whitehouse.gov, includes social media links through which the administration can carry out direct and instantaneous communications, and it hosts several features that promise greater interactivity and transparency.[17] Through this portal the public can get videos, pictures, and blog postings on real-time presidential events, read about what is happening in the administration, peruse President Obama's remarks, see presentations from executive branch officials, track important legislation, follow the president's schedule, view his public addresses, and sign up to stay connected through social communications networks like Facebook, Flickr, LinkedIn, MySpace, Twitter, and Vimeo. Routine administration practices, governmental restrictions on postings and links, and obsolescent technologies bequeathed by previous presidents hampered early efforts to realize fully the kind of robust, interactive White House site Obama promised on the campaign trail.[18] In addition, even though it is more interactive than earlier White House pages, it nonetheless comes up short in providing the open, freewheeling exchanges commonly associated with today's web-based media. As Obama's New Media director admitted, the site was still very much an ongoing experiment. Nonetheless, this experiment had gone well enough to prompt some journalists, concerned about how the administration used web-based social media to manage and target its message, to mock this whole operation as "state run media 2.0."[19]

President Obama thus not only possesses solid rhetorical skills and an aptitude for moving his policy preferences by carrying out public relations campaigns, but he combines those with an intuitive sense of the importance of harnessing the power of new communications technologies to ratchet up his outside game. As a result, he was certainly well-prepared to mount a public campaign on behalf of the stimulus plan he pushed in response to the economic crisis he inherited.

The Economic Crisis and Obama's Response: The President-Elect Makes History

In December 2007, the economy entered into the deepest recession since the Great Depression. Over the course of 2008, several major banks failed, credit markets froze, stock prices plummeted, the housing market deteriorated, the number of business failures spiraled upwards, and the ranks of the unemployed swelled as the economy contracted. In the waning days of the presidential campaign, the Bush administration and Congress agreed to a $700 billion program—"one of thelargest-ever government interventions in the nation's economy"—which enabled the Treasury Department to bail out banks, get credit flowing, and calm an increasingly skittish Wall Street.[20] Concern about the economy, however, continued to grow, notwithstanding this mammoth infusion of funds. Consumer spending plunged, major domestic automobile manufacturers veered toward bankruptcy, and the world economy continued its downward slide. By the time Obama won the election and started plotting his transition to office, the economy was shrinking faster than at any time in the last quarter of a century.[21] The stark reality of this severe contraction crystallized support for governmental action. Political momentum to do something started to build as the chair of the Federal Reserve, Ben Bernanke, and a range of professional economists weighed in on behalf of a fiscal stimulus to prevent an already teetering economy from tipping into a depression.[22]

Obama had little time to savor his victory over Sen. John McCain (R-AZ). Within weeks of the election, he became an "instant president."[23] Besides attending to the transition's normal challenges of holding national security and policy briefings, filling staff positions, and meeting with executive branch officials, Obama attacked the crisis. He subsequently told Jonathan Alter: "I explicitly rejected FDR's strategy [in the weeks after the 1932 election] of not taking any ownership of what needed to be done during the transition."[24] His activities included first, helping President Bush lobby Congress for additional Troubled Asset Relief Program (TARP) funds, and then working with his own economic advisors and congressional party to map out a politically palatable stimulus plan large enough to shore up a rapidly eroding economy.

The president-elect also turned to addressing the nation about its economic woes. In his initial postelection press conference, Obama stressed that, given the recent jump in the unemployment rate, he preferred a "stimulus package sooner rather than later," though he promised that "if it does not get done in the lame-duck session" he would make it his first order of business.[25] He echoed those views a day later in his first weekly Saturday address, where he reassured listeners that his

Transition Economic Advisory Board was well along in preparing policy options on the crisis that would enable him to "hit the ground running on January 20th."[26]

While they pressed the lame duck Congress to take action, Obama and his team started doing the political spadework required to take office. Both he and his chief-of-staff designate, Rahm Emanuel, wanted to move quickly so that they could build momentum for subsequent legislative action on executive branch nominees and high priority initiatives on the budget, health care, and the environment. They informed Capitol Hill colleagues that they sought a completed bill on the president's desk and ready for his signature by Inauguration Day. Obama and his advisors agreed that to have the desired effect the package had to be at least $800 billion; and even though some economists were pushing for a package almost twice that size, they decided the legislation's upper limit could not, for political reasons, exceed a trillion dollars. Congressional Democrats concurred. Once Obama reached tentative agreement on principles with his party's leaders, he deferred to Congress. Democratic leaders and relevant committees, not Obama, therefore assumed responsibility for hammering out the bill's details.[27]

As congressional Democrats translated these principles into policy, Obama turned to selling the recovery plan. Here existing public opinion presented the president-elect with some choice opportunities. Views on the economy had grown increasingly pessimistic; almost 90% of those surveyed in the last weeks before the election rated "the condition of the national economy" as "bad" or "very bad," with a similar ratio responding that it would stay the same or worsen.[28] Popular sentiment also favored taking ameliorative action; close to 70% of those polled agreed it was "important," "very important," or "critical" for the government to pass some sort of stimulus.[29]

On the other hand, polls signaled that Obama had his work cut out for him. Some surveys, for instance, revealed that the heretofore unprecedented amounts of money that the government had already committed to propping up the banks and the automobile industry had touched off concerns about governmental spending and deficits. A postelection poll found nearly half of the American public "very concerned" about the growing "size of the federal budget deficit," with another third indicating it was "somewhat concerned."[30] A high percentage of the public also did not trust government to provide a calibrated response. One postelection survey, for instance, showed a majority believing government would "spend too much" in its effort to "boost the economy."[31] Then again, although there was support for some type of policy response, many suspected that government lacked the financial wherewithal to act. Even before the expenditure of all TARP funding had been authorized, and the deal to save the automobile industry had been consummated, nearly half of those surveyed surmised that the government could not, given the growing deficit, afford a fiscal stimulus large enough to jumpstart the economy.[32]

Obama made history as he juggled transition activities with a full-throttled public relations campaign commonly associated with sitting presidents. In the weeks leading up to the inauguration, he proceeded strategically in making the case for his incoming administration. Aides to the transition team conducted polls and convened focus groups to help Obama and his Democratic supporters in Congress better "frame" a plan to maximize public support. Their findings showed that describing it as a "recovery" package and as an "investment" plan rather than a "stimulus" or "infrastructure" spending bill resonated better with a public wary about governmental waste and eye-popping deficits.[33] Stressing the fragility of the economy and the grave dangers it faced, he rhetorically elevated the long-term costs of temporizing or failing to act with enough fiscal vigor. And in mounting that public relations campaign Obama and his team implemented a communications strategy that integrated newer social media platforms with more conventional outlets.

Obama regularly used his weekly Saturday address to make the case for his "recovery" plan. On November 15, 2008, he became the first president-elect to have his weekly radio message simultaneously video streamed to the public, and he used that historic occasion to highlight once again America's "economic crisis." Pointing to ten consecutive months of job losses and a recent spike in unemployment claims, he reiterated his call for Congress to make an immediate "down-payment" on a recovery plan while stressing that this crisis presented an opportunity to create a more competitive and greener economy through "long-term investments" that had been "neglected for too long."[34]

President-elect Obama followed up this appearance with nine more weekly radio and YouTube addresses before Inauguration Day. More than half of those focused specifically on his recovery plan or touched on some aspect of the economic crisis. This included even his Thanksgiving address in which he paused to underscore the seriousness of the economic crisis confronting the United States, discuss the need for "bold" action, and outline the steps he had already taken since the election.[35]

Besides his radio and YouTube addresses, Obama enlisted more traditional venues to push his economic recovery package, and his communications team supplemented these with strategic postings on change.gov's blog. He appeared, for instance, with Tom Brokaw on *Meet the Press* in the first week of December. There he discussed his incoming administration and addressed, among other things, the economic downturn and the policy that his White House would pursue. The next week he sat for an interview with *Time* magazine, where he reiterated the problems of the American economy and outlined benchmarks his transition team had set for his administration's domestic and foreign policies. His communications operation included both these sessions with the media, along with his web and radio addresses, on change.gov's blog.[36] They also added regular weekly postings of interviews with his economic advisers, videos of the president-elect's meetings with other political officials, including Democratic members of Congress and the nation's governors.[37] This kept the focus on the economic crisis and the incoming administration's plans to deal with it.

President-elect Obama made his way to the Capitol at the start of the 111th Congress for face-to-face negotiations with party leaders to launch his plan on the Hill.[38] He then resumed his public relations campaign, traveling to George Mason University on the outskirts of the Beltway, to give his first formal speech since winning the presidency. There he made his case for the American Recovery and Reinvestment Act recently introduced in Congress. The speech helped put the spotlight back on the incoming administration, which subsequently saw its news coverage triple over what it had been the preceding week.[39] In giving a high-profile, headline-grabbing speech, Obama ostensibly intended to nudge Congress along in its work. After all, congressional Republicans, registering concerns that the price tag of Obama's recovery plan was mushrooming out of control, had started floating some of their own initiatives.[40] Meanwhile, Democrats were showing signs they were getting bogged down working out such a large, complicated relief bill. They had already pushed back the deadline for completing the package to the February 13 recess and, by the way things were going, it looked as though even that date was no longer a realistic target.[41]

Obama used this speech to build pressure for a swifter response, and he proceeded by portraying his plan in ways that were especially mindful of the different currents of public opinion that set the parameters for his case.[42] Enlisting language that resonated with a public worried about the state of the economy, the president-elect checked off, in near litany-like fashion, economic indicators that pointed to a historic decline. He framed the problem in unusually stark language, warning his audience that the window of opportunity was quickly closing. "[I]f we don't take dramatic actions as soon as possible, [the] recession … could linger for years," producing double-digit unemployment rates while dulling the nation's "competitive edge." For those who did not trust the government to act responsibly, he promised a "whole new approach to meeting our most urgent challenges." The government would make investments, not simply disburse money, and it would do so in ways shorn of provincial political calculations, that is, "transparently, [under the guidance of] independent experts whenever possible." There would be no backroom deals "behind a veil of secrecy," and he pledged the plan would be "free from earmarks and pet projects." He further tried to allay concerns of those preoccupied with a growing deficit. He thus accentuated the economy's fragility, and although he acknowledged his plan would increase the deficit, he warned that failure to act boldly would result in "an even greater deficit of jobs, incomes and confidence in our economy." Only government, he declared, had the capacity to stop the downward spiral. Moreover, he promised that any deficit spending would be temporary and used only to finance the long-term capital investments necessary to rebuild the American economy and make it more competitive in world markets.[43]

Obama's communications operation posted a video of the George Mason speech on change.gov. Days later, they added videos of various members of his economic policy staff. The first included Dr. Christina Roemer, Obama's designated nominee to head the Council of Economic Advisors, who discussed a report that projected the Recovery Act would create or save three to four million jobs. This posting included a link to the report, which also indicated that without a sizable injection of funds into the economy the unemployment rate would top out at well above 9%, a point that the GOP would seize on later as the public relations battle unfolded.[44] The next day Obama's New Media shop posted another video in which lower profile transition team staffers outlined the different policy components of the president-elect's plan.[45]

Obama continued his public campaign through his final days as president-elect. On January 15, 2009, congressional Democrats officially announced tentative details of the recovery plan they were sending to committee, and the president-elect traveled to the Cardinal Fastener and Specialty Co., Inc. in Bedford Heights, Ohio the following day to stump for it.[46] Surveys taken these last few days before the inauguration were especially promising for Obama and his congressional allies. Polls revealed a majority of the respondents approving of a stimulus on the order of nearly $800 billion, with less than a quarter believing such a proposal went "too far." Polling data also indicated Republicans had serious cause for concern. A NBC News/*Wall Street Journal* poll showed 68% of the respondents believed GOP lawmakers should compromise on some of their economic principles and work with the incoming administration to pass the stimulus.[47]

The First Campaign

Republicans tried to regain their footing as the stimulus package took shape in Congress in the weeks following the inauguration. Though united in their opposition to the type of sweeping spending plan preferred by the president and his Democratic allies, they found themselves in a tenuous position. Having recently lost control of the White House, they now confronted a rhetorically gifted president, and both he and his stimulus plan were polling well. The president in his negotiations with Republicans also signaled that, even though he promised to bring change to the tenor of Washington politics, he intended to wield the political capital provided to him by his sizable electoral victory and popularity. He drove home this point at a meeting convened with congressional leaders early in his administration. With House Democrats moving an economic stimulus through committee and Republicans making noise about an absence of bipartisanship, President Obama brought together chamber leaders to build consensus on behalf of a bill he could sign into law before the President's Day recess.[48] Republicans voiced their alarm about the Democrats' stimulus package's escalating costs and vented their frustrations over their lack of input in the process. House Minority Whip Eric Cantor (R-VA) presented the president with a packet outlining some of the GOP's economic policy alternatives. President Obama acknowledged that none of their ideas "looked outlandish or crazy." Still, he rejected their initiatives, especially their hard line stance against tax increases, bluntly reminding them: "I won [the election]."[49]

Democrats had other strategic advantages. They had increased their ranks with the recent election and now had sizable majorities in both chambers. And even though their numbers included a somewhat larger contingent of potential defectors, like the House's "Blue Dogs," they still managed a united front. Indeed, in the early weeks of the administration so many Blue Dogs "turned tail" and supported Pelosi that several in the blogosphere started to make cracks about how the Speaker had "neutered" them, turning them into a pack of fawning "poodles."[50] With House rules favoring a fairly unified Democratic majority, the one hundred and seventy-eight Republicans in that chamber thus had scant room to maneuver. Meanwhile, though Republican prospects were more auspicious in the Senate, where rules and procedures gave them leverage, even there the party saw its options constrained as Democrats, joined by two Independents, found themselves with a near filibuster proof majority.

Opening a Public Relations Front on the Hill

With momentum for action on a stimulus building inside Hill chambers, lawmakers engaged the president in the public relations campaign. This was perhaps clearest among House Republicans. They had been laying the groundwork necessary to realize their objectives well before the 111th Congress started moving on the legislation. Lacking formal institutional powers, they knew they had few options other than seeking outside reinforcements. As Minority Leader John Boehner (R-OH) later explained, "I have been trying to get my Republican colleagues to understand that we are not in the legislative business any more. We don't have enough numbers and obviously [Democrats] are not interested in allowing us to participate. If we are going to do our job in terms of being the party that we will call better solutions … the only way we can affect this process is to communicate better with the American people."[51] A number of Republican senators, on the other hand, seemed more inclined in these earlier stages to want to use their institutional leverage to shape legislation as it made its way through their chamber. Sen. Charles Grassley (R-IA), the ranking member on the Senate Finance panel, betrayed this sentiment, noting that he perceived the Republican role as one of being the "loyal opposition, emphasis on loyal."[52]

House GOP leaders bolstered communications staffs and reconfigured their party's public relations operation to reflect the new political realities they had to negotiate. Now Boehner was confronting a Democratic president, who possessed the strategic advantages of his office in using the news to govern. The minority leader added a communications staffer to work specifically with the White House press corps to ensure members of that beat had "constant access to the Republican message."[53] Minority Whip Cantor adjusted his office's responsibilities, focusing his efforts more on marketing the party's ideas as opposed to the whip's more traditional task of tallying members' votes. He thus assumed greater authority for developing and popularizing his party's policy response to the economic crisis, and he beefed up his own messaging operation, even adding an aide to his office to handle new media communications.[54] "A primary goal," as one of his staffers told *The Washington Times*, "is making sure everything we do somehow translates into a link on the Internet."[55]

Meanwhile, the newly installed Republican Conference Chair Mike Pence (R-IN) stepped up his office's booking operation. He enlisted more than a third of his conference's members in rapid response groups ("tiger teams") and worked to get them placed on cable television and talk radio shows, where they could promote the GOP's positions.[56] In an effort to grow audiences for the GOP's messages, he added a staffer to work on "outreach to minority communications," and he institutionalized within the Conference a new media operation to disseminate

Republican views through increasingly popular venues like Facebook, Twitter, and YouTube.[57]

As they shored up their public relations operations, Republicans developed a policy alternative they could offer in response to their opponents' legislative initiatives. With Minority Whip Cantor taking the lead, House Republicans sketched out their own version of a stimulus plan. While it had little chance of succeeding, it gave them something around which they could unite to provide a clear message. It also inoculated them against the charge that they were being obstructionists. To that end, Cantor and his group pared back demands for more substantial tax cuts advocated by the some members of the conference and instead included "things" in their proposal they believed the president might accept.[58] The scheme they devised, and one which many GOP senators endorsed in principle, tilted toward tax relief and was about half as expensive as their opponents' plan. It also promised that expenditures for infrastructure would be offset by corresponding cuts in other governmental programs, and it included a home buyers' credit to stabilize the housing market.[59]

With the Democrat's recovery legislation making its way through the House, Republicans started their publicity campaign. Minority Whip Cantor publicized his party's initiative by posting a web page, which could be hyperlinked with others' websites, outlining the principles of their recovery plan. GOP members also used their online offices to issue press releases on their alternative solution and posted editorials that endorsed it.[60] Minority Leader Boehner, assisted by his own political action committee, the Freedom Project, adopted an increasingly popular Internet search strategy many businesses use to push their products and hook consumers. This "Google" strategy also coincided with one used by FreedomWorks, the antitax organization led by the former Texas representative and Republican leader, Richard Armey. It involved linking the Republicans' alternative recovery plan with selected search terms like *stimulus*, thus ensuring that folks surfing the web to read about the economic crisis and the sorts of policy responses it engendered would, with a single click of the mouse, automatically receive a political ad showcasing the GOP's proposals.[61]

The First Round

President Obama went public to press for the more substantial package he preferred just as his opponents were unveiling and marketing their ideas. With House Democrats moving their legislation through committees and to the floor for a vote, Obama used his January 24 Saturday address, his first as president, both to make history and to present his party's case. This marked the first time a White House video-streamed a Saturday address directly to the American people, and it proved highly popular, ultimately becoming the week's most downloaded YouTube news video.[62] The president used this occasion to drive home once again his overarching theme. He cited rising unemployment claims to advocate for a bold, swift response to prevent a "bad situation" from becoming "dramatically worse." He promised to reboot the American economy through long-term investments in critical "priorities" of education, energy, health care, and infrastructure and to hold government accountable for its expenditures. In conjunction with that last point, Obama tried to reassure those "skeptical about the size and scale" of the plan, announcing for the first time that his administration planned to launch a website, Recovery.gov, geared to promoting greater transparency in governmental expenditures.[63]

President Obama edged back from the stage after making this last appeal before the scheduled House vote. Still hoping to bring some Republican lawmakers on board, he perhaps feared a more aggressive public relations campaign might turn them away and stiffen their resistance. He opted instead to apply a more personal touch to bring them around.[64] Meanwhile, Obama's White House communications operation was slow getting out of the box. Existing rules that restricted the use of political lists, combined with a shortage of experienced personnel to handle digital communications, kept the administration from fully applying the tactics successfully employed in the campaign to get out its message directly and mobilize its supporters.[65] With Obama following a more personal, "soft-sell" approach on the Hill, the administration put its most formidable voice on the sidelines. Unfortunately for Democrats, no one else appeared to take up the slack in closing the deal with the American public. *Newsweek* correspondent Michael Hirsh concluded that the administration was fighting a war without any generals: "it's engaged in a Pickett's Charge—without the benefit of being led by Pickett."[66] At the same time, Democratic allies got little pressure to sell the plan. Sam Stein, of the liberal online site the Huffington Post, later wrote that a Democratic official conceded to him that the party's "communications shops" received no directions to "push back on the negative, push the positive, or undercut Republicans" on the stimulus.[67]

This presented the Republicans with a choice opportunity, and they exploited it by taking their case outside their chambers. Here they treaded carefully, for they wanted to avoid taking on a popular president in the first weeks of his administration. They instead concentrated their fire on the bill and its congressional supporters. Inadvertently, Obama provided them with an opening they could pry. In trying to sell the package to a public concerned about waste in government, the president emphasized that recovery expenditures would be determined by merit, not politics, and that they would be targeted only to those activities and programs that promised to strengthen the nation's infrastructure and make America more competitive in the global economy. In fact, early on he raised the stakes when he vowed the bill would contain no earmarks. But Democrats, feeling little direct pressure from the White House in writing the bill, ignored his commitments. They inserted several narrowly focused projects that ostensibly did not pass the president's test. *The Wall Street Journal* mocked the Democrats' package as "a 40-Year Wish List," as it ticked off expenditures for the National Endowment for the Arts, the Smithsonian, a National Mall Restoration Project, programs to combat sexually transmitted diseases and smoking, coupons to obtain digital television convertor boxes, tax breaks for Hollywood, and a host of other items ostensibly unrelated to stimulating the economy and rebuilding the nation's infrastructure.[68]

Republicans seized on these projects. They strategically invoked them to discredit their opponents, separate Obama from his party, and shield themselves from charges they were thwarting a popular president. Minority Leader Boehner publicly complimented the president for pressing Congress to act on the economy and then attacked the opposition for its "wasteful spending."[69] One Republican House member put it this way: "It's not so much his [President Obama's] effort, it's what the House has done with this bill, what Pelosi has done with this bill."[70] They blamed Democrats, and especially Speaker Nancy Pelosi (D-CA), for hijacking the legislation and larding it up with frivolous expenditures or pet projects that would do little to bring the country out of its economic doldrums. Some even branded it the "Nancy Pelosi stimulus" or the "Pelosi Pork Package."[71] Many of these criticisms, in turn, were echoed by hosts of politically charged talk shows and writers at partisan websites, who used substantial amounts of time to discuss and criticize the plan and in the process shaped the news narrative.[72]

While leaders and members on both sides of the aisle went outside their chambers and engaged with the media, Republicans were especially energetic in their efforts to drive a message.[73] Several lawmakers, for instance, posted comments on *The Hill's Congress blog*, a site that affords lawmakers opportunities to stake out positions on issues and matters pending in Congress and whose postings are also made available through links to other sites, RSS feeds, and Twitter. A dozen lawmakers, including Minority Leader Boehner, submitted posts on the plan to *Congress blog* in the week following the president's address. All but two came from House Republicans. Taken together, these criticized their opponents' bill as loaded with waste, presented their preferred alternative of less spending and more tax relief, and attacked what they presented as Democrats' heavy-handed tactics in drafting the bill.[74]

On January 29, the House passed the legislation, without a single Republican vote, by a margin of 244-188.[75] Republicans mounted an aggressive outreach to cable news shows that coincided with this House vote, and though they did not have that terrain to themselves, they certainly overshadowed their Democratic opponents. We conducted a search of cable and television newscasts from the day the president gave his Saturday address on January 24 until January 30, the day after the House cleared its version of the bill, and found GOP lawmakers, both senators and representatives, eclipsing their opponents in total bookings on cable news shows by a ratio of roughly 1.7 to 1.[76] The GOP advantage for representatives was about 1.5 to 1; for senators, it was about 2 to 1. Democratic aides conceded that their party was being outhustled on the cable news circuit. One senior staffer told Greg Sargent, the *Washington Post's Plumline* blogger, "Republicans are winning this thing right now because more of them are shouting louder, not because of what they are shouting," adding that "moving forward, we need to be much more aggressive in deploying our folks. We need to saturate the airwaves like it is the week before an election."[77] Whatever the reason for these differences in the coverage, the Republican edge in television interviews left some in the Democratic base nonplussed. Indeed, differences between the two parties in cable news discussions at one point became so stark and unnerving that *ThinkProgress*, a blog associated with the liberal Center for American Progress, started monitoring and publicizing Republicans' advantage in the cable news wars. This prompted Democrats to promise a redoubling of their efforts to raise their public profile.[78]

The GOP also turned to other forums to disseminate members' messages. House Republicans posted their talking points on their Conference web page's newsroom. There they also included favorable press coverage they received. The Republican National Committee, meanwhile, amplified congressional party members' efforts by sponsoring a "district by district message campaign" conducted through local media, bloggers, and talk radio.[79]

Although the administration handily won the first round in the House, Democrats had cause for concern. The news narrative seemed to be slipping from their grasp. Already some in the media surmised that the president and congressional Democrats were "losing the stimulus message war," and even the president's Chief of Staff, Emanuel, confessed in a *Wall Street Journal* interview that the White House and its allies had for a few days ceded control of the message.[80] Speaker Pelosi, meanwhile, had been visibly thrown off balance as she publicly tried to defend the more questionable pieces in the legislation. Her difficulties in addressing concerns raised by Republicans, moreover, were magnified in this new media world. The *PEJ New Media Index*, for instance, reported that a video of her struggling to describe how expenditures to prevent STDs would actually promote greater economic growth was the third most viewed political news YouTube video of the week.[81]

Perhaps of even greater concern, popular sentiment seemed to be turning against the bill, eroding the Democrats' earlier advantage. Two public opinion polls showed support for the stimulus had declined, and opposition to it had increased, by double digits. One of those polls also indicated that Republicans had made substantial headway on their argument that tax relief, not spending, was the best way to combat the recession.[82] Another poll showed that nearly a third of the respondents believed that the bill contained "too much pork spending."[83] Some Democrats blamed the president for their eroding fortunes. "There's no message out of the White House," one Democratic representative lamented. Others blamed themselves, even acknowledging they had made the bill an easy public relations target for the GOP to hit.[84]

On the Road Again

Now on the defensive, the president and his congressional allies fought back. On February 2, the House Democratic Congressional Campaign Committee initiated a targeted ad campaign against twenty-eight Republicans who voted against the package.[85] House Democratic leaders, meanwhile, applied pressure to rank-and-file members to have them make the case for the bill. One news account, for instance, noted that at a closed door meeting Speaker Pelosi exhorted her colleagues to "sell, sell, sell" the bill, warning them that the upcoming days would be critical in shifting perceptions on it.[86] Another indicated that Democratic lawmakers planned to make their case back home by providing constituents with information on the money that would flow into their districts and states once the president signed the bill.[87]

President Obama, meanwhile, also showed signs of concern about the "cable chatter" surrounding the bill. As he later admitted to Jonathan Alter, "I have to say it [the Republican response to the stimulus] took me by surprise."[88] Some members of his administration even conceded that they had lost a week by not giving the stimulus the "air cover" that it needed.[89] Consequently, the president abandoned his soft-sell, bipartisan approach, which so far had yielded few dividends.

Shortly after the House vote, Obama's team deployed its much vaunted campaign tactics in an effort to mobilize support for the legislation. They sent out e-mails through Organizing for America, a grassroots group they had relied on during the campaign and that was now located in the Democratic National Committee. In those electronic communications, they asked individuals to host "Economic Recovery House Meetings." The president prepared a five minute video address on the Democrats' plan. Obama's team intended to use these more than 3,500 neighborhood recovery parties to screen the video, which became the second most viewed YouTube news video of the week, and build support for the Democratic plan pending in the Senate.[90]

Beginning February 3, the president commenced a week-long communications blitz to parallel the direct social media strategy. This intense public relations effort also coincided with the Senate finishing up its work on the legislation. Obama launched his publicity campaign by giving Oval Office interviews to five networks—ABC, CBS, CNN, Fox, and NBC. There he acknowledged early miscues that had diverted the public's attention away from his recovery and reinvestment policy. In particular, he singled out his own failure to vet properly all of his administration's nominees, including former Senator Tom Daschle, who had to withdraw as the designated nominee to head the Department of Health and Human Services and spearhead the president's upcoming health care initiative. Obama also used these sessions to pivot back to the weakening economy and the need to pass the recovery legislation currently pending in the Senate.[91] He followed these with a more partisan, high-profile, February 5 *Washington Post* op-ed, which he used both to defend the recovery plan from charges leveled against it by Republicans and their allies and to argue for its "urgency."[92] The president then used his February 7 Saturday radio and YouTube addresses both to highlight a recent increase in unemployment and to criticize Republican economic policies of the past eight years and argue on behalf of the Democratic bill.[93] The following Monday he traveled to Elkhart, Indiana, a city symbolically important because it had been especially hard hit by the recession. There he held a campaign style, town hall meeting to present his case and to generate news attention. Later, he gave his first prime time press conference where he again addressed the state of the economy and reiterated his call for the need to act quickly. He followed his press conference with an appearance on ABC's *Nightline*, an interview with sixteen reporters from regional news providers, and a trip to Fort Myers, Florida to hold another town hall event to stump for his plan and keep the pressure on Congress.[94]

The Senate, meanwhile, worked to get a bill to send to conference. In the week leading up to its vote on February 10, when the chamber passed the legislation, lawmakers again took to the airwaves. Overall, the number of appearances that House members booked during this time was negligible, as attention shifted to the Senate. Republican senators managed to edge out their opponents by a ratio of slightly less than 1.5 to 1. Even discounting appearances by Sen. Ben Nelson (D-NE), Sen. Olympia Snowe (R-ME), Sen. Susan Collins (R-ME), and Sen. Arlen Specter (R-PA), who were involved in crafting a bipartisan deal to pass the bill and send it to conference committee, the ratio remained roughly the same.

As lawmakers worked out the conference report, Rep. Tom Price (R-GA), the head of the economically conservative Republican Study Committee, posted on YouTube the first of a series of videos attacking the bill. With the assistance of a staffer, he filmed a video outside the Speaker's office, denouncing the behind-the-scenes deals involved in putting the finishing touches on the bill. It received 30,000 hits and was hyperlinked to other sites across the web.[95]

The legislation cleared Congress on February 13. Television bookings for both Democrats and Republicans during the time that the bill made its way through conference and on to the president were fairly equal, with each side averaging roughly ten appearances per day. On the day the bill cleared the Congress, House Republicans posted on their Conference's online site a series of videos of floor speeches given by members in opposition to the bill. Rep. Price added another video, linked to by some evening news (ABC) accounts and several blogs, showing him trying to wade through the 1,073 page bill he had received shortly before midnight the day before. Meanwhile, Senate Democrats posted a video on their web page, "Creating Jobs and Investing in America's Future," interviewing five senators on how the bill would facilitate the nation's economic recovery.[96]

On February 17, the president and Vice President Joseph Biden flew to Denver, the city where the president had received his nomination, and in a ceremony that was broadcast live and video-streamed on WhiteHouse.gov he signed the bill into law. As the president made his way west to sign the legislation, Democrats made their way home to sell it to the voters and attract some local news attention. The House Democratic Caucus reported 214 of its members scheduled 750 events in their constituencies that week. Freshman Democrats, by themselves, planned 120 sessions devoted specifically to discussing the stimulus legislation.[97]

Overall, in the weeks leading to the bill's enactment, from January 24 through February 17, slightly more than a fifth of House Republicans and slightly less than a fifth of House Democrats appeared at least once on television shows to discuss the stimulus bill. Meanwhile, roughly three-fourths of Republican senators and slightly more than three-fifths of Democratic senators had taken to the air at least once to present their positions. During this time, individual members on both sides also used their own online offices to publicize their positions. As we noted earlier, members of Congress use these sites both to speak directly to interested publics and to amplify their voices by courting the attention of other news providers. Their online media releases, which most offices make available through real-time news feeds and assorted social media platforms, also provide data that can be tapped to determine how effective parties were in getting their members to address the legislation and to stay on message. With that in mind, we analyzed online press releases issued by members from January 15, the day Democrats first unveiled the outlines of the bill, until February 17, the day the president signed it into law. We were able to access roughly 90% of the House (N=395) and Senate (N=90) online press archives. Of the 395 House sites we examined, 161 were Republican and 234 were Democratic. The Senate sites included 40 Republicans and 50 Democrats. We examined press releases to determine whether they supported the party's position and whether or not they cited specific benefits for the district/state or state they represented. In House releases we also looked for statements pertaining to whether or not the legislation included instances of pork or other waste.

House Republicans were especially effective in getting their members to speak from the same page when it came to their statements. Out of the 161 House Republican sites, 90% included press releases on the stimulus, and nearly all of these were consistent with the GOP's message in opposition to the bill. Of perhaps even greater importance, over half of the House Republican offices issued press releases citing specific instances of pork or wasteful projects in the bill. House Democrats were almost equally successful in addressing the bill and staying on message. Roughly 90% of them issued press releases on the stimulus, and of these only a negligible number (less than 2%) were at odds with the party's theme. In addition, of the House Democrats who issued press releases, roughly three-fifths cited particular benefits their districts would receive. Ironically, in claiming credit for the local goods provided they perhaps diluted their overall message and reinforced the perception that the legislation was laden with particular benefits. A headline of an article posted by ProPublica's Christopher Weaver at the HuffingtonPost captured the Democrats' paradox: "Congress Brags About 'Pork' in Pork Free Bill."[98]

On the Senate side, roughly 90% of the GOP sites examined included press releases on the stimulus. Republicans were effective in keeping all their membership on the party's message, save for the three members who voted for the bill—Sen. Olympia Snowe (R-ME), Sen. Susan Collins (R-ME), and Sen. Arlen Specter (R-PA). While some Democrats occasionally noted misgivings about the legislation, saying things like "not the bill I would have written" or "not the bill I would have preferred," over 95% issued press releases on the stimulus and of these nearly 85% made arguments that stressed the need for, or urgency of, the legislation.

With the party fairly united, both in its deeds and its words, the president brought to fruition a landmark piece of legislation that he had been spearheading almost from the day he got elected. Republicans, however, would shortly claim Obama's victory was a pyrrhic one. Indeed, Rep. Mike Pence (R-IN) told those in attendance at the 2009 Conservative Political Action Conference later that month that "[w]e lost that legislative battle [on the stimulus], but we won the argument."[99] While that might have overstated the results, there was evidence to support his contention. Most polls showed a majority of the people still favoring the policy, but they also revealed support was soft and that Democrats had failed to close the deal. One NBC News/*Wall Street Journal* survey indicated that a rather sizable 66% of those polled indicated that the bill "will help only a little" or "will not help at all."

That same poll also asked respondents to cite the legislation's greatest failings. The top three items named were: "too much pork-barrel spending" (36%); "does not provide enough tax cuts to individual taxpayers" (21%); and "spending is focused on the wrong areas" (21%).[100] At the same time, the legislation also created the perception, which fueled Tea Party uprisings later in the year, that the administration lacked the discipline to restrain governmental growth. One senior GOP Senate staffer told Salon.com that Republicans wake up every morning knowing their message: "Obama's spending too much."[101] It appeared that Republicans had hit on a theme that resonated with the American people. This, along with the public's lukewarm support for the policy, suggested that the public relations battle to shape how the legislation would be interpreted and understood was far from over.

The Battle Continues

Earlier we found that high-pitched public relations battles on a policy can occasionally continue well beyond the day that a bill has been signed into law. Events surrounding the recovery legislation provide a textbook case of this. In the months following the president's approval of the legislation, the issue for both parties was especially ripe to use for their messaging operations. First, public sentiment on the issue was unsettled. This suggested it could still be nudged one way or the other. Second, the two sides were internally cohesive but clearly divided on the policy, thus making it easier for them to stay on message. The issue therefore represented a choice opportunity for the two sides both to shape perceptions of their respective parties' brands and to determine the trajectory and the accompanying narrative of the Obama presidency. Success in doing that, in turn, promised to help them as they tried to influence the policy agenda and advance their electoral fortunes before the 2010 midterm elections.

Shortly after the president signed the bill, the White House and congressional Democrats took several steps to shape popular sentiment on the legislation in ways that worked to their strategic advantage. First, the president symbolically highlighted the program's salience and tried to reassure those concerned about pork-barrel projects and waste by naming Vice President Biden to oversee its implementation. The administration and the congressional party also created online resources to disseminate, without any intermediary or filter, their interpretation of the stimulus and to claim credit for any benefits that it produced. The White House and Senate Democrats maintained separate pages on their portals—White.House.gov and Democrats.Senate.gov—to publicize, through videos, pictures, interactive maps, blogs, and online newsrooms, the policy's achievements and significant milestones. House Democrats, meanwhile, included information on the recovery policy on the Democratic Caucus website (Dems.gov) in a section dedicated to discussions pertaining to their performance on the economy. House Democrats also periodically cross-linked on their Caucus site their members' press releases on stimulus-funded projects in their constituencies. Many congressional Democrats in their online offices also inserted hyperlinks to these White House and party pages, which were updated to include new achievements.

Finally, Democratic lawmakers headed back home to try to shore up support for the policy by delivering the message directly to their constituents. They timed this local communications blitz to coincide with the day that the tax cuts in the legislation went into effect, the first day of April. As they went back home, congressional Democrats intended to saturate their constituencies with media appearances and town hall meetings. To assist those newly elected members still learning the ropes, congressional leaders helped set up events, like town hall meetings and media spots, through which members could market the legislation and explain to their publics what it promised to accomplish.[102]

Republicans, meanwhile, tried to undercut their partisan opponents. This required that they first provide a more inviting alternative, and second, point to the policy's failure to reach the goals or fulfill the claims set down by the president. To ward off charges that they were only interested in carping about the Democrats' actions, House Republicans established a "Solutions Center" within the Whip's office. The online site, as described by one staffer, was a "one-stop" shopping center for programmatic solutions to public problems. This gave them a forum through which they could provide an alternative and better define their image. It also gave them a place to which Republican officials across the country could turn for ideas, thus enabling them to sharpen their overall message on what they promised to provide in dealing with problems like increasing joblessness and a declining economy.[103]

Republicans likewise turned to online party sites in the Senate (Republican. Senate.gov) and the House (GOP.House.gov) to post, regularly and in a controlled and unfiltered way, information and clips that both highlighted the stimulus's shortcomings in realizing its goal of driving down unemployment, which was described on the Republican.Senate.gov's "Leader Board" as the "broken jobs promises," and pointed to what the GOP believed to be frivolous expenditures and egregious instances of waste.

The two parties waged a spirited public relations campaign to define the policy as they headed into their summer recess. Here, in selling its package the administration had unwittingly presented Republicans with an opening. By early summer, the unemployment rate broke 9% and continued to climb, creating a public relations quandary for Democrats. Indeed, as we noted earlier, the president's own head of the Council of Economic Advisors, Dr. Christina Roemer, had once promised that the administration's proposal would keep unemployment below 9%. The spike in unemployment prompted the president to try to tamp down expectations and redefine what made for success. Thus, for instance, shortly after unemployment hit 9.5%, the president gave a longer than usual weekly Saturday address to "reframe the public's expectations for the spending program."[104]

Republicans, in turn, pounced on the increase in the jobless rate, invoking it to diminish the policy. They developed a simple yet catchy message they would echo all the way up to the 2010 election. Minority Leader Boehner fired an opening salvo on July 1 by releasing a "light-hearted" video that captured the attention of a plethora of news organizations and online political sites, many of which provided links to it. Narrated by Georgia Republican Congressman Lynn West-moreland, it featured the Minority Leader with a bloodhound, Elle Mae, looking for the jobs the president, vice president, and speaker had promised. As Minority Leader Boehner and Elle Mae traversed the countryside the two found plenty of instances of fraud, waste, and inefficiency, but no new jobs.[105] Over the next several weeks, House GOP members vigorously pursued that theme of asking about the jobs. The House Conference posted a YouTube video, "Done Its Job," on July 8, and another, "Obama v. Obama on the Stimulus," on July 14, which highlighted how the administration had failed to achieve its promise of job creation.[106] A week later one hundred and thirty-four House Republicans, roughly 75% of the Conference, took to the floor in their one-minute addresses to ask: "Where are the jobs?"[107] They then spliced those together in a video, "House Republicans Ask: Where Are the Jobs?," and posted it on the Conference's website on July 22.[108] They followed that with a series of other videos bearing that leitmotif.[109] These claims, in turn, correlated with existing public sentiment. Some polls conducted at the end of the month showed that 57% of the respondents believed the program had "no impact," with another 13% indicating that they believed it had made the economy "worse."[110]

With support for the stimulus declining and unemployment heading toward 10%, Democrats pushed back. They tried to embarrass publicly and pressure those Republicans who criticized the stimulus but welcomed and even occasionally touted the money that flowed back to their own districts and states.[111] The Democratic National Committee joined in by running ads in GOP leaders' districts and states that outlined the benefits and jobs the stimulus had provided there.[112]

By the end of the year, nearly ten months after the stimulus package had cleared the Congress, the struggle to define it showed no signs of abating. Republicans pounded Democrats on the waste and fraud engendered by the stimulus. Party leaders like Boehner sent e-mails to reporters that highlighted instances of financial improprieties in some of the programs, and they provided rank-and-file members with data and talking points on these as they went back home.[113] This coincided with a high-profile report released by Sen. Tom Coburn (R-OK) and Sen. John McCain (R-AZ) that pointed to questionable expenditures.[114]

On the one year anniversary of the legislation's signing, the partisan battle to define the policy again came into sharp relief. From the perspective of the administration, polling data were hardly reassuring. At best, they showed the public evenly divided in their support of what the White House and Democrats had accomplished.[115] The president took to the public stage to interpret and ultimately defend the policy. The White House also used that day to announce that the vice president and members of the administration planned to visit thirty-five communities to showcase projects funded by the stimulus. Minority Leader Boehner marked the anniversary by joining with Minority Whip Cantor to challenge Speaker Pelosi and Majority Leader Steny Hoyer (D-MD) to a televised debate on jobs and by releasing a video that highlighted the president's "broken promises." He also posted a report that questioned the soundness of the plan, pointed to several instances of waste, and that asked, once again: "Where are the jobs?"[116] That same day, the House Education and Labor Committee released a video based on Apple's popular "there's an app for that" advertisement for its iPhone: "America's Economic Recovery: There's an Act for That." The video highlighted the legislation's different policy benefits.[117] Congressional Democrats received assistance from the Democratic National Committee; it released a "happy anniversary video" targeting ninety-three GOP lawmakers who claimed credit for the benefits flowing from the very law they opposed and openly castigated.[118] Meanwhile, congressional Republicans and their allies countered with such a flurry of critical press releases that a *Washington Post* account noted that "those who say the federal stimulus program didn't create jobs have ignored a crucial sector of the economy: critics of the package, who right now are enjoying record production levels and full employment."[119] Minority Leader Cantor followed with a video news release, "Rhetoric vs. Results," that highlighted alleged stimulus failures by juxtaposing what the president promised to what his plan had so far delivered.[120]

Though stimulus money continued to flow over the next several months, the unemployment rate continued to climb. People frustrated with government bailouts, the growing deficit, and the recent health care reform continued to drive Tea Party protests. With some polls now showing that a majority of the population had turned against the stimulus, and with the midterm election just around the corner, congressional Democrats grew increasingly skittish. For Republicans, the stimulus was now a central piece of their communications. As one GOP staffer told *The Washington Independent*: "We're hitting this message every day.... Where's the jobs? Where's the jobs? Where's the jobs? [Democrats] can't answer that." [121] Democrats, however, tried to regroup. As the campaign season got underway, the administration announced, with much fanfare, its "Recovery Summer," a six week national tour intended to draw the spotlight to notable projects funded by the stimulus. Those traveling around the countryside to trumpet the measure's success included the president, Vice President Biden, and a number of high ranking executive branch officials.[122]

Republicans, meanwhile, continued their assault. As the "recovery summer" drew to a close, Sen. Tom Coburn (R-OK) and Sen. John McCain (R-AZ) issued a press release, including a video, of another of their high profile reports on the stimulus. Entitled "Summertime Blues," the report and corresponding video highlighted items in the stimulus that would give "taxpayers the blues."[123] And there were certainly more videos to come, including one Minority Leader Boehner posted right before the election that juxtaposed still photos of the president with a number of television personalities pointedly asking: "Where are the jobs?"[124] With time running out and the economy showing few signs of life in generating employment, there was little left for Democrats to do. Surveying the electorate's mood on the economy, a blogger at National Journal.com summed up their dilemma: "Despite Stimulus Results, Public Relations Battle Largely Lost," a point that Pelosi later conceded in diagnosing the midterm results as a referendum on the jobs question.[125]

Lessons Learned

This case, while not exhaustive, is instructive on several fronts. First, as we suggested in chapter 6, strategic opportunities to mount public relations campaigns frequently present themselves in the rhythm of the policy process. President Obama certainly hit the ground running in preparing his economic policy agenda and then pressing his case for the legislation. Focusing on the crisis early, and then working within the parameters of existing popular sentiment, he took to a variety of different forums to make the case for a sizable stimulus package. By the time he took the oath of office, he had strong Democratic majorities in Congress working on his behalf, and he had gained public backing for the kind of measure he had promoted. Yet by deferring to Congress and by trying to build bipartisan support for the bill, he created an opportunity for a united Republican party. In stepping to the sidelines, assuming a "soft-sell" approach, he made it possible for a cohesive Republican congressional party to seize the public relations initiative to make the case that the stimulus was a pork-laden package that simply spent too much.

Samuel Kernell notes that when presidents started to enlist on a regular basis a public relations strategy to advance their initiatives "opponents tended to hunker down and hope that the campaign would fail or its effects would dissipate before final action was taken," though some pressure groups did join the air wars and try to neutralize the president's public appeals through costly television advertisements. Although the White House did receive pushback from these ads and even from chamber leaders who worked the weekend talk show circuit, the president enjoyed a "real institutional advantage over congressional actors."[126] Presidents, to be sure, still retain that upper-hand. Nonetheless, as this case suggests, congressional opponents now find that by engineering public relations campaigns in this new media world they can sometimes reduce the president's marginal advantage. Contemporary presidents who "go public" confront a strategic context different from that of their predecessors.[127] Although presidents still command considerable attention on the public stage and have at their disposal many new ways to communicate their views, they now share that stage with multiple actors who can also tap the power of new technologies and coordinate their public relations efforts to create an echo chamber that can on occasion significantly constrain the White House's ability to shape public support for its positions, in ways they would have been unable to in the past.

In his book on presidential leadership, George Edwards observes that while presidents have a difficult time moving public opinion they still carry on with a "faith" that they are capable of shaping popular sentiment through calculated appeals.[128] The example of the stimulus suggests that in this new strategic context presidents have good reason to be motivated by uncertainty and fear as much as by "faith" in their own abilities. In today's environment, where parties are unified and able to strike a coherent public chord, presidents now have powerful incentives to skip negotiations with members across the aisle in order to avoid ceding control of the public arena to their opponents.[129] Indeed, what lesson did President Obama learn as he watched his recovery package get picked apart by Republicans on cable news shows and in their press releases as he worked behind the scenes to build a deal? As he confided to Alter, it was clear and simple: "when trouble hits, get out of Dodge [the Beltway]."[130]

Getting out of Dodge, however, poses other challenges. Among these is that when presidents go public they run the risk of overpromising and elevating expectations.[131] That, in turn, provides the opposition congressional party with an easy target on which they can concentrate their attack as they launch their own public relations campaigns. This was something the Obama administration unhappily discovered when the jobless rate eclipsed the 9% ceiling his advisors promised the unemployment rate would not exceed if Congress passed the bill.

The example of the stimulus also underscores the significance the House minority assigns to an outside strategy in today's environment, and it points to the role internal party cohesion, partisan policy differences, and the interinstitutional context play in shaping and determining the efficacy of outside strategies. House Republicans initiated and drove the message operation because they had few other strategic options. United in their preferences on the issue, and working within an institution the majority controls, they turned to an outside strategy and mounted an effective publicity campaign. It also became easier for them to partner with Senate Republicans, who for the most part generally shared their views. Additionally, since Democrats controlled the White House, neither Senate nor House Republicans had any compelling reason to soften their arguments or restrain their public relations activities, let alone work with the president to realize any sort of agreement. This represents a classic case of what Tim Groeling had in mind when he noted that under conditions of "unified government" a minority party is "paradoxically aided by its institutional weakness" in its communications activities.[132]

This chapter's case also points to some challenges that congressional parties confront in orchestrating a public relations operation, even when they are fairly cohesive in their preferences. Congressional Democrats were also fairly united in support of the policy and thus were generally able to eschew dissension in their public communications on it. Still, even that is not always enough to mount a successful publicity campaign. Democrats, after all, were slow to step up to the plate and drive the message as the president edged away from the public stage shortly after the legislation was introduced in Congress. This early lapse perhaps reflects a challenge for legislators of the party that controls the other end of Pennsylvania Avenue. Patrick Sellers has speculated that members of the party that holds the White House may be more inclined to be "free riders" when it comes to selling their partisan message. Because they feel they can rely on the president to take their case to the American public, they have fewer incentives to mount aggressive public relations activities than do their opponents.[133] It should, of course, probably be added that this is more likely if presidents are popular, as Obama was during those first several months in office. Yet even as congressional Democrats sensed that the news narrative was turning against them, thus increasing their incentives to define and sell the stimulus, they had a hard time regaining their footing, and even when they succeeded they did not always help their larger cause. One problem here was that as the party did manage to get its members selling the package to their different constituents, it inadvertently created an opening for Republicans and their allies. In particular, by reminding their audiences of the ways the act helped their communities, their "credit claiming" rhetoric centering on local material benefits played into, and perhaps reinforced, Republicans' arguments that the policy was filled with waste and pet projects.[134]

Finally, as we saw in the previous chapter, communications operations on a policy do not always end when a bill is signed into law. When public opinion is unsettled and congressional are parties are unified and preoccupied with shoring up their images, they, like presidents, have incentives to resurrect past decisions and wage public battles in an effort to redefine and even on occasion to repeal them. And as they take that up they now also have available to them, as this case makes clear, a number of communications tools they can deploy at strategically timed points to drive the discussion in ways that help them move toward their goals.

8 Thinking Constitutionally
Challenges of Deliberating While Turned Inside Out

Before the clock had struck eight a.m. on the second day of the 112th Congress, House Majority Leader Eric Cantor (R-VA) had appeared on five national television shows. He then participated in a local Richmond radio program, while his office posted a YouTube video of his cable appearance on Fox the day before. Later that day, he joined other members to read the Constitution on the House floor, an event his office streamed live through Facebook.[1] This sort of media activity is not new for Representative Cantor, who puts "a high value on *policy* communications" and whose office staffers admit that it "drives our top-line strategy because we know we are not only talking to each other, we are also speaking to Americans around their kitchen tables."[2] Nor is such activity unusual for today's leaders and contingents of members who turn to publicity to help their parties and themselves carry out their legislative work. As we have seen, many members routinely use a multitude of communications venues to fulfill personal and partisan goals. And while one audience of these communications efforts includes other legislators, executive branch officials, and attentive elites, another regularly encompasses, and engages, the American people themselves. As such, it signals a fundamental transformation in the constitutional system and of Congress's role within that system.

Certain changes from earlier times are obvious. One, members and the parties to which they belong now regularly communicate with each other and other political actors through the media. And two, lawmakers routinely use publicity and media in what is perhaps a more novel way as they try to bring popular sentiment to bear on their institution's processes and outcomes, involving citizens and their parties in conversations in ways they had not been in the past.

While transformations in communications technology may account for part of today's more public style of congressional behavior, such changes do not explain all aspects of it. Legislators are not reluctant to invite public opinion into their lawmaking councils; rather, as we have shown, members and the parties to which they belong have made such activity integral to their governing style. The claim that the media and public relations have moved from the periphery to the center of much of today's congressional politics seems uncontestable. That this development is compatible with the vision underlying the Constitution, however, is far less clear.

Constitutional vs. Public Deliberation

When the Framers drafted Article One of the Constitution, they were not simply interested in Congress as an end in itself. Instead, their larger goal was to design the institution to make distinctive contributions to the constitutional order they were founding. They were focused, then, on the larger political system of which the Congress was a part, and they fashioned the legislature to work in ways that would serve the ends of the regime. It is this concern that we have in mind when we say that we want to think constitutionally about Congress. To what extent, in other words, does today's more public Congress make the contributions to the "common welfare" that only a legislature can make? Ultimately, this leads us to focus on the institution's deliberative capacities.

The Framers believed that they were devising a more energetic constitutional system that fostered deliberation, and in their view Congress played a central role in providing those deliberative processes, a point with which many contemporary observers agree.[3] It is with that in mind that we turn to reflect on how the increased emphasis on public and partisan communication impacts Congress's ability to meet its intended obligations. Here we are particularly interested in exploring whether or not the kinds of activities and discourse promoted by today's more public Congress encourage the institution to make its distinctive deliberative contribution to the polity.

Perhaps the most obvious way that what we have identified as the public Congress breaks with older understandings of American politics is the way it celebrates direct and constant communication between national legislators and citizens. While lawmakers have always been in contact with their constituents, for the most part these communications in the past were meant to keep people broadly aware of political developments and to aid members' reelection efforts. Members of Congress were discouraged, most of the time, from bringing publicity to bear on the day-to-day committee and floor conversations that members had with each other and with executive branch officials as they worked to pass legislation. Passing laws was intended to be a deliberative event, and for deliberation to occur the American people in their collective capacity generally could not be regular and constant participants in that part of the congressional process.

This goal of inhibiting the direct participation of the public in the crafting of legislation was not primarily rooted in a distrust of ordinary people. It instead reflected the understanding that most citizens have neither the leisure nor the inclination to become knowledgeable about public issues. Simply put, according to this older understanding, most people do not have the time they need to listen to arguments on a range of complicated questions, nor do they have the means to explore and assess the quality of the evidence introduced in policy discussions. Moreover, proponents of this older perspective believed that many people are not naturally inclined to give a sympathetic hearing to ideas with which they disagree, especially if those disagreements touch on issues that stir powerful emotions or disturb entrenched interests. In this view, the principal concern is not that most people lack the ability to deliberate. Rather, it is that the context of most peoples' lives does not include the conditions that deliberation requires. The Framers wanted to set the national government's decision-making structure in an arena where argument and the sharing of ideas had a better chance of shaping policy than stump speeches and votes.[4]

They were convinced that deliberation enhanced the chances that policy would meet the dual demands of competency and justice. Competency means that policy decisions are based on an accurate understanding of often complicated and technical questions. Justice, in a country that aspires to represent all of its citizens, includes the notion that most people must be able to see some of their goals reflected in policy decisions. Not all of their goals must always be realized, of course, but people have to believe that over time and on balance government decisions are sufficiently responsive to their concerns.

Accommodation and compromise are thus cardinal political virtues in this older understanding, not only because policymakers often *must* compromise, since they lack the power to ignore the views of others, but also because, and perhaps primarily because, an inclination to compromise reflects a deep commitment to the proposition that all citizens are equal and that they all deserve to have some part of their hopes and goals reflected in the laws that govern them. This is one way that a Founder's perspective differs from a partisan's point of view. Partisans yearn for a political system that allows them to win political battles. Founders, at least the founders of a regime that aspires to the belief that all people are equal, seek to design a political system that will sometimes frustrate and defeat their own private political goals.

Our Founders placed policymaking decisions in a constitutional arena because they were convinced that the people in their collective capacity lacked the time, expertise, and inclination to meet the demands of a deliberative politics.[5] Constitutional officers were, of course, elected by, accountable to, and representative of the people, but they were charged with the task of creating laws through a series of interactions with other constitutional officers located in the legislative and executive branches. In this sense, the Constitution should not only be read as a list of "do's and don'ts," of specific powers that are either granted to, or withheld from, the government, but as an articulation of a "way" to order public affairs. In this sense, the Constitution is the source of a "constitutional politics," wherein the regular, day-to-day operation of its offices, and the manner in which its officers interact, is at the heart of the American political experience.

This older view elevates the Constitution's offices to a place of preeminence in the regular politics of ordinary times. Under this paradigm, the Constitution's officers, not the people themselves, should be the ones who usually make policy decisions. And those decisions will usually be shaped by the views and interests of the other constitutional officers with whom they interact. These offices are, by design, intended to represent people in myriad ways. The constituencies of the House, Senate, and president differ in size, for example, and in geographic location and in diversity, and all three institutions operate under different time constraints imposed by their terms. They thus altogether represent the American people simultaneously and variously. But while they are rooted in popular opinion and consent, they flower in the interplay with other constitutional officers.[6] *Deliberation* is the term we use to describe the interplay of these officers and it is in this sense that "constitutional politics" is "deliberative."[7]

The interaction of constitutional officers can take a variety of forms. Sometimes it will involve conversations in a formal or an informal setting where participants share information that supports their policy preferences—say, an executive official appearing before a congressional subcommittee, or a representative having lunch with a senator. Other participants are thus provided with the chance to assess, explore, and question the quality of that information and to point to other information that the first participant had not had the chance, or chose not to consider. In these settings, policymakers begin to learn why their colleagues hold the policy preferences that they do, and they are given the opportunity to reassess their own positions, and possibly to refine them or even to change their minds.

Sometimes this interaction will involve threats to do something without taking the view, or even the reasons behind the view, of others into account. They can threaten to stop talking, for instance, or to refuse to stop talking (filibuster), or to call for a vote, stage a walk-out, or issue an executive order. That can prompt counterthreats, such as holding up an unrelated bill, investigating an agency's budget, delaying a nomination, or exercising a veto.

This process is deliberative in many ways. Its pace is often measured, even slow, as various constitutional officers representing the people in overlapping yet distinctive ways engage over a period of time to persuade each other to take their policy preferences into account. And it is deliberative in that it often requires policymakers to defend their policy preferences by pointing to arguments and reasons that others find credible, or at least not obviously flawed. Other constitutional officers usually have the time, the resources, and the expertise to examine this kind of evidence and to assess its merit. This discourages, though it certainly does not preclude, chicanery, fabrication, and a rush to judgment based on partial or erroneous evidence. Moreover, the process reveals not only what participants' policy goals are but how much they value them. Are they willing, for instance, to pursue one objective without compromise, even if it means that they may lose another due to a veto or budget cut? This has the effect of encouraging officers to consider any one of their policy goals as part-and-parcel of a whole array of other goals that they, and the country, hope to pursue. Hence the process encourages them to broaden their understanding of governance as something involving decisions on a host of intertwined issues instead of as a set of discrete, separate, stand-alone decisions.

The deliberative nature of this process is enhanced by the regular interaction of officeholders. This provides them with the chance to get to know each other: to see displayed one another's acumen, diligence, sense of humor, and temperament. They may come to know each other's interests: Are they religious? Do they hunt? Collect stamps? They learn one another's personal circumstances: Are they married? Have kids? Feel any tension between the demands of their job and being a parent? They discover each other's tastes: in food, music, or fashion. They find out something of their personal histories: Did they have alcoholic parents? Been a crime victim? Play high school sports? This regular interaction of constitutional officers creates the conditions necessary for allowing policymakers to know each other in a more completely human way, providing them with the chance to see one another as something other than, more than, a political ally or opponent. Another way to say this is that this process creates the conditions necessary for collegiality.

Collegiality, in turn, can foster respect for, though not necessarily agreement with, other officeholders, and more broadly, for the people those other officers represent. Collegiality can deepen the deliberative character of policymaking by encouraging lawmakers to listen to each other, in part because they have come to respect one another. Thus this process nurtures officeholders' inclination to listen to those they disagree with and so encourages them to give some kind of a hearing to the views of those citizens with whom they may have many and profound disagreements.[8] And as they assess and examine the arguments that are presented by their legislative colleagues, they are provided with the opportunity to reexamine their own views, and so perhaps can deepen and refine their understanding of public affairs.[9]

American Politics: Then and Now

The more closed "baronial" Congress supported a kind of congressional politics that resembled something like the above. As we discussed in chapter 3, policymaking in this period was largely an internal, institutional activity and most policy decisions stemmed from the behind-the-scenes conversations members had with each other, and with executive branch officials and actors from concerned interests. Members were encouraged to develop policy expertise on a few subjects, and the norm of committee reciprocity rewarded that expertise with influence. Members were encouraged to speak respectfully of each other and of the Congress and discouraged from using inflammatory language in public. This was a Congress that valued collegiality more than confrontation, and it was relatively common for lawmakers to socialize with one another. While most legislators sought publicity for electoral purposes, only a few mavericks sought it to influence policy. Junior members served as apprentices, deferred to senior colleagues' decisions, and learned the myriad folkways of the Hill's culture. A small group, the "oligarchs" or "barons," presided over this Congress, managing key institutional resources to exercise control. For the most part, they rewarded members who projected a calm, low-key, moderate public presence and punished those who did not, prompting members to conform to their chambers' informal requirements. Members' ambitions and activities were thus tethered to, and made to serve, the needs and purposes of their institution.

Chapter 3 describes why and how this system unraveled. Suffice it here to say that today's institution, the public Congress, has upended and reversed the older understanding of the proper relationship between lawmakers, the media, and the American people. Today, it is no longer frowned upon for lawmakers to conduct public relations campaigns while carrying out the duties of their office; indeed, given the needs of parties to get out their messages, it is expected and even rewarded as communications acumen has become an important part of the route to power and prestige. Members, as we have shown, have built up formidable resources to take their messages outside chamber walls, and the parties have adapted structures and strategies to help them harness their members' communications activities so as to advance their programmatic and partisan goals. And as our case studies illustrate, congressional parties now find public relations campaigns aimed directly at the American people an integral component in policymaking calculations and activities.

While this new understanding of the proper relationship between congressional members and their constituents began to increase the frequency and expand the aims of members' publicity activities, it also began to change the pace and tone of congressional discourse. In today's variegated, competitive, and more partisan breaking-news environment, speed and drama increase the chances that any one political actor's voice will be heard amidst all the others clamoring for attention. Speed is important, because once a news story appears, it can be picked up almost instantly by a plethora of other media and in a matter of hours start to dominate and shape the country's political conversation. Policymakers are under tremendous pressure to respond as fast as they can, in order to increase their chances of managing the news narrative. Similarly, the media need to report breaking stories quickly in order to stay up-to-date and relevant with their audiences. In this environment, participants in both the political sphere and news world have less time to examine and assess different political actors' claims.

The experience of Shirley Sherrod, an African American woman who was forced to resign from the Department of Agriculture in the summer of 2010, is a revealing example of how the contemporary pace of media-driven political events can impact even seasoned political officials' judgments. On July 19 at 11:20 a.m., a conservative blogger posted an edited video clip of Ms. Sherrod that made it appear that she acknowledged discriminating against a white farmer in carrying out her official duties. Others picked up the story, and about an hour-and-a-half after the first posting, FoxNation ran the clip under the headline: "Caught On Tape: Obama Official Discriminates Against White Farmer." By late afternoon, more mainline news providers were covering it, and it was being discussed by Fox's Bill O'Reilly and Sean Hannity, as well as by a former White House press secretary, CNN, Tea Party officials, Rush Limbaugh, and a growing chorus of others. Department of Agriculture officials, the White House, and presumably the president felt compelled to act before the narrative spiraled beyond their control. Less than nine hours after the story first broke, the White House asked Ms. Sherrod to resign, and the NAACP President tweeted he was "appalled" by her actions. It turns out that the video had been edited and that the story she told about the white farmer had taken place twenty-four years earlier. The truth is she helped him save his farm and had become friends with his family. Her intent was to demonstrate that it is always unjust to treat people differently based on race.[10] The larger point of this episode, for our purposes, is that it illustrates the speed with which the contemporary Washington community sometimes responds to political developments, and it reveals how the links between today's different media platforms intersect to drive stories in ways that sometimes overwhelm the cognitive capacities of those who wield power.

Not only do more members talk more frequently in the media than they used to, many talk differently as well. The substance and the tone of congressional rhetoric are now more regularly combative and confrontational, more likely than in the past to stress ideological messages and disparaging remarks. Partly this stems from our competitive, fast-paced media environment. Scandal, conflict, and drama are much more likely to attract coverage than more tempered discourse.[11] Moreover, speaking in this way is likely to win the attention of those citizens who are most passionately attached to the issue being discussed, and so dramatic rhetoric can generate votes, campaign volunteers, and money, thus serving the parties' interests.[12]

Some worry that today's rhetoric promotes and excites divisive passions that inhibit civil discourse and can lead to political violence, a point alluded to in accounts covering the attempted assassination of Rep. Gabrielle Giffords (D-AZ) in January 2011.[13] There is some reason to believe that members of Congress are endangered today in ways that they were not when their public rhetoric was more sedate. The Senate Sergeant at Arms told reporters that threats against members increased by 300% in the first few months of 2010. Capitol Hill police testified their hazardous material response teams responded to 128 suspicious packages in 2008 and 152 such packages in 2009. During that same period, the number of sweeps to secure areas where congressional meetings took place jumped from 568 to 3,868, and the number of bomb sweeps doubled, going from 970 to 1,808. Seven members of Congress received death threats in 2009 serious enough to warrant FBI investigations, and when the man who left a voice message for Rep. Heath Shuler (D-NC) promising that, "If you vote for that stimulus package, I'm gonna kill you" was asked about his motives, he told the FBI that "I was trying to work the political scene."[14]

Coverage given to Rep. Paul Broun (R-GA) captures both the tone of some contemporary congressional rhetoric and the reactions it generates. Rep. Broun often calls President Obama a socialist.[15] Shortly after the 2008 election, he said he feared "the president would impose a Gestapo-like security force to impose a Marxist dictatorship." And while he was attending the 2011 State of the Union address he tweeted: "Mr. President, you don't believe in the Constitution. You believe in socialism." Later, Rep Broun alerted the Secret Service that one of his constituents asked him at a town hall meeting, "Who's going to shoot Obama?"[16] While Rep Broun characterized the question as "abhorrent," some might think that publicly likening the president to a Marxist dictator who employs fascist brutalities to transform the state helps create a climate of opinion that induces some to believe that the country would be well served by political violence.

Needless to say, no one side has a monopoly on such rhetoric in today's Capitol Hill community. Indeed, as Rep. Broun was accusing the president of carrying out a socialist agenda, a member from the Democratic side of the aisle, who once called a female adviser in Federal Reserve Chair Ben Bernanke's office a "K Street whore" on a talk radio show, was depicting his GOP opponents as "foot-dragging, knuckle-dragging Neanderthals." The congressman, Rep. Alan Grayson (D-FL), ultimately took to the floor of the House to charge that the Republican's health care plan amounted to telling sick people to "die quickly," a stance that earned him a fair amount of attention on both sides of the ideological divide that defines the cable news circuit and the blogosphere, though it most certainly did little to promote collegiality in the institution in which he served.[17]

Assessing Deliberation

By explaining why we think that the more traditional, hierarchical Congress perhaps on occasion created a kind of politics whose forms resembled the deliberative processes described by the Framers, we do not thereby conclude that it was superior to the style of the contemporary Congress. Compared to its current counterpart, there is no doubt that the older Congress was slower paced, its public rhetoric less vituperative, its members more collegial and bipartisan, and its decision-making apparatus more insulated from untutored public opinion.

Yet for all of that, and for all of the worry today about political violence, it was that older time that experienced the assassination of a sitting president, and of a major presidential candidate, and the grievous wounding of another. It was then that Martin Luther King, Medger Evers, and Malcolm X were shot to death. It was then that civil rights workers were murdered in Mississippi, college students shot down at Kent State, children blown up while attending church. It was then that police turned water hoses and dogs and batons on citizens who were marching peacefully for what they understood to be their natural and constitutional rights. Cities all over the country erupted in riots during this era, in part because many were frustrated that the government turned a deaf ear to their concerns about civil rights and the Vietnam War. This was the time when a major party was able to select its presidential nominee only because a city's entire police force used tear gas and billy clubs to keep thousands of protesters from storming the hotel where its delegates met. And this was when tax-paying African American citizens were only able to enter some public universities because they had armed federal protection.[18]

This was also a time when constitutional officers failed their institutions. In the previous decade, they had allowed Senator Joseph McCarthy (R-WI) to smear the reputations and ruin the careers of citizens. Members of Congress failed to examine presidential claims during the Vietnam War and passed the Gulf of Tonkin Resolution. The activities of executive branch agencies like the CIA and FBI were left unchecked, while the IRS was encouraged to audit some citizens only because they were a president's political opponents. And it was at the end of this era that an individual who served his entire career in high constitutional offices in both the legislative and executive branches resigned from the presidency in disgrace.

The point here is to recall that as interested as they were in establishing a deliberative political system, deliberation itself was not the Framers' most important objective. It was, rather, a means to an end, and that end was to create what they took to be a just government. Sensitive to the ways that participatory democracy can threaten that kind of society, the Framers aimed for a political system th modulated the impact of popular opinion on government decisions. The challenge they faced was to make government simultaneously open to, and insulated from, popular opinion. The violence and policy fiascos of the post-World War II era may indicate that at some point in those years this balance was lost, that perhaps constitutional officers had become too insular, too removed from the most important policy goals of too many of the citizens.

This draws our attention to ways in which the more participatory style of contemporary congressional politics perhaps enhances the deliberative goals of the country's original design. It was while the current system was being constructed that a more expansive and welcoming public space was carved out for those citizens whose opinions, interests, and rights were often stifled and ignored by a more closed Congress—Catholics, Jews, women, racial minorities, young adults, and increasingly, gay men and lesbians and the physically and mentally impaired. It is under the auspices of this more participatory political order that the country's constitutional offices were opened to these citizens who had been ignored and discriminated against. This era has a more capacious understanding of who the Constitution refers to in its opening three words, and this is another way that it realizes the aspirations of the founding regime more completely than the one that preceded it.

Changes in the contemporary media similarly add to the country's chances of engaging in a deliberative politics. At the same time that a small number of baron-like legislators had a powerful impact on the Congress, a handful of news providers exercised an almost hegemonic control over political reporting. Many observe that as older, traditional news companies lost their ability to act as gatekeepers, to define the parameters of what constitutes political news, the subject and tone of political reporting changed. It became coarser, more focused on scandal, conflict, and gossip than on serious and careful explorations of public questions.[19] While this observation merits attention, it obscures another dimension to these developments that bears on our ability to assess the deliberative character of American politics.

Consider the way that the press covered the private lives of Presidents Kennedy and Clinton in these two time periods. Clinton's private indiscretions were vigorously investigated; Kennedy's were not. Let us assume the media elite decided not to report Kennedy's infidelities for a variety of reasons, including: while the indiscretions were widely suspected, it was difficult to find sources to verify them; that such affairs are private activities that do not bear on a president's public responsibilities; and hence reporting these liaisons would be to traffic in gossip, not news, and would pander to the public's interest in salacious stories. All of these are reasonable on their face for stonewalling an investigation into these incidents, and this is not the place to separate rumor from fact regarding Kennedy's life. Nonetheless, it has been established that he had an affair with Judith Exner while she was simultaneously involved with the organized crime boss, Sam Giancana.[20] That a sitting president would take such risks might lead some to question his judgment and wonder if he had the temperament to meet successfully the duties of his constitutional office. The country had the opportunity to have that debate 'n the 1990s. A small group of political and media elites deprived the country of at opportunity thirty years earlier. The contemporary media expand the number of citizens whose "opinions, passions and interests" have the chance to influence politically relevant conversations and so shape the laws under which they live, and in this way it enhances the country's commitment to the democratic and deliberative political project started by the founding generation. [21]

Yet if the postwar Congress was overly insulated from public opinion, the danger facing the new Congress may be that it is overly exposed to it. As we have demonstrated, public relations campaigns carried out by congressional parties are an important dimension of our politics today, one that reinforces trends ushered in by American presidents. That is not to say that such campaigns are mounted on all issues or that they are always successful. As our cases studies suggest, congressional parties think strategically in determining whether, when, and how they carry out their messaging activities. There are still issues that provoke fissures within congressional parties, giving them few incentives to mount publicity campaigns. Our cases also show that, despite their best efforts, congressional parties struggle to surmount the collective action challenge of getting their folks out on the issues, keeping them on message, and coordinating their public relations campaigns with their partisan colleagues across the Washington community. Nonetheless, these sorts of campaigns have become an important part of today's Congress and, at some points, even assume center stage, using members' precious time and diverting their attention away from many of their legislative responsibilities. An aide to Minority Leader Nancy Pelosi once betrayed just how heavily communications campaigns weigh on today's congressional parties when asked about the Democrats' legislative plans. The staffer replied: "It's not about governing. We're focused on message."[22] Recall that this was exactly the same point Minority Leader John Boehner made when, at the start of the Obama administration, he told his folks they were in the communications, not the legislative business. What this suggests is that in today's Congress preoccupation with publicity on behalf of parties seriously weakens the capacity of members to identify with the duties of the offices they hold. They thus run the risk of no longer being able to, in Hugh Heclo's words, "think institutionally."[23]

Beyond that, recall that these congressional communications operations are events engineered to shape and excite popular sentiment. As they organize and execute these campaigns, congressional parties and the presidents whose lead they have followed increasingly adopt the language of marketing executives: they are creating and controlling a message and building a brand that resonates with some important constituencies. This is the language of commercial sales, and its aim, of course, is to persuade. Still, while this language and that goal are a part of a deliberative discourse, deliberation also seeks to explore and assess, to understand as well as to persuade. Lawmakers and other constitutional officers engaged in deliberation are thus open to the possibility that they have something to learn, and so they listen to those with whom they currently disagree and even adjust their views in light of what they hear. They seek not only to reflect public opinion, but also to test and uplift it.

Highly coordinated town hall meetings—public relations events—that members frequently hold signify some of the threats that current congressional communication practices pose for deliberative politics. Members assemble citizens, and deliver a scripted message in the hopes of ginning up support and additional media coverage for their party's positions. While this may present the façade of allowing the public's voice to be heard, it leaves the public's opinion unexplored and unchallenged. Policy conversations dominated by passionate citizens chanting slogans do not create the kind of environment that encourages them, or their representatives, to think their way through important public matters. Moreover this process leaves many citizens vulnerable to being manipulated with partially true or perhaps even false information. This sort of discourse seems ill-suited to the goal of being guided by the "cool and deliberate sense of the community" to create policies that seek, in the words of the Preamble to the Constitution, "to secure the blessings of liberty."[24]

We do not mean to overstate the case. We do not claim, for instance, that the contemporary Congress is unequivocally inimical to deliberation. Nor do we claim that there was some past "golden" age when our representatives' debate sought only the public good, untainted by any partisan or personal consideration. We mean to paint a more complicated picture. The shift from the more isolated baronial order to today's public Congress reveals the endemic tension between the goals articulated by our nation's Founders. That generation sought to establish a polity rooted in popular consent, yet wanted its government's decision-making apparatus to be shaped by opinion that was "refined" and thus more reflective than is commonly found among the people.[25] If the Congress of the midtwentieth century was perhaps too isolated from the policy desires of the citizens of that time, today's legislators may be so attached to them that their ability to improve and correct public opinion may be diminished.

Yet as we have shown, these communication practices are deeply embedded in American political life and culture. Indeed, that is one of the reasons we undertook this study. We are convinced that understanding the role that the media and public relations play in congressional politics and in interbranch relations provides us with a vantage point from which other, interrelated features of the American polity come into view. The congressional behavior that we have described and analyzed grew out of a reaction to internal institutional reforms, to the changing rhetorical behavior of presidents, to the proliferation of interest groups, to the ideological polarization of the two major parties, and to economic and technological changes in modern media. Any attempt to change or redirect these congressional communication campaigns will thus also have to contend with these powerful forces that over the last fifty years swept through and reshaped the political landscape. Additionally, any attempt at reform will need to take place in the context of awareness of the conflicting tension inherent in the project launched by the founding generation of Americans and embedded in the Constitution; that is, how do we sustain a politics that is based on popular rule and yet provides policymakers with some distance from public opinion? It is in this sense that the country is once again confronting the question raised in 1787: How do we construct a public life whereby laws are the product of a deliberative discourse that, while open and robust, "does not disgrace the cause of truth"?[26]

Notes

Chapter 1

1. Timothy E. Cook, *Governing with the News: The News Media as a Political Institution* (Chicago: University of Chicago Press, 1998); George Edwards III, *Campaigning by Governing: The Politics of the Bush Presidency* (New York: Pearson Longman, 2007); and Samuel Kernell, *Going Public: New Strategies of Presidential Leadership*, 3rd ed. (Washington, DC: CQ Press, 1997).
2. Tim Groeling, *When Politicians Attack!: Party Cohesion in the Media* (Cambridge, UK: Cambridge University Press, 2010), 2 (emphasis in the original).
3. Richard Fenno, *Congressmen in Committees* (Boston: Little Brown, 1973).
4. Scott Galloway and Doug Guthrie, "Digital IQ Index: U.S. Senate," *L2*, August 18, 2010, http://www.l2thinktank.com/senatedigitaliq/; and Jennifer Bendery and Christina Bellantoni, "Social Media Goes Viral on Capitol Hill," *Roll Call*, February 6, 2011.
5. Speaker John Boehner's online office, http://www.youtube.com/johnboehner.
6. Kathleen Hunter and Jessica Brady, "Democrats Look to Past to Chart Future," *Roll Call*, January 24, 2011.
7. Christina Bellantoni, "GOP Surpasses Dems on Twitter," *Washington Times*, February 17, 2009. Posted on GOP.gov, http://www.gop.gov/wtas/09/02/19/gop-surpasses-dems-on-twitter.
8. Patrick O'Connor, "Boehner Lost Vote, Won Power," *Politico*, January 29, 2009, http://www.politico.com.
9. Nancy E. Roman, *Both Sides of the Aisle* (New York: Council on Foreign Relations, 2005), 17.
10. Carl Hulse, "House Democrats Rapidly Unleash Sharp Attacks," *New York Times*, January 8, 2011, http://www.nytimes.com/2011/01/09/us/politics/09memo.html.
11. For an overview of this normative foundation, see Eric Uslaner, *The Decline of Comity in Congress* (Ann Arbor: University of Michigan Press, 1993), chap 2.
12. Groeling, *When Politicians Attack*, chap. 1.
13. Ibid.
14. Interview conducted by the authors, August 2004. We conducted interviews with a broad cross-section of members' and parties' communications staffers—13 Democrats and 13 Republicans—during August 2004 and August 2005. We also conducted interviews with three representatives from the DC press corps and news service. Interviews were taped and all interviewees were granted anonymity.
15. See Groeling, *When Politicians Attack!*; and Patrick Sellers, *Cycles of Spin: Strategic Communications in the U.S. Congress* (New York: Cambridge University Press, 2010).
16. Barbara Sinclair, *Party Wars: Polarization and the Politics of National Policy Making* (Norman: University of Oklahoma Press, 2006), chap. 7.

17. Alexander Hamilton, John Jay, and James Madison, *The Federalist Papers*, ed. George Carey and James McClellan (Indianapolis, IN: Liberty Fund, 2001), no. 10, 42–49; and no. 63, 327.

18. Joseph Bessette, *The Mild Voice of Reason: Deliberative Democracy and American National Government* (Chicago: University of Chicago Press, 1994), 28–29. For an alternative view, see Gary Mucciaroni and Paul Quirk, *Deliberative Choices* (Chicago: University of Chicago Press, 2006), 4–5.

19. *Federalist*, no. 70, 363.

20. Bessette, *The Mild Voice of Reason*, 49–55.

21. *Federalist*, no. 51, 269.

22. Jeffrey K. Tulis, *The Rhetorical Presidency* (Princeton, NJ: Princeton University Press, 1987), 37–38.

23. See Stephanie Burkhalter, "Message Discipline in Floor Deliberation in the Contemporary Congress: Study of the Estate Tax Repeal" (paper prepared for the American Political Science Association Annual Conference, Washington, DC, September 1–5, 2005).

24. Leroy N. Rieselbach, *Congressional Reform: The Changing Modern Congress* (Washington, DC: CQ Press, 1994), chap. 2.

25. Groeling, *When Politicians Attack!*, chap. 2. See also Sellers, *Cycles of Spin*.

26. Samuel Kernell, *Going Public: New Strategies of Presidential Leadership* (Washington, DC: CQ Press, 1997), 2.

27. George Edwards, *The Strategic President: Persuasion and Opportunity in Presidential Leadership* (Princeton, NJ: Princeton University Press, 2009), chap. 3.

28. This theme is developed by Tulis, *The Rhetorical Presidency*, 9–13.

Chapter 2

1. "President Bush's Top Economic Adviser, Lawrence Lindsey Talks about Bush Tax Cut Plan," *Good Morning America*, ABC, February 5, 2001; Lori Nitschke, "Tax Plan Destined for Revision," *CQ Weekly*, February 9, 2001: 318–21; Federal News Service, "Press Conference with Senate Minority Leader Senator Tom Daschle (D-SD) and Senator Kent Conrad (D-ND)," February 5, 2001; "President Bush Pushes Tax Cut Proposal," *Inside Politics*, CNN, February 5, 2001; and "Bush's Tax-Cut Plan," *Hardball with Chris Matthews*, MSNBC, February 5, 2001.

2. "Democrats Attack Bush Tax Cut Proposal," *Inside Politics*, CNN, February 6, 2001; Richard W. Stevenson, "Bush To Propose Making a Tax Cut Effective in 2001," *New York Times*, February 6, 2001; Doug Bandow, "The Capitol Eye: Tax Cuts for Taxpayers," *Copley News Service*, February 6, 2001; and Tania Anderson, "Area Democrats Want Tax Cuts Toned Down," *Worcester Telegram and Gazette*, February 6, 2001.

3. "Treasury Secretary Paul O'Neill Discusses President Bush's Tax Cut Proposal," *Business Center*, CNBC, February 7, 2001; "House Leaders Back Bush Tax Cut Plan on Steps of Capitol Hill," *Live Event*, CNN, February 7, 2001; and "Will Bush's Tax Plan Survive Congress?," *Hannity & Colmes*, Fox, February 7, 2001.

4. Federal News Service, "The White House Regular Briefing," February 8, 2001; "Republican Leadership Welcomes Bush's Tax Cut Proposal," *Live Event/Special*, CNN, February 8, 2001; and "Pros and Cons of the President's Tax Cut Plan," *Talk of the Nation*, National Public Radio, February 8, 2001.

5. "One of the Largest Tax Cut Proposals Ever Sent to Congress," *News Day*, CNN, February 8, 2001.

6. "Delivering the Plan," *The News Hour with Jim Lehrer*, PBS, February 8, 2001; "Representative Dick Armey on Bush's Tax Cut Proposal and Clinton's Pardon of Marc

Rich," *Hardball With Chris Matthews* MSNBC, February 8, 2001; "Representative Barney Frank on Clinton's Pardoning of Marc Rich and Bush's Tax Cut," *Hardball With Chris Matthews*, February 8, 2001; "Does George W. Bush Want to Cut Taxes by too Much or too Little?," *The Spin Room*, CNN, February 8, 2001; and "Interview with Pat Toomey," *Special Report with Brit Hume*, Fox, February 8, 2001.

7. Tim Groeling and Samuel Kernell, "Congress, the President, and Party Competition via Network News," in *Polarized Politics: Congress and the President in a Partisan Era*, ed. Jon R. Bond and Richard Fleisher (Washington, DC: CQ Press, 2000), 76.

8. Barbara Sinclair, *The Transformation of the U.S. Senate* (Baltimore: Johns Hopkins University Press, 1989), chap. 10; and Timothy Cook, *Governing with the News: The News Media as a Political Institution* (Chicago: University of Chicago Press, 1998).

9. Richard Fenno, *Congressmen in Committees* (Boston: Little, Brown, 1973).

10. Tim Groeling, *When Politicians Attack!: Party Cohesion in the Media* (New York: Cambridge University Press, 2010); and Patrick Sellers, *Cycles of Spin: Strategic Communication in the U.S. Congress* (New York: Cambridge University Press, 2010).

11. Sellers, *Cycles of Spin*, 215–16

12. Cook, *Governing with the News*, 121, 122.

13. Shanto Iyengar, "Overview," in *Do the Media Govern?: Politicians, Voters, and Reporters in America*, ed. Shanto Iyengar and Richard Reeves (Thousand Oaks, CA: Sage, 1997), 319–20.

14. Samuel Kernell, *Going Public: New Strategies of Presidential Leadership* (Washington, DC: CQ Press, 1997), 2.

15. Ibid., 2.

16. Jeffrey Cohen, *The Presidency in the Era of 24-Hour News* (Princeton, NJ: Princeton University Press, 2008).

17. George C. Edwards III, *The Strategic President: Persuasion and Opportunity in Presidential Leadership* (Princeton, NJ: Princeton University Press, 2009).

18. Martha Joynt Kumar, *Managing the President's Message: The White House Communications Operation* (Baltimore: Johns Hopkins University Press, 2007).

19. Cohen, *The Presidency in the Era of 24-Hour News*, 200.

20. Deborah Stone, *Policy Paradox: The Art of Political Decision Making* (New York: Norton, 1997), 133.

21. Remarks by President George W. Bush on Iraq at the Cincinnati Museum Center, Cincinnati Union Terminal, October 7, 2002, http:www.whitehouse.gov/news/releases.

22. Cook, *Governing with the News*, 126–27.

23. Richard Neustadt, *Presidential Power and the Modern Presidents* (New York: Free Press, 1990). Clinton quoted in Lawrence R. Jacobs, "The Presidency and the Press: The Paradox of the White House Communications War," in *The Presidency and the Political System*, ed. Michael Nelson (Washington, DC: CQ Press 2006), 284.

24. Cook, *Governing with the News*, 129.

25. Kernell, *Going Public*, chap. 1–2. That does not mean they always succeed in transforming opinion. See George C. Edwards III, "The Limits of the Bully Pulpit," in *Readings in Presidential Politics*, ed. George C. Edwards III (Belmont, CA: Thomson Wadsworth, 2006), 183–211.

26. Quoted in Howard Kurtz, "In His Own Words: A Portrait of Ronald Reagan Emerges in Excerpts from His Diaries," *Washington Post, National Weekly Edition*, May 7–13, 2007, 13.

27. Quoted in Andrew Taylor, "Obama: Catastrophe Coming if Congress Doesn't Act," *The Associated Press State and Local Wire*, February 4, 2009.

28. Kernell, *Going Public*, 37.

29. Timothy E. Cook, *Making Laws and Making News: Media Strategies in the U.S. House of Representatives* (Washington, DC: Brookings Institution, 1989); and Karen

Kedrowski, *Media Entrepreneurs and the Media Enterprise in the U.S. Congress* (Cresskill, NJ: Hampton Press, 1996).

30. David Von Drehle, "A Mastodon Takes on Global Warming," *Time*, June 11, 2007, 36–38, 41.

31. Jeff Kosseff, "Hooley Likes Open-Door Approach to Problems," *The Oregonian*, August 30, 2006.

32. John Broder, "Democrats Oust Longtime Leader of House Panel," *New York Times*, November 21, 2008; and Faye Fiore, "For Better or Worse, He's On It," *Los Angeles Times*, July 17, 2006, http://articles.latimes.com/2006/jul/17/nation/na-waxman17.

33. Daniel Libit, "Bachmann Turns to Overdrive," *Politico*, October 20, 2008, http://www.politico.com

34. Quoted in Carroll J. Doherty, "Congressional Affairs: How Will Congress Navigate the New Media Maelstrom," *CQ Weekly*, March 20, 1989, 682–86.

35. Ann Compton, "Speed Over Substance," *Media Studies Journal: Media and Congress* 10 (Winter 1996): 26.

36. David Mayhew, *America's Congress: Actions in the Public Sphere, James Madison through Newt Gingrich* (New Haven, CT: Yale University Press, 2000), 232.

37. See Cook, *Making Laws and Making News*; *Governing with the News*, 150; and Kedrowski, *Media Entrepreneurs and the Media Enterprise*.

38. Timothy Cook, "PR on the Hill: The Evolution of Congressional Press Operations," in *Congressional Politics*, ed. Christopher Deering (Chicago: Dorsey Press, 1989), 83.

39. Stephen Hess, *News and News Making* (Washington, DC: Brookings Institution, 1996), 67.

40. Fenno, *Congressmen in Committees*.

41. Roger H. Davidson and Walter J. Oleszek, *Congress and Its Members* (Washington, DC: CQ Press, 2004), 153.

42. Cook, *Governing with the News*, 150–56.

43. Cook, "PR on the Hill," 72.

44. Quoted in Michael Sandler, "A Parting of the Ways at the Border," *CQ Weekly*, March 27, 2006, 828–35.

45. He had ten clips from cable news shows on which he appeared from March 1 to May 1, 2007 posted on his website as of May 1, 2007.

46. Quoted in David M. Drucker, "Immigration Foes Retooling Caucus," *Roll Call*, March 12, 2007.

47. Sandler, "A Parting of the Ways at the Border," 828–35.

48. Sinclair, *Transformation of the U.S. Senate*, 193; and Cook, "PR on the Hill," 72.

49. Kimberly Hefling, "Anti-War Congressman Continues to Make News," *Associated Press*, December 8, 2005.

50. Quoted in Maeve Reston, "Murtha Commands Spotlight Over Iraq Policy: A Veteran Backbencher Becomes an Anti-War Darling," *Pittsburgh Post-Gazette*, December 26, 2005.

51. Maeve Reston, "Murtha Put War at Top of Agenda in House," *Pittsburgh Post-Gazette*, November 20, 2005.

52. Trudy Rubin, "Murtha's Call a Turning Point in War," *The Times Union*, December 1, 2005.

53. Melissa Drosjack, "Supreme Court's Decision to Uphold Partial Birth Abortion Ban Gives Bush Victory," Foxnews.com, http:www.foxnews.com/story/0,2933,266789,00.html.

54. James M. Lindsay, "Congress and Foreign Policy: Why the Hill Matters," *Political Science Quarterly* 107 (Winter 1992–93): 624. Timothy Cook finds that this strategy of going public can help legislators realize several goals simultaneously. See Cook, "PR on the Hill," 73–74. For a consideration of how other senators have tried to use publicity to shape the executive's actions, see Sinclair, *The Transformation of the U.S. Senate*, 199–201.

55. Quoted in Nadine Cohodas, "Press Coverage: It's What You Do That Counts," *CQ Weekly*, January 3, 1987, 29–33.
56. Tip O'Neill, "Rules for Speakers," in *The Speaker: Leadership in the U.S. House of Representatives*, ed. Ronald M. Peters Jr. (Washington, DC: CQ Press, 1994), 220.
57. Cook, "PR on the Hill," 72.
58. Quoted in Cohodas, "Press Coverage: It's What You Do That Counts," 29–33.
59. See Kedrowski, *Media Entrepreneurs and the Media Enterprise.*
60. Hedrick Smith, *The Power Game* (New York: Random House, 1988), 139.
61. Burdett Loomis, *The New American Politician: Ambition, Entrepreneurship and the Changing Face of Political Life* (New York: Basic Books, 1988), 97, 98–99.
62. See Burdett Loomis, "Senate Leaders, Minority Voices: From Dirksen to Daschle," in *The Contentious Senate: Partisanship, Ideology and the Myth of Cool Judgment*, ed. Colton C. Campbell and Nicol Rae (Lanham, MD: Rowman and Littlefield, 2001), 98; and Janet Hook, "Behind Daschle's Mild Manner Is a Man on the Move," *CQ Weekly*, June 11, 1994, 1491–94.
63. Connie Bruck, "The Politics of Perception," *The New Yorker*, October 9, 1995, 62–63.
64. Alan Ehrenhalt, "Media, Power Shifts Dominate O'Neill's House," *CQ Weekly*, September 13, 1986, 2131–38.
65. David Mayhew, *Congress: The Electoral Connection* (New Haven, CT: Yale University Press, 1974).
66. Timothy E. Cook, "Press Secretaries and Media Strategies in the House of Representatives: Deciding Whom to Pursue," *American Journal of Political Science* 32 (November 1988): 1053–55.
67. Ross K. Baker, *House and Senate* (New York: Norton, 2001), 123–25.
68. Martin Weinberger, "Coverage—The Void at Home," *Media Studies Journal* 10 (Winter 1996): 104.
69. Rep. Earl Blumenauer, "Staying the Course is No Longer an Option," *The Oregonian*, November 21, 2005.
70. Jeffrey L. Katz, "Studios Beam Members from Hill to Hometown," *CQ Weekly*, November 29, 1997, 2946–47.
71. Matthew Harris, "Rep. Sanchez Launching TV Show," *Orange County Register*, April 26, 2007, http://articles.ocregister.com/2007-04-26/news/24693229_1_sanchez-health-care-military-spending.
72. http://mikepence.house.gov/. Pence has been a leading figure in the conservative Republican Study Committee (RSC).
73. http://grassley.senate.gov/.
74. TweetCongress, http://tweetcongress.org/.
75. See Steven S. Smith and Gerald Gamm, "The Dynamics of Party Government in Congress," in *Congress Reconsidered*, ed. Lawrence C. Dodd and Bruce I. Oppenheimer (Washington, DC: CQ Press, 2005), 185–201.
76. Brian Friel and Richard E. Cohen, "The Congressional Jigsaw," *National Journal*, February 28, 2009, 37.
77. Nelson W. Polsby, *How Congress Evolves: Social Bases of Institutional Change* (New York: Oxford University Press, 2004); David Rohde, *Parties and Leaders in the Postreform House* (Chicago: University of Chicago Press, 1991); Gary Jacobson, "Party Polarization in National Politics: The Electoral Connection, " in *Polarized Politics: Congress and the President in a Partisan Era*, ed. Jon R. Bond and Richard Fleisher (Washington, DC: CQ Press 2000), 9–30; Bruce I. Oppenheimer, "Deep Red and Blue Congressional Districts: The Causes and Consequences of Declining Party Competitiveness," in *Congress Reconsidered*, ed. Lawrence C. Dodd and Bruce I. Oppenheimer (Washington, DC: CQ Press, 2005), 135–58; and Paul Quirk, "The Legislative Branch: Assessing the Partisan Congress," in *A Republic Divided*, ed. The Annenberg Democracy Project (New York: Oxford University Press, 2007), 130–31

78. See Richard E. Cohen, Kirk Victor, and David Bauman, "The State of Congress," *National Journal*, January 10, 2004, 82–105.

79. Barbara Sinclair, "Parties and Leadership in the House," in *The Legislative Branch*, ed. Paul J. Quirk and Sarah B. Binder (New York: Oxford University Press, 2005), 226; and Barbara Sinclair, "The New World of U.S. Senators" in *Congress Reconsidered*, ed. Lawrence C. Dodd and Bruce I. Oppenheimer (Washington, DC: CQ Press, 2005), 13–16.

80. Daniel Lipinski, "Congressional Party Agendas: Creation, Content, and Communication" (paper presented at the 2000 Annual Meeting of the American Political Science Association, Washington, DC, August 30–September 3), 5; and Patrick J. Sellers, "Winning Media Coverage in the U.S. Congress," in *U.S. Senate Exceptionalism*, ed. Bruce I. Oppenheimer (Columbus: Ohio State University Press, 2002), 134.

81. Cook, *Making Laws and Making News*; Barbara Sinclair, *Legislators, Leaders, and Lawmaking: The U.S. House of Representatives in the Postreform Era* (Baltimore: Johns Hopkins University Press, 1995); Barbara Sinclair, "The Senate Leadership Dilemma: Passing Bills and Pursuing Partisan Advantage in a Nonmajoritarian Chamber," in *The Contentious Senate: Partisanship, Ideology, and the Myth of Cool Judgment*, ed. Colton C. Campbell and Nicol C. Rae (Lanham, MD: Rowman and Littlefield, 2001), 72–73.

82. This discussion is based on Roger H. Davidson, "The Emergence of the Postreform Congress," in *The Postreform Congress*, ed. Roger H. Davidson (New York: St. Martin's Press, 1992), 21–22; Roger H. Davidson, "The Presidency and Congressional Leadership," in *Rivals for Power: Presidential–Congressional Relations*, ed. James A. Thurber (New York: Rowman and Littlefield, 2002), 83–85; Barbara Sinclair, "Leadership Strategies in the Modern Congress," in *Congressional Politics*, ed. Christopher J. Deering (Chicago: Dorsey Press, 1989), 135–54; Barbara Sinclair, "House Majority Party Leadership in an Era of Constraint," in *The Postreform Congress*, ed. Roger H. Davidson (New York: St. Martin's Press, 1992), 91–99; Barbara Sinclair, *Legislators, Leaders, and Lawmaking: The U. S. House of Representatives in the Postreform Era* (Baltimore, MD: The Johns Hopkins University Press, 1995); and Rhode, *Parties and Leaders in the Postreform House*.

83. Davidson, "The Emergence of the Postreform Congress," 22.

84. Steven S. Smith, "The Senate in the Postreform Era," in *The Postreform Congress*, ed. Roger H. Davidson (New York: St. Martin's Press, 1992), 183–87.

85. Steven S. Smith, "Parties and Leadership in the Senate," in *The Legislative Branch*, ed. Paul J. Quirk and Sarah A. Binder (New York: Oxford University Press, 2005), 264.

86. Charles O. Jones, *The Minority Party in Congress* (Boston, Little Brown, 1970); and Sellers, *Cycles of Spin*.

87. Barbara Sinclair, "Parties and Leadership in the House," in *The Legislative Branch*, ed. Paul J. Quirk and Sarah A. Binder (New York: Oxford University Press, 2005), 249; Barbara Sinclair, *Unorthodox Lawmaking: New Legislative Processes in the U.S. Congress* (Washington, DC: CQ Press., 1997); and Gary Cox and Matthew McCubbins, *Legislative Leviathan* (Berkeley: University of California Press, 1993). The considerable extent to which the majority has used its prerogatives to control the institution is chronicled in Thomas E. Mann and Norman J. Ornstein, *The Broken Branch: How Congress is Failing America and How to Get It Back on Track* (New York: Oxford University Press, 2006).

88. Steven S. Smith and Gerald Gamm, "The Dynamics of Party Government in Congress," in *Congress Reconsidered*, 8th ed., ed. Lawrence C. Dodd and Bruce I. Oppenheimer (Washington, DC: CQ Press, 2005), 181–205.

89. Quoted in Michael Crowley, "Oppressed Minority: The Miserable Lives of the House Democrats," *The New Republic*, June 23, 2003, 19.

90. E. E. Schattschneider, *The Semisovereign People* (Hinsdale, IL: Dryden Press, 1975); and Patrick Sellers, "Manipulating the Message in the U.S. Congress," *Press/Politics* 5 no.1 (2000): 24; and Sinclair, "Parties and Leadership in the House," 249.

91. Eve Fairbanks, "Children of the Revolution," *The New Republic*, December 31, 2008, 18; Sean Lengell, "House GOP Persists in Protest of Energy Stalemate; Cites Constituents' Demands for Action Now," *The Washington Times*, August 11, 2008; and Steven T. Dennis, "Boehner: GOP Has Pelosi on the Run," *Roll Call*, August 11, 2008.

92. Sellers, "Manipulating the Message in the U.S. Congress," 24.

93. Groeling and Kernell, "Congress, the President, and Party Competition via Network News," 77; and Groeling, *When Politicians Attack*, chap. 1.

94. See, for instance, Mark Sanford, "The GOP Has Damaged Its Brand," *Washington Times*, March 4, 2009.

95. C. Lawrence Evans, "Committees, Leaders, and Message Politics" in *Congress Reconsidered*, 7th ed., ed. Lawrence C. Dodd and Bruce I. Oppenheimer (Washington, DC: CQ Press, 2001), 217–43.

96. C. Lawrence Evans and Walter J. Oleszek, "Message Politics and Senate Procedure," in *The Contentious Senate: Partisanship, Ideology, and the Myth of Cool Judgment*, ed. Colton C. Campbell and Nicol C. Rae (Lanham, MD: Rowman and Littlefield, 2001), 107–27.

97. See, for example, David Drucker, "Health Care Battle Flares Anew," *Roll Call*, June 9, 2010.

98. Bruce Bimber, *Information and American Democracy: Technology in the Evolution of Political Power* (Cambridge, UK: Cambridge University Press, 2003).

99. Martin Wattenberg, "The Changing Presidential Media Environment," in *Readings in Presidential Politics*, ed. George Edwards III (Belmont, CA: Thomson Wadsworth, 2006), 224, 228.

100. Jeffrey E. Cohen, "News That Doesn't Matter: Presidents, the News Media, and the Mass Public in an Era of New Media," in *Readings in Presidential Politics*, ed. George Edwards III (Belmont, CA: Thomson Wadsworth, 2006), 241–44. Several studies point to the President's advantage in news coverage: see Elmer E. Cornwell, "Presidential News: The Expanding Public Image," *Journalism Quarterly* 36 (Summer 1959): 275–83: Alan P. Balutis, "Congress, the President and the Press," *Journalism Quarterly* 53 (Autumn 1976): 509–515; Robert E. Gilbert, "President Versus Congress: The Struggle for Public Attention," *Congress and the Presidency*, 16 (Autumn 1989): 83–102; and Lynda Lee Kaid and Joe Foote, "How Television Coverage of the President and Congress Compare," *Journalism Quarterly* 61 (Spring 1985): 59–65. For a discussion of the "routines" followed by news organizations, see W. Lance Bennett, *News: The Politics of Illusion* (New York: Pearson Longman, 2005), chap. 5.

101. Some like Sen. William Fulbright (D-AR) were so concerned that news coverage had dramatically increased presidential leverage that they considered enacting legislation requiring television stations to provide equal access to Congress "at all times." See "Equal Time for Congress: Congressional Hearings, 1970," in *Congress and the News Media,* ed. Robert O. Blanchard (New York: Hastings House, 1974), 103–128; and Thomas Curtis, "The Executive Dominates the News," in *Congress and the News Media*, ed. Robert O. Blanchard (New York: Hastings House, 1974), 100–103.

102. Matthew A. Baum and Samuel Kernell, "Has Cable Ended the Golden Age of Television?" *American Political Science Review* 93 (March 1999): 99–114.

103. Cohen, "News That Doesn't Matter," 245.

104. Bennett, *News*, 104.

105. Doris A. Graber, *Mass Media and American Politics* (Washington, DC: CQ Press, 2006), chap. 12.

106. Cohen, "News That Doesn't Matter," 246.

107. Matthew Baum, "Sex, Lies and War: How Soft News Brings Foreign Policy to the Inattentive Public." *American Political Science Review* 96 (March 2001): 91–109; and The Pew Research Center for the People and the Press, "The Daily Show: Journalism, Satire or Just Laughs," May 8, 2008, http://pewresearch.org/pubs/829/the-daily-show-journalism-satire.

108. Kenneth Jost, "Talk Show Democracy," *CQ Researcher*, April 29, 1994, 10.

109. Data and information contained in this paragraph come from "The New Washington Press Corps: As Mainstream Media Decline, Niche and Foreign Outlets Grow," *Pew Research Center's Project for Excellence in Journalism*, February 11, 2009, http://www.journalism.org/analysis_report/new_washington_press_corps.

110. These are identified as some of the most popular blogs. See Bara Vaida, "Bloggin On," *National Journal*, October 6, 2007, 24–30.

111. The result, as one Washington reporter put it, is that "almost nothing that happens in Washington is fresh in the next day's paper unless it breaks at 10 o'clock at night." Quoted in Katherine Q. Seelye, "In Trying Times, Papers Retreat From Washington," *The New York Times*, January 8, 2007.

112. Pew Research Center, "Internet Overtakes Newspapers as News Sources," *The Pew Research Center for the People and the Press*, December 23, 2008, http://people-press.org/report/479/internet-overtakes-newspapers-as-news-source. See also the Pew Research Center, "Internet's Broader Role in Campaign 2008," *The Pew Research Center for the People and the Press*, January, 11, 2008, http://people-press.org/report/384/internets-broader-role-in-campaign-2008.

113. Julian E. Zelizer, *On Capitol Hill: The Struggle to Reform Congress and Its Consequences, 1948–2000* (Cambridge, UK: Cambridge University Press, 2004), 231.

114. Barbara Sinclair, *Party Wars: Polarization and the Politics of National Policymaking* (Norman: University of Oklahoma Press, 2006), 334–43. See also Groeling, *When Politicians Attack!* 194–97.

115. Sinclair, *Party Wars,* 225, 231.

116. Allen was caught on a camera phone at a campaign event applying a racially offensive term to a person associated with his opponent's campaign. The video was posted on the web and picked up by various media outlets. Allen was subsequently defeated by Sen. Jim Webb (D-VA) in his reelection bid. Lott was captured on video by C-SPAN making a favorable remark regarding Sen. Strom Thurmond's (R-SC) presidential campaign as a segregationist Dixiecrat. Lott's comments were kept alive by bloggers and picked up by news organizations, all of which touched off a furor that prompted Lott to resign as his party's Senate floor leader. Don Imus applied a racially offensive term to the Rutgers women's basketball team on his radio/television show. This was caught by a media watchdog group and put on the web. The story was kept alive by netroot chatter and featured prominently in radio and television accounts for the next several days. He was ultimately fired by both employers, CBS (radio) and MSNBC (cable television). All three figures, however, managed to rehabilitate their careers. Lott eventually came back to be elected Minority Whip before he vacated his Senate seat and Imus returned to radio and cable television. Allen, meanwhile, remained involved in politics and is currently planning to mount a bid to return to the Senate seat he once held.

117. "After Imus." *USA Today*, April 16, 2007.

Chapter 3

1. Hedrick Smith, *The Power Game* (New York: Random House, 1988), 134, 135.

2. Nelson Polsby, "Political Change and the Character of the Contemporary Congress," in *The New American Political System*, ed. Anthony King (Washington, DC: AEI Press, 1990). There is a rich and voluminous literature covering these changes and

the forces that produced them. See, for example, Julian Zelizer, *On Capitol Hill: The Struggle to Reform Congress and Its Consequences* (Cambridge, UK: Cambridge University Press, 2004); Nelson W. Polsby, *How Congress Evolves: Social Bases of Institutional Change* (Oxford, UK: Oxford University Press, 2004); Ronald M. Peters, *The American Speakership: The Office in Historical Perspective* (Baltimore: Johns Hopkins University Press, 1997); Barbara Sinclair, *The Transformation of the U.S. Senate* (Baltimore: Johns Hopkins University Press, 1989); James Sundquist, *The Decline and Resurgence of Congress* (Washington, DC: Brookings Institution, 1981); and Roger H. Davidson, "The Emergence of the Postreform Congress," in *The Postreform Congress*, ed. Roger H. Davidson (New York: St. Martin's Press), 3–23. For a discussion of the role of reforms in bringing about changes, see Leroy Rieselbach, *Congressional Reform: The Changing Modern Congress* (Washington, DC: CQ Press, 1994); and Eric Schickler, *Disjointed Pluralism: Institutional Innovation and the Development of the U.S. Congress* (Princeton, NJ: Princeton University Press, 2001).

3. Ronald Brownstein, *The Second Civil War: How Extreme Partisanship Has Paralyzed Washington and Polarized America* (New York: The Penguin Press, 2007); Barbara Sinclair, *Unorthodox Lawmaking: New Legislative Processes in the U.S. Congress* (Washington, DC: CQ Press, 2000); and Thomas E. Mann and Norman Ornstein, *The Broken Branch: How Congress is Failing America and How to Get it Back on Track* (Oxford, UK: Oxford University Press, 2006).

4. Scholars have identified these three groups of legislators as constituting the key leaders in this congressional era. See, for example, Robert Peabody, *Leadership in Congress: Stability, Succession, and Change* (Boston: Little, Brown, 1976), chap. 2; and Randall B. Ripley, *Power in the Senate* (New York: St. Martin's Press, 1969).

5. See Peters, *American Speakership*, chap. 3; and Ripley, *Power in the Senate*, chap. 3.

6. James MacGregor Burns, "The Deadlock of Democracy," in *Congressional Reform: Problems and Prospects*, ed. Joseph Clark (New York: Crowell, 1965), 68.

7. Ripley, *Power in the Senate*, chap. 3–5.

8. James Sundquist, *Decline and Resurgence of Congress*, 176–79. Ronald Peters refers to the House of Representatives as "feudalistic" in *The American Speakership*, chap.3. For an assessment of Congress as a responsible body during this era, see Rieselbach, *Congressional Reform*, chap. 2.

9. George Goodwin, Jr., "Subcommittees: The Miniature Legislatures of Congress," in *The Congressional System: Notes and Readings*, ed. Leroy N. Rieselbach (North Scituate, MA: Duxbury Press, 1979), 113. James Dyson and John Soule show that the House enacted about 90% of bills reported by committees in this era. See their article "Congressional Committee Behavior on Roll Call Votes: The U.S. House of Representatives, 1955–1964," *Midwest Journal of Political Science*, 14 (November 1970): 626–47. See also Richard Fenno, "The Internal Distribution of Influence: The House," in *The Congress and America's Future*, ed. D. B. Truman (Englewood Cliffs, NJ: Prentice Hall, 1964), 65; and William S. White, *Citadel: The Story of the U.S. Senate* (New York: Harper, 1957), esp. chap. 14.

10. See Peters, *The American Speakership*, chap. 3; Joseph Cooper and David W. Brady, "Institutional Context and Leadership Style: The House from Cannon to Rayburn," *American Political Science Review* 75 (June 1981): 411–25; and Howard E. Shuman, "Lyndon B. Johnson: The Senate's Powerful Persuader," in *First Among Equals: Outstanding Senate Leaders of the Twentieth Century*, ed. Richard A. Baker and Roger H. Davidson (Washington, DC: CQ Press, 1991), 199–235.

11. Nelson Polsby, *Congress and the Presidency* (Englewood Cliffs, NJ: Prentice-Hall, 1964), 43–45, 49–52.

12. Burns, "The Deadlock of Democracy," 66; and Richard Fenno, Jr., "The House Appropriations Committee as a Political System: The Problem of Integration," in *Congressional Reform: Problems and Prospects*, ed. Joseph Clark (New York: Crowell, 1965), 247–75.

13. Quoted in Charles Clapp, *The Congressman: His Work as He Sees It* (Washington, DC: Brookings Institution, Anchor Edition, 1964), 326–27.

14. Arthur Krock, *New York Times*, April 8, 1958. See also George Goodwin Jr., "The Seniority System in Congress," *American Political Science Review* 53 (June 1959), 412–36.

15. See, Burns, "The Deadlock of Democracy," 67; White, *Citadel*, 180; Joseph Clark, "Coda: Making Congress Work," in *Congressional Reform: Problems and Prospects*, ed. Joseph Clark (New York: Crowell, 1965), 347; Nicholas A. Masters, "Committee Assignments in the House of Representatives," *American Political Science Review* 55 (June 1957): 345–57; Clapp, *The Congressman*, 250; Herbert Asher, "The Changing Status of the Freshman Representative," in *Congress in Change: Evolution and Reform*, ed. Norman J. Ornstein (Westport, CT: Praeger, 1975), 234; and Sundquist, *The Decline and Resurgence of Congress*, 176.

16. White, *Citadel*, 240. See also Clapp, *The Congressman*, 251.

17. Joseph Clark, "Congress: Environment or Hereditary?," in *Congressional Reform: Problems and Prospects*, ed. Joseph Clark (New York: Crowell, 1965), 245.

18. J. Leiper Freeman, *The Political Process: Executive-Bureau-Legislative Committee Relations* (Garden City, NY: Doubleday, 1955); and Douglas Cater, *Power in Washington* (New York: Random House, 1964). See also, Theodore J. Lowi, *The End of Liberalism* (New York: Norton, 1979).

19. Quoted in Clapp, *The Congressman*, 25.

20. Fenno, "The House Appropriations Committee as a Political System," 271, 266; and Barbara Hinckley, *Stability and Change in Congress* (New York: Harper and Row, 1971), 65.

21. Quoted in Clapp, *The Congressman*, 13–19. See, also, Hinckley, *Stability and Change in Congress*, 65.

22. Matthews, *U.S. Senators and Their World*, 99–101. Rayburn is quoted in Lewis L. Gould and Nancy Beck Young, "The Speaker and the Presidents: Sam Rayburn, the White House, and the Legislative Process, 1941–1961," in *Masters of the House: Congressional Leadership Over Two Centuries*, ed. Roger H. Davidson, Susan Webb Hammond, and Raymond W. Smock (Boulder, CO: Westview Press, 1998), 182.

23. Clapp, *The Congressman*; Fenno, "The House Appropriations Committee as a Political System," 259; Nelson W. Polsby, "Congress, Publicity and Public Policy," in *Congress and the News Media*, ed. Robert O. Blanchard (New York: Hastings House, 1974), 131–34; Matthews, *U.S. Senators and Their World*; and Sinclair, *The Transformation of the U.S. Senate*, chap. 2.

24. Matthews, *U.S. Senators and Their World*, chap. 5; and Herbert Asher, "The Learning of Legislative Norms," *American Political Science Review* 67 (June 1973): 499–513.

25. Fenno, "The House Appropriations Committee as a Political System," 269, and for his broader discussion of this point, see 263–71. See also Hinckley, *Stability and Change in Congress*, 62–63; Masters, "Committee Assignments in the House of Representatives," 352; Herbert Asher, "The Learning of Legislative Norms," in *The Congressional System: Notes and Readings*," 2nd ed., ed. Leroy Rieselbach (North Scituate, MA: Duxbury Press, 1979) 166, 170–71; Clapp. *The Congressman*, 13–32; and Charles S. Bullock III, "House Committee Assignments," in *The Congressional System: Notes and Readings*, ed. Leroy N. Rieselbach (North Scituate, MA: Duxbury Press, 1979), 80–81. Current scholarship suggests these norms, while important, were not as inviolate as earlier portraits of Congress suggested. See David Brady and Morris Fiorina, "Congress in the Era of the Permanent Campaign," in *The Permanent Campaign and Its Future*, ed. Norman J. Ornstein and Thomas E. Mann (Washington, DC: American Enterprise Institute/Brookings Institution, 2000), 146–48.

26. Fenno, "The House Appropriations Committee as a Political System," 265.

27. Ibid., 253; and Hinckley, *Stability and Change in Congress*, 66–67, 199.

28. Richard F. Fenno, Jr. "The Senate through the Looking Glass: The Debate over Television," *Legislative Studies Quarterly* 14 (August 1989): 315. One senator told Donald R. Matthews that being in the Senate was "like living in a small town." See Matthews, *U.S. Senators and Their World*, 92.

29. Masters, "Committee Assignments in the House of Representatives," 352 (emphasis added).

30. Eric Uslaner, *The Decline of Comity in Congress* (Ann Arbor: University of Michigan Press, 1993), chap. 1–2.

31. Fenno, "The Senate through the Looking Glass," 314–15.

32. Daniel M. Berman, *In Congress Assembled: The Legislative Process in the National Government* (New York: Macmillan, 1964), 45–47; and Norman O. Ornstein, "The Open Congress Meets the President," in *Both Ends of the Avenue: The Presidency, the Executive Branch and Congress in the 1980s*, ed. Anthony King (Washington, DC: American Enterprise Institute 1983), 391.

33. Zelizer, *On Capitol Hill*, chap. 3.

34. Ralph K. Huitt, "The Outsider in the Senate: An Alternative Role," *American Political Science Review* 55 (September, 1961): 566–75.

35. Hinckley, *Stability and Change in Congress*, 66.

36. Douglass Cater, *The Fourth Branch of Government* (Boston: Houghton Mifflin, 1959), 67.

37. Robert Caro, *The Years of Lyndon Johnson: Master of the Senate* (New York: Knopf, 2002), 563–64; and Reedy, *The U.S. Senate: Paralysis or a Search for Consensus?* (New York: Crown, 1986), 22–25.

38. Clapp, *The Congressman*, 22–23.

39. Matthews, *U.S. Senators and Their World*, 94.

40. Ibid., chap. 9.

41. Robert D. Novak, *The Prince of Darkness: 50 Years Reporting in Washington* (New York: Crown Forum, 2007).

42. See Peabody, *Leadership in Congress*, 43–44.

43. Sen. Everett Dirksen (R-IL) and Rep. Charles Halleck (IN) and later Gerald Ford (R-MI) hosted the "Ev and Charlie" and "Ev and Jerry" shows. See Burdette Loomis, "Senate Leaders, Minority Voices: From Dirksen to Daschle," in *The Contentious Senate: Partisanship, Ideology, and the Myth of Cool Judgment*, ed. Colton Campbell and Nicol C. Rae (Lanham, MD: Rowman and Littlefield, 2001), 91–106.

44. Randall B. Woods, *LBJ: Architect of American Ambition* (New York: Free Press, 2006), 238.

45. Cater, *Fourth Branch of Government*, 66.

46. Quoted in Matthews, *U.S. Senators and Their World*, 207.

47. Timothy Cook, *Governing with the News: The News Media as a Political Institution* (Chicago: University of Chicago Press, 1998), 120.

48. See, for instance, Clapp, *The Congressman*, 14–15 and 439–43; and Hinckley, *Stability and Change in Congress*, 46–50.

49. Nelson Polsby, "The Institutionalization of the House of Representatives," *American Political Science Review* 62 (March 1968): 144–68; and David Mayhew, *Congress: The Electoral Connection* (New Haven, CT: Yale University Press, 1974).

50. Joseph S. Clark, *Congress: The Sapless Branch* (New York: Harper & Row, 1964), 76.

51. Clapp, *The Congressman*, chap. 8; and Matthews, *U.S. Senators and Their World*, chap. 8–9.

52. Hinckley, *Stability and Change in Congress*, 46–50.

53. As Zelizer notes, Richard Russell (D-GA), the acknowledged leader of the old bulls of the southern Democrats in the Senate, kept a sign in his office that read: "You ain't learning nothing when you are talking." See *On Capitol Hill*, 23.

54. Ronald Garay, *Congressional Television: A Legislative History* (Westport, CT: Greenwood Press, 1984), 52; and H. G. Dulaney and Edward Hake Phillips, *Speak, Mister Speaker* (Bonham, TX: Sam Rayburn Foundation, 1978), 458–59.
55. Peabody, *Leadership in Congress*, 91.
56. Samuel Kernell, *Going Public: New Strategies of Presidential Leadership*, 3rd ed. (Washington, DC: CQ Press, 1997), 4.
57. George Reedy, *The U.S. Senate*, 86.
58. Joseph Cooper, "The Twentieth-Century Congress," in *Congress Reconsidered*, 7th ed., ed. Lawrence C. Dodd and Bruce Oppenheimer (Washington, DC: CQ Press, 2001), 340, 345; and Mildred Amer, "Freshmen in the House of Representatives and Senate by Political Party: 1913–2005," *Congressional Research Service Report for Congress* (June 16, 2005), 1–5.
59. Sinclair, *Transformation of the U.S. Senate*, 14–25.
60. Polsby, *How Congress Evolves*, chap. 1–2; Sinclair, *The Transformation of the U.S. Senate*, chap. 3; and Zelizer, *On Capitol Hill*, chap. 3.
61. Richard Bolling, *Power in the House: A History of the Leadership of the House of Representatives* (New York: E. P. Dutton, 1968), 196.
62. See Arthur G. Stevens, Jr., Arthur H. Miller, and Thomas Mann, "Mobilization of Liberal Strength in the House, 1955–1970: The Democratic Study Group," *American Political Science Review* 68 (June 1974): 667–81; Zelizer, *On Capitol Hill*, 53–60; and Sundquist, *The Decline and Resurgence of Congress*, 376.
63. John G. Stewart, "Two Strategies of Leadership: Johnson and Mansfield," in *Classics of Congressional Politics*, ed. Herbert F. Weisberg, Eric S. Heberlig, and Lisa M. Campoli (New York: Addison Wesley, Longman, 1999), 329–45; David W. Rohde, Norman J. Ornstein, and Robert L. Peabody, "Political Change and Legislative Norms in the U.S. Senate, 1957–1974," in *Studies in Congress*, ed. Glenn R. Parker (Washington, DC: CQ Press, 1985), 147–88; and Donald A. Ritchie, "Twentieth-Century Senate Reform: The View From the Inside," in *The Contentious Senate: Partisanship, Ideology, and the Myth of Cool Judgment*, ed. Colton C. Campbell and Nicol C. Rae (Lanham, MD: Rowman and Littlefield, 2001), 141–42.
64. Sinclair, *The Transformation of the U.S. Senate*, chap. 3; and Ripley, *Power in the Senate*, chap. 3.
65. Schickler, *Disjointed Pluralism*, chap. 5.
66. For a discussion of all of this, see Schickler, *Disjointed Pluralism*, chap. 5; Rieselbach, *Congressional Reform*, chap. 3; Polsby, *How Congress Evolves*, 59–74; Zelizer, *On Capitol Hill*, chap 8–9; Roger Davidson, "Subcommittee Government: New Channels for Policy," in *The New Congress*, ed. Thomas E. Mann and Norman J. Ornstein (Washington, DC: American Enterprise Institute, 1981), 99–133; and Michael Malbin, "Delegation, Deliberation, and the New Role of Congressional Staff," in *The New Congress*, ed. Thomas Mann and Norman J. Ornstein (Washington, DC: American Enterprise Institute, 1981), 134–77.
67. Davidson, "The Emergence of the Postreform Congress," 11.
68. Barbara Sinclair, "The New World of U.S. Senators," in *Congress Reconsidered*, 8th ed., ed. Lawrence C. Dodd and Bruce I. Oppenheimer (Washington, DC: CQ Press, 2005), 3; and Bert A. Rockman, "The New Institutionalism and the Old Institutions," in *New Perspectives on American Politics*, ed. Lawrence C. Dodd and Calvin Jillson (Washington, DC: CQ Press), 143.
69. Rieselbach, *Congressional Reform*, chap. 2; and Barbara Sinclair, *Unorthodox Lawmaking: New Legislative Processes in the U.S. Congress*, 2nd ed. (Washington, DC: CQ Press, 2000).
70. Samuel C. Patterson, "The Semi-Sovereign Congress," in *The New American Political System*, ed. Anthony King (Washington, DC: American Enterprise Institute, 1978), 177.

71. James Ceaser, "Political Parties—Declining, Stabilizing, or Resurging?," in *The New American Political System*, ed. Anthony King (Washington, DC: AEI Press, 1990), 118–22.

72. Hugh Heclo, "Campaigning and Governing: A Conspectus," in *The Permanent Campaign and Its Future*, ed. Norman J. Ornstein and Thomas E. Mann (Washington, DC: American Enterprise Institute/Brookings Institution, 2000), 19.

73. Gary C. Jacobson, "Parties and PACS in Congressional Elections," in *Congress Reconsidered*, 4th ed., ed. Lawrence C. Dodd and Bruce I. Oppenheimer (Washington, DC: CQ Press, 1989), 117–52; and Christopher J. Bailey, *The Republican Party in the U.S. Senate, 1974–1984: Party Change and Institutional Development* (New York: Manchester University Press, 1988), 44–45.

74. John T. Tierney and Kay Lehman Schlozman, "Congress and Organized Interests," in *Congressional Politics*, ed. Christopher J. Deering (Chicago: Dorsey Press, 1989), 197–219.

75. Robert H. Salisbury, "The Paradox of Interest Groups in Washington—More Groups, Less Clout," in *The New American Political System*, ed. Anthony King (Washington, DC: AEI Press, 1990), 204–5. See also Sinclair, *Transformation of the U.S. Senate*, chap. 4.

76. William M. Lunch, *The Nationalization of American Politics* (Berkeley: University of California Press, 1987), chap. 7.

77. Salisbury, "The Paradox of Interest Groups in Washington," 208–12.

78. Tierney and Scholzman, "Congress and Organized Interests," 197–219; Jacobson, "Parties and PACS in Congressional Elections," 121, 143; and John R. Wright, *Interest Groups and Congress: Lobbying, Contributions, and Influence* (New York: Longman, 2003).

79. Davidson, "Subcommittee Government," 131–32.

80. Michael K. Moore and John R. Hibbing, "Situational Dissatisfaction in Congress: Explaining Voluntary Departures," *Journal of Politics* 60 (November 1988): 1088–1107.

81. Daniel J. Reagan and Donald L. Davison, "Ambition, Reform, and Retirement from the U.S. House of Representatives, 1957–1984," *The Political Chronicle* 5 (Winter 1994): 9–15.

82. Zelizer, *On Capitol Hill*, 162.

83. Burdett Loomis, *The New American Politician* (New York: Basic Books, 1988), chap. 4.

84. Michael Robinson, "Three Faces of Congressional Media," in *The New Congress*, ed. Thomas E. Mann and Norman J. Ornstein (Washington, DC: American Enterprise Institute), 70–71.

85. Quoted in Alan Ehrenhalt, "Media, Power Shifts Dominate O'Neill's House." *CQ Weekly*, September 13, 1986, 2131–38. See also Bailey, *The Republican Party in the U.S. Senate*, 35–37.

86. Loomis, *The New American Politician*.

87. Quoted in Hedrick Smith, *The Power Game* (New York: Random House, 1988), 135.

88. See Timothy Cook, *Making Laws and Making News: Media Strategies in the U.S. House of Representatives* (Washington, DC: Brookings Institution, 1989). For a discussion of campaigning as a way of governing, see Hugh Heclo, "Campaigning and Governing,", 1–37.

89. Richard F. Fenno, *Congressmen in Committees* (Boston: Little, Brown, 1973); and David Mayhew, *Congress: The Electoral Connection* (New Haven, CT: Yale University Press, 1973).

90. Quoted in Loomis, *The New American Politician*, 101.

91. For a discussion of how members could use the media to advance their interests, see Karen Kedrowski, *Media Entrepreneurs and the Media Enterprise in the U.S. Congress*

(Cresskill, NJ: Hampton Press), 1996; Cook, *Making Laws and Making News*; Timothy Cook, "PR on the Hill," in *Congressional Politics*, ed. Christopher Deering (Chicago: Dorsey Press, 1989), 62–89; Barbara Sinclair, *The Transformation of the U.S. Senate*, chap. 10; and Loomis, *The New American Politician*, chap. 4.

92. Garay, *Congressional Television: A Legislative History*; and Fenno, "The Senate Through the Looking Glass," 313–48.

93. John Hibbing and Sue Thomas, "The Modern United States Senate: What is Accorded Respect?" *The Journal of Politics* 52 (February 1990): 143.

94. Kernell, *Going Public*.

95. Larry Berman, "Looking Back on the Reagan Presidency," in *Looking Back on the Reagan Presidency*, ed. Larry Berman (Baltimore: Johns Hopkins University Press, 1990), 7.

96. Kernell, *Going Public*, 144–54; and Barbara Sinclair, *Legislators, Leaders, and Lawmaking: The U.S. House of Representatives in the Postreform Era* (Baltimore: Johns Hopkins University Press, 1995), 149.

97. Quoted in George Galloway, *History of the House of Representatives* (New York: Crowell, 1961), 259.

98. Kernell, *Going Public*, 18.

99. Quoted in Bailey, *The Republican Party in the U.S. Senate*, 110–11.

100. Tierney and Schlozman, "Congress and Organized Interests," 215.

101. Fred I. Greenstein, "Change and Continuity in the Modern Presidency," in *The New American Political System*, ed. Anthony King (Washington, DC: American Enterprise Institute, 1978), 71.

102. The characterization of the political system as "atomized" comes from Anthony King, "The American Polity in the Late 1970s: Building Coalitions in the Sand," in *The New American Political System*, ed. Anthony King (Washington, DC: American Enterprise Institute, 1978), 391. For a discussion of presidents' response to this more fragmented political context, see Kernell, *Going Public*.

103. Stephen Skowronek, *The Politics Presidents Make: Leadership from John Adams to George Bush* (Cambridge, MA: Belknap Press of Harvard University Press, 1993), 54–55; and Theodore J. Lowi, *The Personal President: Power Invested, Promise Unfilled* (Ithaca, NY: Cornell University Press, 1985). Of course, the story of this development is at the heart of Kernell's *Going Public*.

104. Quoted in James Q. Wilson, *Bureaucracy: What Government Agencies Do and Why They Do It* (New York: Basic Books, 1989), 259.

105. Stephen Hess, *News and Newsmaking* (Washington, DC: Brookings Institution, 1996), 62.

106. Quoted in Brownstein, *The Second Civil War*, 123.

107. Ibid., 195–200.

108. Material in this paragraph follows the ideas presented by David W. Rohde, *Parties and Leaders in the Postreform House* (Chicago: University of Chicago Press, 1991); and Sinclair, *Legislators, Leaders, and Lawmaking*.

109. Sinclair, *Legislators, Leaders, and Lawmaking*; Barbara Sinclair, "Leadership Strategies in the Modern Congress," in *Congressional Politics*, ed. Christopher Deering (Chicago: Dorsey Press, 1989), 135–54; Barbara Sinclair, "House Majority Party Leadership in an Era of Legislative Constraint," in *The Postreform Congress*, ed. Roger H. Davidson (New York: St. Martin's Press, 1992), 91–111; and Daniel J. Palazzolo, "From Decentralization to Centralization: Members' Changing Expectations for House Leaders," in *The Postreform Congress*, ed. Roger H. Davidson (New York: St. Martin's Press, 1992), 112–26.

110. Barbara Sinclair, "House Majority Party Leadership in an Era of Legislative Constraint," in *The Postreform Congress*, ed. Roger H. Davidson (New York: St. Martin's Press, 1992), 99–101; Alan Ehrenhalt, "Media, Power Shifts Dominate O'Neill's House."

111. William F. Connelly, Jr., *Congress' Permanent Minority: Republicans in the U.S. House* (Lanham, MD: Littlefield Adams, 1994), 47.

112. Steven S. Smith, "Parties and Leadership in the Senate," in *The Legislative Branch*, ed. Paul J. Quirk and Sarah A. Binder (New York: Oxford University Press, 2005), 255–78.

113. Barbara Sinclair, "The Senate Leadership Dilemma: Passing Bills and Pursuing Partisan Advantage in a Nonmajoritarian Chamber," in *The Contentious Senate: Partisanship, Ideology, and the Myth of Cool Judgment*, ed. Colton C. Campbell and Nicol Rae (Lanham, MD: Rowman and Littlefield, 2001), 72–73.

114. Barbara Sinclair, *Party Wars: Polarization and the Politics of National Policy Making* (Norman: University of Oklahoma Press, 2006), 309, 310–23.

115. Andrew Rich, *Think Tanks, Public Policy, and the Politics of Expertise* (Cambridge, UK: Cambridge University Press, 2004), chap. 2; and Sinclair, *Party Wars*, 325–34.

116. Sinclair, *Party Wars*, chap. 9.

117. Ibid., chap. 8–9. For a discussion of party labels as "brand names," see Tim Groeling, *When Politicians Attack: Party Cohesion in the Media* (Cambridge, UK: Cambridge University Press, 2010), chap. 1.

118. Quoted in David Cloud, "Speaker Wants His Platform to Rival the Presidency," *CQ Weekly*, February 4, 1995, 333.

119. Ornstein, "The Open Congress Meets the President," 391–92.

Chapter 4

1. Nelson Polsby, *How Congress Evolves: Social Bases of Institutional Change* (New York: Oxford University Press, 2004), 4.

2. Roger Davidson, "The Emergence of the Postreform Congress," in *The Postreform Congress*, ed. Roger H. Davidson (New York: St. Martin's Press, 1992), 4–5, 8–9.

3. Interviews with authors, August 2004 and August 2005.

4. Lauren Whittington, "The Obscure Caucus: Invisible Men," *Roll Call*, September 8, 2003.

5. Timothy E. Cook, "Press Secretaries and Media Strategies in the House of Representatives: Deciding Whom to Pursue," *American Journal of Political Science* 32 (November 1988): 1049.

6. Michael Malbin, "Delegation, Deliberation, and the New Role of Congressional Staff," in *The New Congress*, ed. Thomas Mann and Norman Ornstein (Washington, DC: American Enterprise Institute, 1981), 141–42.

7. For a discussion of the "characteristics" ascribed to institutionalized organizations see Nelson Polsby, "The Institutionalization of the U.S. House of Representatives," *American Political Science Review* 62 (March 1968): 144–68.

8. Donald R. Matthews, *U.S. Senators and Their World* (New York: Vintage Books, 1960), 84.

9. Charles L. Clapp, *The Congressman: His Work as He Sees It* (Washington, DC: Brookings Institution, 1963), 60, 61.

10. Data on staffing personnel gathered by the authors from Charles B. Brownson, *Congressional Staff Directory* (Mt. Vernon, VA: Congressional Staff Directory, , 1962)

11. Robert H. Salisbury and Kenneth A. Shepsle, "U.S. Congressman as Enterprise," *Legislative Studies Quarterly* 6 (November 1981): 560–61.

12. The House of Representatives did not guarantee the minority party committee staff until 1975 and the Senate did not change its rules and provide for minority staffing of committees until 1977. See James Sundquist, *The Decline and Resurgence of Congress* (Washington, DC: Brookings Institution, 1981), 406.

13. Data come from the 1962 *Congressional Staff Directory*.

14. For an overview of staff allocated to offices, see Norman J. Ornstein, Thomas E. Mann, and Michael Malbin, *Vital Statistics on Congress, 1999–2000* (Washington, DC: AEI Press, 2000), chap. 5.

15. Susan H. Miller, "News Coverage of Congress: The Search for the Ultimate Spokesman," *Journalism Quarterly* 54 (Autumn 1977): 464.

16. Ibid; and Ross K. Baker, *House and Senate* (New York: Norton, 2001), 152–67. See also Donald R. Matthews, *U.S. Senators and Their World*, chap. 9.

17. Matthews, *U.S. Senators and Their World*, 197.

18. William White, *Home Place: The Story of the U.S. House of Representatives* (Boston: Houghton Mifflin), 43.

19. Matthews, *U.S. Senators and Their World*, 109; and Ronald Garay, *Congressional Television: A Legislative History* (Westport, CT: Greenwood Press, 1984), 37.

20. George Reedy, *The U.S. Senate: Paralysis or a Search for Consensus* (New York: Crown, 1986), 25, 26–27.

21. Robert L. Peabody, Norman J. Ornstein, and David W. Rohde, "The United States Senate as a Presidential Incubator: Many Are Called but Few Are Chosen," *Political Science Quarterly* 91(Summer 1976): 253; and William J. Rorabaugh, *The Real Making of the President: Kennedy, Nixon, and the 1960 Election* (Lawrence: University of Kansas Press, 2009).

22. Nelson W. Polsby, "Political Change and the Character of the Contemporary Congress," in *The New American Political System*, 2nd ed., ed. Anthony King (Washington, DC: AEI Press), 35.

23. Of course, the Senate's Democratic Policy Committee (DPC) and Republican Policy Committee (RPC), both of which were created to provide the parties with centralized forums through which they could develop legislative proposals, indirectly served members' communications activities. Yet neither one these two Senate policy committees had on board anyone whose formal responsibility was centered on working with the press. For a discussion of the role of these, see Hugh A. Bone, "An Introduction to the Senate Policy Committees," *American Political Science Review* 50 (June 1956): 339–59.

24. Data taken from the 1962 *Congressional Staff Directory*.

25. Robert Caro, *The Years of Lyndon Johnson: Master of the Senate* (New York: Knopf); Robert Dallek, Lone Star Rising: Lyndon Johnson and His Times (New York: Oxford University Press, 1991), chap. 14; Lewis Gould and Nancy Young, "The Speaker and the Presidents: Sam Rayburn, the White House, and the Legislative Process," in *Masters of the House: Congressional Leadership Over Two Centuries*, ed. Roger H. Davidson, Susan Webb Hammond, and Raymond W. Smock (Boulder, CO: Westview Press, 1988); Ronald M. Peters, *The American Speakership: The Office in Historical Perspective* (Baltimore: Johns Hopkins University Press, 1997), chap. 3; and Joseph Cooper and David. W. Brady, "Institutional Context and Leadership Style: The House From Cannon to Rayburn," *American Political Science Review* 75 (June 1981): 411–25.

26. Caro, *The Years of Lyndon Johnson*, chap. 13–14; and Howard E. Shuman, "Lyndon B. Johnson: The Senate's Powerful Persuader," in *First Among Equals: Outstanding Senate Leaders of the Twentieth Century*, ed. Richard A. Baker and Roger H. Davidson (Washington, DC: CQ Press, 1991), 219–20.

27. Doris Kearns, *Lyndon Johnson and the American Dream* (New York: Harper & Row, 1976), 128–29; and Julian E. Zelizer, *On Capitol Hill: The Struggle to Reform Congress and Its Consequences, 1948–2000* (Cambridge, UK: Cambridge University Press, 2004), 41.

28. Paul Healy, "Mansfield of Montana," *Saturday Evening Post*, October 1974, 10.

29. Joe. S. Foote, "The Speaker and the Media," in *The Speaker: Leadership in the U.S. House of Representatives*, ed. Ronald M. Peters Jr. (Washington, DC: CQ Press, 1994), 136–37, 141.

30. Edward and Frederick H. Schapsmeier, *Dirksen of Illinois: Senatorial Statesman.* (Urbana: University of Illinois Press, 1985); Byron Hulsey, *Everett Dirksen and His Presidents: How a Senate Giant Shaped American Politics* (Lawrence: University Press of Kansas, 2000); and Burdett Loomis, "Everett M. Dirksen: The Consummate Minority Leader," in *First Among Equals: Outstanding Senate Leaders of the Twentieth Century*, ed. Richard A. Baker and Roger H. Davidson (Washington, DC: CQ Press, 1991), 249–51.

31. Foote, "The Speaker and the Media," 142.

32. Data calculated from the 1962 *Congressional Staff Directory*.

33. Michael J. Robinson, "Three Faces of Congressional Media," in *The New Congress*, ed. Thomas Mann and Norman Ornstein (Washington, DC: American Enterprise Institute, 1981), 65.

34. *Congressional Staff Directory*, 1962; Charles B. Brownson, *Congressional Staff Directory* (Mt. Vernon, VA: Congressional Staff Directory, 1983); and *Congressional Staff Directory* (Washington, DC: Congressional Quarterly, 2005). Data calculated by authors.

35. Timothy Cook, "PR on the Hill: The Evolution of Congressional Press Operations," in *Congressional Politics*, ed. Christopher Deering (Chicago: Dorsey Press, 1989), 63–66.

36. Ornstein et al., *Vital Statistics on Congress, 1999–2000*, 131.

37. Data from 1962, 1983, and 2005 *Congressional Staff Directory* calculated by authors.

38. Jonathan D. Salant, "The Budget: More Hill Cutbacks Coming; Support Services Eyed," *CQ Weekly*, February 11, 1995, 433–34.

39. The House GOP redoubled communications efforts by bringing committee public relations staffers into its partisan communications operations. See Jackie Kucinich, "Boehner Expands GOP Communications Plan," *Roll Call*, April 13, 2009.

40. Hedrick Smith, *The Power Game* (New York: Random House, 1988), 524–28; Alan Ehrenhalt, "Congress and the Country: Speaker's Job Transformed Under O'Neill," *CQ Weekly*, June 22, 1985, 1247; John Aloysius Farrell, *Tip O'Neill and the Democratic Century* (Boston: Little, Brown, 2001), chap. 24; and Barbara Sinclair, *Legislators, Leaders, and Lawmaking* (Baltimore: Johns Hopkins University Press, 1995), 79.

41. *Congressional Staff Directory*, 1983.

42. *Congressional Staff Directory*, 2005.

43. Ibid.

44. Ibid.

45. Ibid. Quoted in Paul Kane, "Reid Hires Senior Aides for 'War Room,'" *Roll Call*, November 29, 2004.

46. *Congressional Staff Directory*, 2005; and *Congressional Staff Directory*, 1983.

47. Walter Oleszek, "Congress and the Internet: Highlights," *CRS Report for Congress*, August 29, 2007, 2–3.

48. This overview is based on Diana Owen, Richard Davis, and Vincent James Strickler, "Congress and the Internet," *The Harvard International Journal of Press/Politics* 4, no.2 (1999): 11–14; Dennis W. Johnson, *Congress Online: Bridging the Gap between Citizens and Their Representative* (New York: Routledge, 2004), chap. 4; and Chris Casey, "Congress and the Internet: Looking Back and Looking Forward," in *Congress and the Internet*, ed. James A. Thurber and Colton C. Campbell (Upper Saddle River, NJ: Prentice Hall, 2003), Afterword. The description of Congress as a "'paper based' institution" comes from U.S. Representative David Dreier, "We've Come a Long Way…Maybe" in *Congress and the Internet*, ed. James A. Thurber and Colton C. Campbell (Upper Saddle River, NJ: Prentice Hall, 2003), 53.

49. Quoted in Johnson, *Congress Online*, 98.

50. Susan Crabtree, "Members Score Poorly in New Tech Survey," *Roll Call*, June 5, 2000.

51. Quoted in Jonathan Weisman, "Lawmakers Gingerly Step Into the Information Age," *CQ Weekly*, November 26, 1997, 2935–39.
52. Rep. David Dreier, "'Virtual Congress' Would Weaken Deliberative Process," *Roll Call*, December 20, 2001. See also Johnson, *Congress Online*, 102; Weisman, "Lawmakers Gingerly Step Into the Information Age"; and Donald Wolfensberger, "Can Congress Cope With IT?: Deliberation and the Internet," in *Congress and the Internet*, ed. James A. Thurber and Colton C. Campbell (Upper Saddle River, NJ: Prentice Hall, 2003), 78–98.
53. Juliet Eilperin, "Internet Caucus Measure Urges Members to Boot Up," *Roll Call*, June 17, 1996.
54. Weisman, "Lawmakers Gingerly Step into the Information Age."
55. Johnson, *Congress Online*, 103.
56. Quoted in Elizabeth Brotherton, "Few Congressional Web Sites Make the Grade," *Roll Call*, February 26, 2007.
57. Dreier, "We've Come a Long Way…Maybe," 57–59. These variations are underscored by recent analyses of virtual offices undertaken by the Congressional Management Foundation (CMF). See Congressional Management Foundation, *Congress Online 2003: Turning the Corner on the Information Age*, http://www.cmfweb.org/index. php?option=com_content&task=view&id=207&Itemid=; Congressional Management Foundation, *2006 Gold Mouse Report: Recognizing the Best Web Sites on Capitol Hill*, 2006, http://www.cmfweb.org/storage/cmfweb/documents/CMF_Pubs/2006 GoldMouseReport.pdf; and Congressional Management Foundation, *2007 Gold Mouse Report: Lessons from the Best Web Sites on Capitol Hill*, 2007, http://www.cmfweb.org/index.php?option=com_content&task=view&id=235.
58. See, for example, the discussion presented in the *2006 Gold Mouse Report*.
59. John McArdle, "Senate Eases Rules on Members' Web Updates," *Roll Call*, January 19, 2006.
60. Elysha Tenenbaum, "Members Try to Keep Up Online," *Roll Call*, March 8, 2006.
61. E. Scott Adler, Chariti E. Gent and Cary B. Overmeyer, "The Home Style Homepage: Legislator Use of the World Wide Web for Constituency Contact," *Legislative Studies Quarterly* 23 (November 1998): 585–95.
62. Tenenbaum, "Members Try to Keep Up Online."
63. See Johnson, *Congress Online*, 6–7.
64. Earlier studies of these websites emphasize their importance for self-promotion. See Owen, Davis, and Strickler, "Congress and the Internet," 10–29; and Johnson, *Congress Online*, chap. 6.
65. Dreier, "We've Come a Long Way…Maybe," 58 (emphasis in the original).
66. The following information on websites is taken from CMF surveys. See *2006 Gold Mouse Report* and *2007 Gold Mouse Report*.
67. *2006 Gold Mouse Report*, 17; *2007 Gold Mouse Report*, 21; and The Partnership for a More Perfect Union, 111th Congress Gold Mouse Project, http://pmpu.org/wp-content/uploads/111GMP-Findings.pdf.
68. We analyzed congressional websites—House (N=432) and Senate (N=100)—from May 15, 2011 through May 21, 2011. Three House seats—CA-36, NY-26, and NV-2—were vacant.
69. Paul Levinson, *New New Media* (Boston: Allyn & Bacon, 2009).
70. Jennifer Lash, "Washington Posts: Members Slow to Catch on to Blogging Phenomenon," *Roll Call*, September 12, 2005.
71. *2007 Gold Mouse Report*, 21.
72. Quoted in Elizabeth Brotherton, "A Different Kind of Revolution; Technology Redefines Constituent Outreach," *Roll Call*, September 10, 2007; and Lash, "Members Slow to Catch on to Blogging Phenomenon."

73. K. Daniel Glover, "Members Who Blog," *National Journal*, January 21, 2006, 36; and Brian Wingfield, "The Latest Initiative in Congress: Blogging," *The New York Times*, February 24, 2005.

74. Michael Doyle, "Blogging Congressman: Mariposa Republican is First from California," *Monterey County Herald*, February 27, 2006.

75. Amy Keller, "Pence Blasts Off to the Blogosphere," *Roll Call*, May 11, 2004; and Jamie Hammon, "Meet the New Blogger; Gillmor Takes to the Blogosphere to Reach Out to Constituents, *Roll Call*, December 6, 2006.

76. Quoted in Andrea Stone, "Blogs—The Hill's Version of Talk Radio," *USA Today*, June 1, 2006.

77. Antoinette Pole, *Blogging the Political: Politics and Participation in a Networked Society* (New York: Routledge, 2010), 93.

78. Bara Vaida, "Blogging On," *National Journal*, October 6, 2007, 24–30.

79. Kim Hart, "On Technology," *The Hill*, November 19, 2009.

80. Emily Yehle, "House Democrats Launch a New Media Caucus," *Roll Call*, May 25, 2010.

81. "PWNED: House GOP Dominates Twitter, YouTube, Social Media in Congress," January 22, 2010, http://republicanleader.house.gov/News/DocumentSingle.aspx? DocumentID=167478.

82. "FYI: House Republicans Add 40,000 Social Media Fans During 6-Week Blitz," http://www.gop.gov/blog/10/06/10/fyi-house-republicans-add-40.

83. J. Newton-Small, "Congress's New Love Affair with Twitter," *InsideTime.com*, February 11, 2009, http://www.time.com/time/politics/article/0,8599,1878773,00. html; Daniel Newhauser, "Congress is All Atwitter," *Roll Call*, January 25, 2010; Dana Milbank, "A Tale of 140 Characters, Plus the Ones in Congress," *Washington Post*, February 25, 2009; and Kim Hart, "On Technology," *The Hill*, November 19, 2009.

84. Doug Beizer, "New Rules Let Congress Use Web Sites Such as YouTube," *FederalComputerWeek*, October 6, 2008, http:few.com/Articles2008/10/06/New-Rules-let-Congress-use-Web-sites-such-as-You-Tube.

85. Matthew E. Glassman, Jacob R. Straus, and Colleen J. Shogan, "Social Networking and Constituent Communications: Member Use of Twitter during a Two-Month Period in the 111th Congress," *Congressional Research Service*, February 3, 2010, 1–17, http://www.fas.org/sgp/crs/misc/R41066.pdf. On the growing importance of Twitter, see also Jay Newton-Small, "Congress's New Love Affair with Twitter," *Time*, February 11, 2009, http://www.time.com/time/politics/article/0,8599,1878773,00. html; and Michelle Cottle, "Congress, The Reality Show," *The New Republic*, May 20, 2009, 5–7;

86. Tony Romm, "'Congress on Facebook' Goes Live," *The Hill's Hillicon Valley*, May 13, 2010, http://washingtonscene.thehill.com/in-the-know/36-news/4089-congress-on-facebook-goes-live.

87. Zachary M. Seward, "More Online Publishing Power in Congress' Hands in 2009," *Nieman Journalism Lab*, January 8, 2009, http:www.niemanlab.org/2009/01/more-publishing-power-in-the-hands-of-congress-in-2009. See also Cottle, "Congress, the Reality Show," 5–7.

88. Calculated by the authors. The percentages were as of May 24, 2010.

89. "Trend Data," Pew Research Center's Internet and American Life Project," 2010, http://www.pewinternet.org/Static-Pages/Trend-Data/Online-Activites-Total.aspx

90. See, for instance, James A. Barnes, "Online Fundraising Revolution," *National Journal*, April 19, 2008, 36–38; and Alexis Simendinger, "New Media as the Message," *National Journal*, April 19, 2008, 40–44.

91. Kris Kotto, "Congress' 'friends' Facebook," *The Hill*, March 11, 2008; Susan Davis "Blunt Stakes Out His Turf; Whip Boosting Outreach to Conservatives, Media

Roll Call, March 27, 2007; "Honoring 75th Anniversary of FDR's Fireside Chat: A Reid Podcast on the Economy," http://democrats.senate.gov./podcasts/051208_podcast_full.cfm; and YouTube: House Republican Leader John Boehner, http://www.youtube.com/user/JohnBoehner. For information on members who tweet, see "TweetCongress," http://tweetcongress.org/.

92. Stephen E. Frantzich, "RepreseNETation: Congress and the Internet," in *Congress and the Internet*, ed. James A. Thurber and Colton C. Campbell (Upper Saddle River, NJ: Prentice Hall, 2003), 39 (emphasis in original).

93. Information on "hits" on Hastert's sites comes from Andrea Stone, "Blogs—The Hill's Version of Talk Radio," *USA Today*, June 1, 2006.

94. This term is taken from a discussion, "New Media Develops Rapidly, *Jim Lehrer News Hour*, PBS, January 1, 2007, http://www.pbs.org/newshour/bb/media/jan-june07/media_01-01.html.

95. Franzich, "RepresNETation," 39.

96. Daniel Lipinski and Gregory Neddenriep, "Using 'New' Media to Get 'Old Media' Coverage: How Members of Congress Utilize Their Web Sites to Court Journalists," *The Harvard International Journal of Press/Politics* 9, no. 1 (2004): 9.

97. For a discussion of the cutbacks, especially as they apply to newspapers, see Paul Farhi, "Under Siege" *American Journalism Review* 28 (February/March 2006): 26–31.

98. Neil Chase, "Feeding the Web While Reporting the Story," *Nieman Reports* 60 (Winter 2006): 64–66.

99. "Journalists Using the Internet More and More," *Quill* 88 (May 2000): 5; and Allison Fass, "Journalists Among the Online Crowd," *New York Times*, March 20, 2000.

100. Stan Ketterer, "Oklahoma Small Dailies, Weeklies Use Internet as Reporting Tool," *Newspaper Research Journal* 25 (Spring 2003): 107–113.

101. Congressional Management Foundation, *Congress Online 2002: Assessing and Improving Capitol Hill Websites*, 70, http://www.cmfweb.org/index.php?option=com_content&task=view&id=206.

102. Ibid.

103. Lipinski and Neddenriep, "Using 'New' Media to Get 'Old' Media Coverage," 18.

104. Levinson, *New New Media,* 56.

105. CRS's recent analysis tweets indicated close to half (46%) of all members' tweets followed in a two-week time frame centered on their coverage in other media. See Glassman, Straus, and Shogan, "Social Networking and Constituent Communication."

106. Roxana Tiron, "Air Force Faces Fire for Controversial Tanker Decision," *The Hill*, March 6, 2008.

107. "Lou Dobbs Tonight," CNN, March 5, 2008.

108. Rep. Tom Tiahrt's website, http://tiahrt.house.gov, May 19, 2008.

109. George Talbot, "Powerful U.S. Rep. John Murtha, Visiting Mobile, Says Northrop, Boeing Should Share Tanker Deal," *Press-Register*, January 30, 2009 http://www.al.com/news/press-register/metro.ssf?/base/news/1233310579113870.xml&coll=3.

110. Cottle, "Congress, The Reality Show," 5.

Chapter 5

1. John Fund, "Flirting With Disaster," *Wall Street Journal*, May 16, 2008, http://online.wsj.com/article/SB121087780413996063.html; and Reid Wilson, "GOP Stunned by Loss in Mississippi," *Real Clear Politics*, May 14, 2008, http://www.realclearpolitics.com/articles/2008/05/gop_stunned_by_loss_in_mississ.html.

2. Alexander Mooney, "Mississippi Election Loss is GOP 'Wakeup Call,'" *CNNPolitics.com*, May 15, 2008, http://www.cnn.com/2008/POLITICS/05/14/miss.election/index.html.

3. Jonathan Weisman and Paul Kane, "After String of Losses, Republicans Face Crisis," *Washington Post*, May 15, 2008; Adam Nagourney and Carl Hulse, "Election Losses Stir Fall Fears for Republicans," *New York Times*, May 15, 2008; Ken Dilanian, "After Losses, Republicans Fear Public has Lost Confidence in Party; Congressman Says Message Deficient," *USA Today*, May 15, 2008; Laura Whittington, "In Defeat, GOP Takes Measure," *Roll Call,* May 15, 2008; and Tom Coburn, "Republicans Are in Denial," May 27, 2008, http://coburn.senate.gov/public/index.cfm/editorialsopinio ns?ContentRecord_id=31711861-802a-23ad-442b-8489d41396d0&ContentType_ id=efd17605-54a8-4be-90b1-f3794c91987a&Group_id=44ab2b65-c608-40a2- 851b-3b51f4e315c9.

4. Tom Davis, "Rep. Davis GOP Memo on How to Win in November," *Real Clear Politics*, May 14, 2008, http://www.realclearpolitics.com/articles/2008/05/post_38. html.

5. John Stanton, "Results Worry Senate GOP," *Roll Call*, May 15, 2008; and George Packer, "The Fall of Conservatism: Have the Republicans Run Out of Ideas," *The New Yorker*, May 26, 2008, 47–55.

6. Dana Milbank, "Agitated? Irritable? Hostile? Aggressive? Impulsive? Restless?," *Washington Post*, May 15, 2008.

7. See Nagourney and Hulse, "Election Losses Stir Fall Fears"; and Weisman and Kane, "After String of Losses, Republicans Face Crisis."

8. Quoted in Dilanian, "After Losses."

9. Jonathan Weisman, "Boehner Leads Effort to Polish GOP 'Brand,'" *Washington Post*, June 1, 2007.

10. Quoted in Paul Kane, "As Losses Mount, GOP Begins Looking in the Mirror," *Washington Post*, May 11, 2008.

11. Quoted in Morton M. Kondracke, "Can GOP Reform to Avoid 'Kennedy Scenario' for 2008?," *Roll Call*, May 22, 2008.

12. David Brooks, "History for Dollars," *New York Times*, June 8, 2010. For a discussion of the importance of brands for parties, see Tim Groeling, *When Politicians Attack! Party Cohesion in the Media* (Cambridge, UK: Cambridge University Press, 2010), chap. 1.

13. Groeling, *When Politicians Attack!*, 22–28.

14. Tim Groeling and Samuel Kernell, "Congress, the President, and Party Competition via Network News," in *Polarized Politics: Congress and the President in a Partisan Era*, ed. Jon R. Bond and Richard Fleisher (Washington, DC: CQ Press, 2000), 73–95. See also Groeling, *When Politicians Attack*, chap. 2.

15. Barbara Sinclair, *Legislators, Leaders, and Lawmaking: The U.S. House of Representatives in the Postreform Era* (Baltimore: Johns Hopkins University Press, 1995); Gerald Gamm and Steven S. Smith, "Emergence of Senate Party Leadership," in *U.S. Senate Exceptionalism*, ed. Bruce I. Oppenheimer (Columbus: Ohio State University, 2002), 211–38; David W. Brady and Mathew D. McCubbins, "Party, Process, and Political Change: New Perspectives on the History of Congress," in *Party, Process, and Political Change in Congress: New Perspectives on the History of Congress*, ed. David W. Brady and Mathew D. McCubbins (Stanford, CA: Stanford University Press, 2002), 1–14; and Groeling, *When Politicians Attack!*, 104–112.

16. Congressional Management Foundation, *2006 Gold Mouse Report: Recognizing the Best Web Sites on Capitol Hill*, http://www.cmfmweb.org/storage/cmfwebdocuments/ CMF_Pubs/2006GoldMouseReport.pdf., 17.

17. Timothy E. Cook, *Governing with the News: The News Media as a Political Institution* (Chicago: University of Chicago Press, 1998), 130.

18. Jeffrey Cohen, "Presidential Leadership in a New Media Age," in *Presidential Leadership: The Vortex of Power*, ed. Bert A. Rockman and Richard W. Waterman (New York: Oxford University Press, 2008), 171–90.

19. "Youngstown Sheet and Tube Co. v. Sawyer," in *The Evolving Presidency: Landmark Documents, 1787–2008*, ed. Michael Nelson (Washington, DC: CQ Press, 2008), 185.

20. Cook, *Governing with the News*, 134; and Shanto Iyengar and Jennifer A. McGrady, *Media Politics: A Citizen's Guide* (New York: Norton, 2007), 174–78.

21. Cook, *Governing with the News*, 134.

22. Lawrence R. Jacobs, "The Presidency and the Press: The Paradox of the White House Communications War," in *The Presidency and the Political System*, ed. Michael Nelson (Washington, DC: CQ Press, 2006), 283–310; and Stephen J. Farnsworth and S. Robert Lichter, *The Mediated Presidency: Television News and Presidential Governance* (Lanham, MD: Rowman and Littlefield, 2005), chap. 5.

23. Elizabeth Bumiller, "Amid Talk of War Spending, Bush Urges Fiscal Restraint," *New York Times*, September 17, 2002.

24. Martha Joynt Kumar, *Managing the President's Message: The White House Communications Operation* (Baltimore: Johns Hopkins University Press, 2007); Martha Joynt Kumar, "The Office of Communications," in *The White House World: Transitions, Organization, and Office Operations*, ed. Martha Joynt Kumar and Terry Sullivan (College Station, TX: Texas A&M University Press, 2003), 252–78; and John Anthony Maltese, *Spin Control: The White House Office of Communications and the Management of Presidential News* (Chapel Hill: University of North Carolina Press, 1994).

25. George C. Edwards III, *Governing by Campaigning: The Politics of the Bush Presidency* (New York: Pearson Longman, 2008), 34–35.

26. Mike Allen and Jonathan Weisman, "Bush Ousts O'Neill and a Top Adviser; Treasury Chief, Key Economic Aide Resign as Jobless Rate Hits 6 Percent," *Washington Post*, December 7, 2002.

27. Barbara Sinclair, *Party Wars: Polarization and the Politics of National Policy Making* (Norman: University of Oklahoma Press, 2006).

28. Gary Lee Malecha and Daniel J. Reagan, "Coverage of the Postreform House Majority Party Leadership: An Expanding or a Shrinking Image," *Congress and the Presidency* 31(Spring, 2004): 53–76.

29. Quoted in Ethan Wallison, "Democrats Plot Counterattack to Presidential Barnstorming," *Roll Call*, March 1, 2001.

30. Patrick Sellers, "Manipulating the Message in the U.S. Congress," *The Harvard International Journal of Press/Politics* 5, no. 1 (2000): 22–31; and Patrick Sellers, "Winning Media Coverage in the U.S. Congress," in *U.S. Senate Exceptionalism*, ed. Bruce I. Oppenheimer (Columbus: Ohio State University Press, 2002), 132–53.

31. Quoted in Erin Billings, "Pelosi Plans Ahead," *Roll Call*, May 14, 2003.

32. Alexander Bolton, "Bungling Meant Leak Letter Leaked," *The Hill*, November 10, 2005. See also Ben Pershing and Paul Kane, "GOP Works to Heal Divisions," *Roll Call*, December 5, 2005.

33. Groeling and Kernell, "Congress, the President, and Party Competition via Network News," 73–95. Parties that control the White House, as Groeling notes, have considerable incentives to keep their folks on message, for the media tend to accentuate public differences between presidents and their parties. See Groeling, *When Politicians Attack*, chap. 3.

34. Ibid., 78–79.

35. Patrick Sellers, *Cycles of Spin: Strategic Communication in the U.S. Congress* (New York: Cambridge University Press, 2010), 63–71; and Sinclair, *Party Wars*, 269.

36. Daniel Lipinski, "Communicating the Party Record: How Congressional Leaders Transmit Their Messages to the Public" (paper Presented at the Annual Meeting of the American Political Science Association, Atlanta, Georgia, September 2–5, 1999); and C. Lawrence Evans, "Committees, Leaders, and Message Politics," in *Congress*

Reconsidered, ed. Lawrence C. Dodd and Bruce Oppenheimer (Washington, DC: CQ Press, 2001), 219–21.

37. Sellars, *Cycles of Spin,* chap. 3; and Sinclair, *Party War,* 265–69.
38. Weisman, "Boehner Leads Effort to Polish GOP 'Brand.'" See also Lauren Whittington, "McCotter Leaves Message Project," *Roll Call,* November 14, 2007.
39. Charge listed on http://policy.house.gov/.
40. David M. Drucker, "Health Care Battle Flares Anew," *Roll Call,* June 9, 2010.
41. William F. Connelly Jr. and John J. Pitney, *Congress' Permanent Minority?: Republicans in the U.S. House* (Lanham, MD: Rowman and Littlefield, 1994).
42. Ronald Peters, "Caucus and Conference: Party Organizations in the U.S. House of Representatives" (paper prepared for delivery at the Annual Meeting of the Midwest Political Science Association, Chicago, Illinois, April 25–28, 2002). For a discussion of GOP's frustrations as the House minority, see Connelly and Pitney, *Congress' Permanent Minority?*
43. Connelly and Pitney, Jr. *Congress' Permanent Minority?,* 43.
44. Peters, "Caucus and Conference." See also Ben Pershing, "Pryce Eyes Message, Potential Challengers," *Roll Call,* February 15, 2006.
45. Available at: http://www.gop.gov/about/pence.
46. Federal News Service, "Rep. Pence Announces Bid for House Republican Conference Chairman," November 17, 2008.
47. Quoted in John R. Parkinson, "Tea Party Favorite Bachmann Seeking Leadership Post," ABC News, November 4, 2010, http://blogs.abcnews.com/thenote/2010/11/tea-party-favorite-bachmann-seeking-gop-leadership-post.html.
48. *Congressional Staff Directory,* ed. Charles B. Brownson (Mt. Vernon, VA: Congressional Staff Directory, 1983).
49. *Congressional Staff Directory* (Washington, DC: Congressional Quarterly, 2005).
50. *Congressional Staff Directory* (Washington, DC: Congressional Quarterly, 2007). That did not include press aides in Putnam's District Office. On Pence's additions, see Richard Cohen, "GOP's Dilemma: Substance Versus Spin," *National Journal,* March 7, 2009, 15.
51. Peters, "Caucus and Conference."
52. *Congressional Staff Directory,* 2007.
53. Jennifer Yachnin, "For Emmanuel, One Title But Lots of Jobs; Frenetic Caucus Chairman Keeps Multitasking," *Roll Call,* May 1, 2007.
54. See Mike Soraghan, "Leaders Want House Freshman to Stay More on Message," *The Hill,* July 20, 2009.
55. Yachnin, "For Emanuel, One Title but Lots of Jobs."
56. David Maraniss and Michael Weisskopf, *Tell Newt to Shut Up!* (New York: Simon & Shuster, 1996), 10. See also Peters, "Caucus and Conference."
57. Sam Dealey, "Rep. J. C. Watts Threatens to Quit Leadership Post," *The Hill,* August 4, 1999.
58. Quoted in Ethan Wallison and Jim VandeHei, "GOP Members Ask: Where's the Message? Budget Battle Splits Leaders, Rank and File," *Roll Call,* October 19, 1998.
59. Lauren Whittington, "McCotter Leaves Message Project," *Roll Call,* November 14, 2007.
60. Erin P. Billings, "Democrats Clash on Communications," *Roll Call,* November 5, 2003.
61. John Bresnahan, "Pelosi Concentrates Power in Office," *Politico,* June 3, 2008.
62. Quoted in Billings, "Pelosi Plans Ahead."
63. Sinclair, *Party Wars,* 269–83.
64. David A. Dulio and Stephan L. Medvic, "The Permanent Campaign in Congress: Understanding Congressional Communications Tactics" (paper prepared for delivery at the Midwest Political Science Association, Chicago, April 3–6, 2003).

65. Daniel Lipinski, "The Outside Game: Congressional Communication and Party Strategy," in *Communications in U.S. Elections: New Agendas,* ed. Roderick P. Hart and Daron R. Shaw (Lanham, MD: Rowman & Littlefield, 2001), 173–75.

66. Susan Davis, "GOP's August Message to Focus on Progress in Iraq," *Roll Call,* August 2, 2007.

67. Steven T. Dennis and Jennifer Yachnin, "Democrats Crank Up Message Machine for Recess," *Roll Call,* December 17, 2007.

68. Daniel Lipinski, *Congressional Communication: Content and Consequences* (Ann Arbor: University of Michigan Press, 2004), 61–63.

69. Connelly and Pitney, *Congress' Permanent Minority?,* 27–30.

70. Betsy Rothstein, "House GOP Theme Team vs. Democrats' Message Group," *The Hill,* March 31, 1999; and Lauren W. Whittington, "Greene Looks Forward to Busy Season," *Roll Call,* June 19, 2000.

71. Rothstein, "House GOP Theme Team."

72. Bree Hocking, "GOP to Hold Seminar on Mastering the Blogosphere," *Roll Call,* March 2, 2006.

73. Jackie Kucinich, "In Minority, Republican Issues Salon Carries On: Weekly Event Offers Insights of Outsiders, *Roll Call,* May 10, 2010.

74. Quoted in ibid.

75. Patrick O'Connor, "Eight Teams Now Man GOP Message Machine," *The Hill,* February 23, 2005.

76. Ben Pershing, "House GOP Conference Forms Message Action Team," *Roll Call,* April 21, 2003.

77. Lyndsey Layton, "Rep. Putnam Stays on Message," *Washington Post,* April 6, 2007; and Richard E. Cohen, "GOP's Dilemma: Substance Versus Spin," *National Journal,* March 7, 2009.

78. Ben Pershing, "GOP Prepares 'War Room,'" *Roll Call,* March 13, 2003; and Patrick O'Connor, "Republicans Establish Immigration War Room," *The Hill,* July 18, 2006.

79. Rothstein, "House GOP Theme Team." See also Daniel Lipinski, "Analyzing Congressional Party Communication Operations from a Formal Perspective" (paper presented at the Annual Meeting of the Midwest Political Science Association, Chicago, April, 2004, 18–19).

80. Douglas B. Harris, "Orchestrating Party Talk: A Party-Based View of One-Minute Speeches in the House of Representatives," *Legislative Studies Quarterly* 30 (February 2005): 129.

81. Ethan Wallison, "Democrats Start 'Rapid-Response' Teams to Check Bush," *Roll Call,* March 12, 2001.

82. Peter Brand, "House Democrats Create 'Message Teams,'" *The Hill,* June 19, 2002.

83. See Susan Crabtree, "Edgy GOP Lawmakers Plot Public Relations Strategy," *CQ Today,* January 28, 2005, http://www.dutkoworldwide.com/downloads/CQ_12805.pdf.

84. Quoted in Ben Pershing, "Speaker Urges GOP to Hit Airwaves Over WMD," *Roll Call,* July 17, 2003.

85. Whittington, "The Obscure Caucus."

86. See http://www.gop.gov/; and Susan Davis, "New Minority Gets a New Messenger," *Roll Call,* February 5, 2007.

87. See http://www.dems.gov/.

88. Sarah A. Binder, "Elections, Parties and Governance," in *The Legislative Branch,* ed. Paul J. Quirk and Sarah A. Binder (New York: Oxford University Press, 2005), 156.

89. Steven Smith, "Parties and Leadership in the Senate," in *The Legislative Branch,* ed. Paul J. Quirk and Sarah A. Binder (New York: Oxford University Press, 2005), 276. See also Barbara Sinclair, "The New World of U.S. Senators," in *Congress Recon-*

sidered, 7th ed., ed. Lawrence C. Dodd and Bruce I. Oppenheimer (Washington, DC: CQ Press, 2001), 1–19; and Barbara Sinclair, "The Senate Leadership Dilemma: Passing Bills and Pursuing Advantage in a Nonmajoritarian Chamber," in *The Contentious Senate: Partisanship, Ideology, and the Myth of Cool Judgment* (Lanham, MD: Rowman and Littlefield, 2001), 65–89.

90. Quoted in Allison Stevens, "Senate GOP Takes P.R. Lesson From House," *The Hill*, February 7, 2001.
91. Alexander Bolton, "Senate GOP Begins Repair of Messaging," *The Hill*, January 17, 2007.
92. Donald C. Baumer, "An Update on the Senate Policy Committee," *P.S.: Political Science and Politics* 24 (June 1991): 175.
93. Sean Q. Kelly, "Democratic Leadership in the Modern Senate: The Emerging Roles of the Democratic Policy Committee," *Congress and the Presidency* 22 (Autumn 1995): 12–15.
94. Sen. Byron Dorgan, "Senate DPC's Role Expands as It Begins New Decade," *Roll Call*, January 30, 2007.
95. John Stanton and Erin P. Billings, "Praise for the 'War Room,'" *Roll Call*, November 27, 2006. See also "A History of the Democratic Policy Committee, 1947–2007, http://dpc.senate.gov/pdf/dpchistory.pdf.
96. Paul Kane, "Reid Hires Senior Aides for 'War Room,'" *Roll Call*, November 29, 2004.
97. Burdett Loomis, "Senate Leaders, Minority Voices: From Dirksen to Daschle," in *The Contentious Senate: Partisanship, Ideology, and the Myth of Cool Judgment*, ed. Colton C. Campbell and Nicol C. Rae (Lanham, MD: Rowman & Littlefield, 2001), 105.
98. Geoff Earle, "Reid Makes It Clear He's No Daschle," *The Hill*, December 1, 2004.
99. *Congressional Staff Directory*, 2007.
100. John Stanton, "Senate Democrats Shift to Local Focus," *Roll Call*, May 10, 2006.
101. Emily Pierce and Jessica Brady, "Reid Expands Schumer's Role in 112th Congress," *Roll Call*, November 16, 2010.
102. David M. Drucker and Steven T. Dennis, "Friction Strains Senate War Room: Reid Aide's Departure Raises Fresh Questions about Schumer's Influence," *Roll Call*, June 14, 2011.
103. Roger H. Davidson and Walter J. Oleszek, "Changing the Guard in the U.S. Senate," *Legislative Studies Quarterly* 9 (November 1984): 652.
104. Bolton, "Senate GOP Begins Repair of Messaging."
105. GOP conference web page, http://src.senate.gov/public/.
106. *Congressional Staff Directory*, 2007.
107. Quoted in Bolton, "Senate GOP Begins Repair of Messaging."
108. John Stanton, "Frist Launches Message Shop," *Roll Call*, January 19, 2006.
109. Bolton, "Senate GOP Begins Repair of Messaging."
110. Ibid.
111. Erin P. Billings, "McConnell Builds Message Center," *Roll Call*, December 5, 2006.
112. http://democrats.senate.gov/; and http://republican.senate.gov/public/?CFID=74146 979&CFTOKEN=66632567.
113. See http://rpc.senate.gov/public/; and http://dpc.senate.gov/.
114. Quoted in Bolton, "Senate GOP Begins Repair of Messaging."
115. John Stanton, "Senate Democrats Shift to Local Focus," *Roll Call*, May 10, 2006; and Bolton, "Senate GOP Begins Repair of Messaging."
116. See Betsy Rothstein, "Sen. Thomas Brings Discipline to GOP Message," *The Hill*, March 21, 2001.
117. Paul Kane, "Gillespie to Help Sell 'Nuke' Plan," *Roll Call*, April 14, 2005.
118. Erin P. Billings, "Parties Step Up Floor Messages," *Roll Call*, April 24, 2007.

119. Ibid.

120. Quoted in Aime Parnes, "GOP Senators Using Online System," *Politico*, May 22, 2008.

121. See the discussion on Senate Democrats "Mirror-Message Teams" in Mark Preston and Susan Crabtree, "Parties Vie for Edge on Education," *Roll Call*, May 6, 2002.

122. John Stanton, "GOP Hatching New Strategy; Senators Adjusting to Obama," *Roll Call*, March 3, 2009.

123. Alexander Bolton, "Senate Republicans Spell Out Disciplined Messages for Recess," *The Hill*, August 10, 2005.

124. John Stanton, "Senate Democrats' Message: Stick to 'Six for '06,'" *Roll Call*, October 31, 2006.

125. Rothstein, "House GOP Theme Team."

126. Barbara Sinclair, "Leadership Strategies in the Modern Congress" in *Congressional Politics,* ed. Christopher J. Deering (Chicago: Dorsey Press, 1989), 151; and Sinclair, "The Senate Leadership Dilemma," 72–76.

127. Bolton, "Senate GOP Begins Repair of Messaging."

Chapter 6

1. "It's the Economy Again! Clinton Nostalgia Sets In, Bush Reactions Mixed," The Pew Research Center for the People and the Press, January 11, 2001, http://people-press.org/reports/pdf/18.pdf.

2. Mike Allen, "Bush Backs Off on Proposal for Medicare Drug Benefit," *Washington Post*, February 28, 2003; Mike Allen, "Bush to Seek New Medicare Drug Plan: Managed-Care Alternative Promoted," *Washington Post,* March 4, 2003; and Mary Agnes Carey, "Medicare Overhaul Proposals Put Difficult Trade-Offs on Table," *CQ Weekly*, March 8, 2003, 563–65.

3. Allen, "Bush to Seek New Medicare Drug Plan"; and Carey "Medicare Overhaul Proposals."

4. Rebecca Adams, "Lawmakers Mindful of Ticking Clock Scramble to Repair Medicare Rift," *CQ Weekly*, April 26, 2003, 999–1000.

5. Larry Lipman, "Key Senators Agree on Medicare Drug Plan," *Cox News Service*, June 5, 2003.

6. Robert Pear, "Senators Reach Agreement on Drug Plan for the Elderly," *New York Times*, June 6, 2003; and Mary Agnes Carey, "Plans for Targeted Benefits Deepen Medicare Debate," *CQ Weekly*, June 7, 2003, 1358–63.

7. "Senator Grassley of Iowa Discusses the Bipartisan Plan to Help Senior Citizens Afford Prescription Drugs," *Capitol Report*, CNBC, June 5, 2003.

8. Pear, "Senators Reach Agreement on Drug Plan for the Elderly"; and Amy Fagan, "Bipartisan Drug-Benefit Pact Made in Senate Finance Panel; Deal Called 'Real Progress' on Medicare Reform," *Washington Times*, June 6, 2003.

9. Robert Pear, "Bush Will Accept Identical Benefits on Medicare Drugs," *New York Times*, June 10, 2003.

10. Rebecca Adams and Mary Agnes Carey, "GOP Bids to Claim Victory on Democrats' Signature Issue," *CQ Weekly*, June 14, 2003, 1455–59.

11. Melissa Seckora, "Conservatives Swipe at Medicare Bill," *The Hill*, June 24, 2003.

12. "Senator Edward Kennedy Discusses the Proposed Drug Benefit and Other Political Issues," *Capitol Report*, CNBC, June 20, 2003.

13. See, for instance, "Senator Bill Frist, Republican Majority Leader, Talks about Prescription Drug Plan for Seniors, Intelligence Hearings on Iraq, and Possible Battle Over Supreme Court Nominee, *Today*, NBC, June 26, 2003; "Interview with John Breaux," *Hannity and Colmes*, Fox, June 26, 2003; and "Interview with John Corzine," *Your World with Neil Cavuto*, Fox, June 26, 2003.

14. See, for example, "Senator Don Nickles of Oklahoma Discussed the Reaction by Some House Republicans to the Senate's Prescription Drug Plan, *Capitol Report*, CNBC, June 19, 2003; and "Medicare Reform Debate Heats Up," *Judy Woodruff's Inside Politics*, CNN, June 24, 2003.

15. "Interview with Tom Daschle," *Hannity and Colmes*, Fox, June 25, 2003; and "Interview with Senator Jay Rockefeller," *Live From the Headlines*, CNN, June 25, 2003.

16. Jonathan Allen and Adam Graham-Silverman, "Hour by Hour, Vote by Vote, GOP Breaks Tense Tie on Medicare," *CQ Weekly*, June 28, 2003, 1614–15. For votes see, "Senate Roll Call on Medicare Legislation," *Washington Post*, June 28, 2003; and "House Roll Call On Medicare Legislation," *Washington Post*, June 28, 2003.

17. Amy Goldstein and Helen DeWar, "Medicare Bills Pass in Congress," *Washington Post*, June 27, 2003; Julie Rovner, "Comparing the House and Senate Medicare Bills," *National Journal*, August 30, 2003, 2618–19; and Marilyn Weber Serafini, "A Prescription for Defeat," *National Journal*, August 30, 2003, 2608–13, 2616–17.

18. David Natiher and Rebecca Adams, "Medicare Rewrite: Prescription for Disappointing Everyone?," *CQ Weekly*, July 5, 2003, 1690–96; and Marilyn Werber Serafini, "A Prescription for Defeat."

19. Jeffrey M. Jones, "Public Endorses Need for Medicare Reform, but Is Skeptical of Recent Legislation," *Gallup News Service*, July 7, 2003, http://www.gallup.com/poll/8770/Public-Endorses-Need-Medicare-Reform-Skeptical-Recent-Legislation.aspx.

20. Democratic Leaders and Menendez (D-N.J) quoted in Erin P. Billings, "Democrats Try to Reclaim Rx Issue," *Roll Call*, July 9, 2003; See also Barbara Sinclair, *Party Wars: Polarization and the Politics of National Policy Making* (Norman: University of Oklahoma Press, 2006), 301.

21. Quoted in Billings, "Democrats Try to Reclaim RX Issue."

22. Chris Cillizza, "DCCC Ads Hit Eight on Drug Vote," *Roll Call*, July 14, 2003; and Sinclair, *Party Wars*, 301–302.

23. Juliet Eilperin, "Democrats' Ads Target GOP on Medicare," *Washington Post*, July 13, 2003; and Sinclair, *Party Wars*, 302.

24. Jennifer Yachnin, "Morning Business," *Roll Call*, July 17, 2003

25. Billings, "Democrats Try to Reclaim Rx Issue." See, for example, "Menendez, House Democrats Announce Prescription Drug Town Halls," July 18, 2003, http://www.dems.gov/index.asp?Type=B_PR&SEC={F881DB72-7965-4E11-9DC7-D8E0D57E7D1D}&DE={CDE2539D-4431-48FE-A30A-62E1C8349B67}; and "Congressmen James E. Clyburn and John Spratt to Host Town Meeting on the Potential Prescription Drug Plan," July 16, 2003, http://www.house.gov/spratt/newsroom/03_04/rx_town_hall.pdf.

26. "House Democratic Leaders Kick Off 'Town Hall' Meetings on Prescription Drug Benefit," *The White House Bulletin.*, July 18, 2003; and "House Democrats Kick Off National Day of Rx Drug Town Hall Meetings," http://democraticleader.house.gov/media/statements.cfm?pressReleaseID=187.

27. For a list of some of the outlets featuring stories, see "Medicare: Obstacles to House–Senate Compromise," *American Health Line*, July 21, 2003. See also Tamera Manzanares, "Seniors Express Concerns at Town Hall Session on Drug Coverage," *Denver Post*, July 20, 2003; Jim Freehan, "Oregon Rep. DeFazio Warns Residents of Higher Costs under New Drug Law," *The Register Guard*, July 21, 2003; Chris Serres, "North Carolina Democrats Attack Medicare Legislation Passed by U.S. House," *The News and Observer*, July 20, 2003; Sandi Doughton, "Prescription-Drug Plans Leave Washington Seniors Confused, Skeptical," *Seattle-Times*, July 20, 2003; and "Senior Citizens Vent Concerns Over Rising Prescription Drug Costs to Democratic Members of Congress," *News Transcripts*, CBS, July 19, 2003.

28. See for example, "Prescription Drug Subsidies for Low-Income Seniors a Hurdle for Final Medicare Bill," Kaisernetwork.org, July21, 2003, http://www.kaisernetwork.org/daily_reports/rep_hpolicy_recent_rep.cfm?dr_cat=3&show=yes&dr_DateTime=07-21-03#18920.
29. Amy Goldstein, "In Home States, Selling Their Take on Medicare Plans," *Washington Post*, August 31, 2003; and Amy Fagan, "Time Seen Eroding Prescription Drug Bill's Backing," *Washington Times*, August 6, 2003.
30. Jeff Flake, "Changing the Course of U.S. Public Opinion," *The Hill*, July 16, 2003.
31. Donald Lambro, "White House, Conservatives Split on Drugs: Activist Groups Fear the $400 Billion in Medicare Funding Sought by the President Only Will Grow, *Washington Times*, June 29, 2003; and Fagan, "Time Seen Eroding Prescription Drug Bill's Backing."
32. Mary Agnes Carey, "Medicare Conference: We Can Get This Done," *CQ Weekly*, October 18, 2003, 2548–50; and Mary Agnes Carey, "Medicare Deal Goes to Wire in Late-Night Vote," *CQ Weekly*, November 22, 2003, 2879–83.
33. Mary Agnes Carey, "Medicare Conference"; and Mary Agnes Carey and Adriel Bettelheim, "Drug Bill Nears Completion," *CQ Weekly*, October 25, 2003, 2621–22.
34. "Interview with Bill Thomas," *This Week with George Stephanopoulos*, ABC, October 19, 2003.
35. "Interview with Bill Frist," *Fox News Sunday*, October 26, 2003.
36. Federal News Service, "News Conference: Medicare Prescription Drugs," October 23, 2003.
37. Henry J. Kaiser Family Foundation and Harvard School of Public Health, "New Survey Finds Most Seniors Favor Reforms that Build on Existing Medicare Program, But Younger Adults are More Favorable Toward Private Plans," http://www.kff.org/medicare/loader.cfm?url=/commonspot/security/getfile.cfm&PageID=14242.
38. Mary Agnes Carey, "Provisions of the Medicare Bill," *CQ Weekly*, January 24, 2004, 238–43.
39. Ibid.; Robert Pear, "Senate Backs Bill: Measure Provides Drug Benefits for Millions of Elderly People," *New York Times*, November 26, 2003; and Amy Goldstein and Helen DeWar, "Medicare Bill Headed to Bush; Senate Vote Clears Way for Drug Benefit," *Washington Post*, November 26, 2003.
40. "Representative Lynn Woolsey Discusses What is Wrong With the Medicare Prescription Drug Benefit Bill," *The News With Brian Williams*, CNBC, November 21, 2003.
41. "Representatives Rosa Delauro and Gil Gutknecht Hold a News Conference on Drug Reimportation," *FDCH Political Transcripts*, November 18, 2003.
42. "Representatives David Dreier and Harold Ford Jr. Discuss Their Perspectives on the Medicare Reform Bill," *Capitol Report*, CNBC, November 25, 2003.
43. "Congress Nearing Medicare Reform," *Lou Dobbs Tonight.*, CNN, November 24, 2003.
44. See, for example, the interview with Sen. Tom Harkin (D-IA) in "Medicare Treatment," *American Morning*, CNN, November 24, 2003.
45. Quoted in Erin P. Billings and Ben Pershing, "Pelosi Issues Warning," *Roll Call*, November 19, 2003.
46. Rep. Charles Rangel (D-NY) quoted in "U.S. Representative Elijah Cummings (D-MD) Holds a News Conference on the Medicare Bill," *FDCH Political Transcripts*, November 21, 2003.
47. "Interview with Senator Edward Kennedy," *American Morning*, CNN, November 24, 2003.
48. "Representatives Discuss GOP Medicare Bill," *Your World with Neil Cavuto*, Fox, November 17, 2003.

49. "Interview with Dan Burton," *Your World with Neil Cavuto*, Fox, November 21, 2003.
50. Mike Pence, "Why I Oppose the Drug Entitlement," *Human Events*, November 24, 2003, 1–8.
51. "Senator Bill Frist Discusses the Work Done on Capitol Hill on the Medicare Prescription Drug Bill," *Capitol Report*, CNBC, November 18, 2003.
52. "Interview with Dennis Hastert," *Fox News Sunday*, Fox, November 23, 2003.
53. "Senator Bill Frist Discusses the Work Done."
54. Carey, "Provisions of the Medicare Bill"; and Jackie Koszczuk and Jonathan Allen, "Late-Night Vote Drama Triggers Some Unexpected Alliances," *CQ Weekly*, November 29, 2003, 2956–63.
55. David E. Rosenbaum, "Bush Signs Law to Cover Drugs for the Elderly," *New York Times*, December 9, 2003; and Sinclair, *Party Wars*, 303.
56. Robert Pear, "Senate Backs Bill: Measure Provides Drug Benefits for Millions of Elderly People," *New York Times*, November 26, 2003.
57. Frank Newport," Senior Citizens Wary of New Medicare Bill," *Gallup News Service*, December 10, 2003, http://www.gallup.com/poll/9883/Senior-Citizens-Wary-New-Medicare-Bill.aspx; and Colleen McMurray, "Medicare Changes Fall Short With Seniors," *Gallup News Service*, January 27, 2004, http://www.gallup.com/poll/10414/Medicare-Changes-Fall-Short-Seniors.aspx.
58. Jonathan E. Kaplan, "GOP Lawmakers Face a Tough Sell to Skeptical Retirees," *The Hill*, February 24, 2004.
59. Quoted in Jonathan E. Kaplan, "GOP Makes Plans to Tout New Rx Law," *The Hill*, December 10, 2003.
60. Quoted in Amy Goldstein and Helen Dewar, "GOP Still Seeking Afterglow of Vote on Drug Benefits; Credit for Huge Expansion of Medicare Eludes Republican Party as Discontent Appears to Spread," *Washington Post*, February 29, 2004.
61. Kaplan, "GOP Makes Plans to Tout New Rx Law."
62. Ibid.
63. Quoted in ibid.
64. Cardin quoted in Amy Goldstein, "Medicare Portrayal Tailored by Parties; In Election Year, Seniors' Support is Key," *Washington Post*, January 11, 2004.
65. Ibid.
66. Mark Preston and Paul Kane, "Daschle, Pelosi Will Try to Pre-empt Bush," *Roll Call*, January 5, 2004. See also "Senator Tom Daschle and Representative Nancy Pelosi Hold a News Conference on President Bush's Upcoming State of the Union Address," *FDCH Political Transcripts*, January 16, 2004.
67. Quoted in Erin P. Billings, "Pelosi Taps Dingell, Rangel for Medicare Road Show" *Roll Call*, February 26, 2004; and Sinclair, *Party Wars*, 304–305.
68. David W. Moore, "Support Drops for New Medicare Law: Few Americans Believe It Will Help Seniors or Financial Security of Medicare," *Gallup News Service*. April 2, 2004, http://www.gallup.com/poll/11176/Support-Drops-New-Medicare-Law.aspx; and "Reactions to the New Medicare Law: Findings Based on Focus Groups with Medicare Beneficiaries," *The Henry J. Kaiser Family Foundation*, June 2004, http://kff.org/medicare/upload/Reactions-to-the-New-Medicare-Law-Findings-Based-on-Focus-Groups-with-People-on-Medicare.pdf.
69. Quoted in "Robin Toner, "Seems the Last Word on Medicare Wasn't," *New York Times*, March 17, 2004.
70. Quoted in ibid.
71. Goldstein, "Medicare Portrayal Tailored by Parties"; Kaplan, "GOP Lawmakers Face a Tough Sell to Skeptical Retirees"; and Sinclair, *Party Wars*, 304.
72. Ben Pershing and Erin P. Billings, "Members Head Home 'on Message,'" *Roll Call*, April 5, 2004.

73. "Gingrey is GOP's Medicare Man," *The Hill*, April 7, 2004.
74. "GOP Steps Up Medicare Publicity in Election-Year," *USA Today*, February 11, 2004, http://www.usatoday.com/news/washington/2004-02-11-gop-medicare_x.htm; and Sinclair, *Party Wars*, 304.
75. See Sinclair, *Party Wars*, 303–305.
76. Quoted in "GOP Steps Up Medicare Publicity in Election-Year."
77. Chris Cillizza, "Drug Battle Reaches Campaign Trail Today," *Roll Call*, May 3, 2004; and Sinclair, *Party Wars*, 305.
78. Ceci Connolly, "New Drug Card for Medicare Touted by GOP; Officials Target Confusion, Frustration Over Program," *Washington Post*, May 4, 2004; and Sinclair, *Party Wars*, 305.
79. "Medicare: Lawmakers Discuss RX Drug Discount Card Program," *American Health Line*, May 4, 2004.
80. Jonathan E. Kaplan, "Dems Mum on Drug Card, GOP Claims," *The Hill*, May 26, 2004.
81. Amy Fagan, "GOP Lawmakers to Tout Successes," *Washington Times*, August 2, 2005.
82. Alexander Bolton, "Senate Republicans Spell Out Disciplined Messages for Recess," *The Hill*, August 10, 2005.
83. Patrick O'Connor, "GOP Lawmakers Star in Public-Service Ads," *The Hill*, September 14, 2005.
84. Quoted in Paul Bedard, "Congress Watch: GOP Plans Medicare Offensive," *U.S. News and World Report*, March 27, 2006, http://www.usnews.com/usnews/news/articles/060327/27congwatch.htm; and Patrick O'Connor and Josephine Hearn, "Recess Spin on Medicare Not Reform," *The Hill*, February 22, 2006.
85. Amy Fagan, "Hill GOP Prescribes Drug Blitz for District Recess; Community Events Aim to Counter Criticism of Medicare Plan," *Washington Times*, April 9, 2006; and Bedard, "Congress Watch."
86. Patrick O'Connor, "Parties Ready Battle Plans for Recess," *The Hill*, June 29, 2006.
87. Karlyn Bowman, "The Medicare Drug Benefit: What Happened?," *Roll Call*, October 19, 2006; and Jeffrey Young, "Drug Benefit Is Popular, but Not Touted Much by GOP," *The Hill*, November 1, 2006.
88. Young, "Drug Benefit Is Popular."
89. "Bush Approval Rating Falls to 28 percent, Lowest Level So Far, in Harris Poll," *The Wall Street Journal*, April 26, 2007, http://online.wsj.com/article/SB117752895118782401.html; and S. A. Miller, "Congress Approval Hits All-Time Low; Gallup Reports Nine-Point Drop Since Last Month," *Washington Times*, August 22, 2007.
90. Carl Hulse, "The Blogs Are Alive With the Sound of Angry Democrats," *New York Times*, August 9, 2007.
91. Martin Kady, "Dems Show No Signs of Letting Up on SCHIP," *Politico*, October 17, 2007.
92. Patrick Sellars, *Cycles of Spin: Strategic Communication in the U.S. Congress* (New York: Cambridge University Press, 2010), 9–10, 31–35. In addition, as the majority their ability to control the chamber worked to their advantage. For a discussion of this advantage see Sinclair, *Party Wars*, chap. 8.
93. Rebecca Adams, "Kids Health Gets Political," *CQ Weekly*, July 23, 2007, 2178–84.
94. Kate Ackley, "Health Insurance for Kids: Who's Coughing Up Cash?," *Roll Call*, June 6, 2007.
95. Liz Mair, "GOP is Right to Mend Health Care Stance," *Politico*, October 29, 2007.
96. Steven T. Dennis and Emily Pierce, "Tough Choices for GOP on SCHIP," *Roll Call*, July 30, 2007.

97. Ryan Grim, "Lauren Aronson: Staffer Becomes Standout under Coach Emanuel," *Politico,* April 23, 2008.
98. Dennis and Pierce, "Tough Choices."
99. Jackie Calmes, "GOP Is Losing Grip on Core Business Vote; Deficit Hawks Defect as Social Issues Prevail; 'The Party Left Me'," *Wall Street Journal,* October 2, 2007.
100. Quoted in "Bush Veto Baffles Some Republicans: Democrats Seeking GOP Allies in Bid to Override Veto of Kid's Health Insurance Bill," CBS News, October 4, 2007, http://www.cbsnews.com/stories/2007/10/04/politics/main3328832.shtml.
101. Quoted in Christopher Lee and Jonathan Weisman, "House Passes Children's Health Bill; Despite Strong Republican Support, Threatened Veto Will Probably Stand," *Washington Post,* September 26, 2007.
102. Tory Newmyer, "Vested Interests," *Roll Call,* June 18, 2007.
103. John Donnelly, "Stage Being Set For Showdown on Healthcare Congress, Bush at Odds on Plan Aiding Children," *Boston Globe,* August 4, 2007.
104. Jonathan Weisman, "Children's Health Bill Approved by House: Insurance Expansion Near Senate Passage but Faces Veto Threat," *Washington Post,* August 2, 2007.
105. See Michael Abramowitz and Jonathan Weisman, "Bush Vetoes Health Measure: President Says He's Willing to Negotiate," *Washington Post,* October 4, 2007.
106. Reid Wilson, "The GOP's SCHIP Dilemma," *Real Clear Politics,* October 9, 2007, http://www.realclearpolitics.com/articles/2007/10/the_gops_schip_dilemma.html.
107. Jeffrey Young and Jackie Kucinich, "Democrats Look to SCHIP as Key Win before August Recess," *The Hill,* August 2, 2007.
108. Quoted in Sean Lengell, "Ads Criticize GOP Votes on SCHIP," *Washington Times,* August 15, 2007.
109. Quoted in Alex Wayne, "Congress Defies Bush on SCHIP," *CQ Weekly Report,* October 1, 2007, 2852–54.
110. Quoted in "Veto This," *The Hill,* September 18, 2007, http://thehill.com/opinion/editorials/6302-veto-this.
111. Martin Kady, "GOP SCHIP Tactics Leave Opening for Dems," *Politico,* September 24, 2007.
112. Abramowitz and Weisman, "Bush Vetoes Health Measure."
113. Mike Shields, "SCHIP Votes Scheduled; Dems Rallying to Override Bush Veto," *Kansas Health Institute,* September 24, 2007, http://www.khi.org/s/index.cfm?aid=854.
114. Robert Pear, "Senate Passes Children's Health Plan," *New York Times,* September 28, 2007; and Matthew Hay Brown, "Boy to Give Radio Address," *Baltimore Sun,* September 29, 2007. Organizers arranged to have the petitions delivered by children to the White House but it refused to accept them. See Chris Frates, "SCHIP Supporters Storm Capitol Hill," *Politico,* October 3, 2007.
115. Jonathan E. Kaplan, "SCHIP Slips as Dems Trip Over Message," *The Hill,* October 3, 2007, http://thehill.com/homenews/news/13257-schip-slips-as-dems-trip-over-message.
116. Quoted in Sheryl Gay Stolberg and Carl Hulse, "Bush Vetoes Health Bill Privately, Without Fanfare," *New York Times,* October 4, 2007; and Martin Kady, "Battle of Sound Bites Reaches Health Care," *Politico,* October 2, 2007.
117. Morton W. Kondracke, "Democrats Gain Ground in Fights Over Budget, SCHIP," *Roll Call,* September 27, 2007.
118. Richard E. Cohen, "What's at Stake for Pelosi?" *National Journal,* October 13, 2007, 39–40.
119. "Nation: DCCC Launches New Round of SCHIP Ads," *Roll Call,* October 2, 2007; Jill Smallen, Jason Dick, and Fawn Johnson, *National Journal,* October 13, 2007, 48; and Richard Wolf, "Republicans Feel Heat in Wake of SCHIP Veto," *USA Today,* October 15, 2007.

120. Suzanne Perry, "Advocacy Campaign Tries Out Blog Ads—Philanthropy.com," *The Chronicle of Philanthropy*, October 18, 2007, 23.
121. Quoted in Stuart Rothenberg, "Have the Republicans Picked Another Losing Fight on SCHIP?," *Roll Call*, October 11, 2007.
122. Quoted in Martin Kady and Patrick O'Connor, "Democrats Lash Back on SCHIP," *Politico*, October 10, 2007.
123. Jennifer Yachnin, "Democrats Boost Spin on Iraq Funds," *Roll Call*, October 10, 2007.
124. Martin Kady, "SCHIP: The Veto Strikes Back? *Politico*, October 23, 2007.
125. John Stanton, "GOP Is Eager for FISA Fight," *Roll Call*, October 15, 2007.
126. See, for instance, Federal News Service, "Weekly Press Briefing with House Minority Leader John Boehner (R-OH), October 4, 2007; Steven T. Dennis and Emily Pierce, "Roadmap," *Roll Call*, October 16, 2007; Trent Lott, "Sustaining the Schip Veto," October 5, 2007, http://www.humanevents.com/article.php?id=22710; and Mike Pence, "Pence Urges President to Veto Massive Increase in SCHIP Program," October 2, 2007, http://www.mikepence.house.gov/index.php?option=com_content&task=view&id=448&Itemid=65.
127. Senator quoted in John Stanton, "Fight Divides GOP; Party Message Worries Some," *Roll Call*, October 9, 2007; and Rothenberg, "Have the Republicans Picked another Losing Fight on SCHIP?"
128. See, for example, Federal News Service, "Press Conference with Senate Majority Leader Harry Reid (D-NV); Senator Max Baucus (D-MT); Senator Chuck Grassley (R-IA); Senator John Rockefeller IV (D-WV); "Senator Orrin Hatch (R-UT)," October 3, 2007; and Steven T. Dennis, "RSC Driving House GOP," *Roll Call*, October 29, 2007.
129. Kady, "Dems Show No Signs of Letting Up On SCHIP."
130. Martin Kady, "House Fails to Muster SCHIP Veto Override," *Politico*, October 18, 2007.
131. Quoted in Jonathan Weisman, "House Passes Revised Children's Health Bill, But Timing Irks GOP," *Washington Post*, October 26, 2007.
132. Jeffrey Young, "Dems Give Up SCHIP Fight Until the 111th," *The Hill*, December 19, 2007, http://thehill.com/leading-the-news/dems-give-up-schip-fight-until-the-11th-2007-12-19.html.
133. Alex Wayne, "Second Attempt to Override Veto on SCHIP Falls Short of Needed Majority," *CQ Weekly*, January 28, 2008, 266.
134. Drew Armstrong, "Health Insurance Program for Kids Will Get Long-Sought Expansion," *CQ Weekly*, February 9, 2009, 309.
135. See Michael Sandler, "2006 Legislative Summary: Immigration Policy Overhaul," *CQ Weekly*, December 18, 2006, 357; Jonathan Weisman, "With Senate Vote, Congress Passes Border Fence Bill: Barrier Trumps Immigration Overhaul," *Washington Post*, September 30, 2006; Dan Balz, "Midterm Election Leaves Political Landscape Blurry," *Washington Post*, November 13, 2006; and Jonathan Weisman, "Backers of Immigration Bill More Optimistic—Lawmakers Cite Sense of Urgency," *Washington Post*, June 2, 2007.
136. Jonathan Weisman, "With Senate Vote, Congress Passes Border Fence Bill," *Washington Post*, September 30, 2006.
137. Michael Sandler, "Negotiators Agree On Immigration Plan," *CQ Weekly*, May 21, 2007, 1518. See also Jonathan Allen, "Immigration Stalemate Obscures Flurry of Activity," *The Hill*, April 6, 2006, 8; David Nather, "Democrats' Turn At Immigration Split," *CQ Weekly*, March 5, 2007, 636; and Darryl Fears and Spencer Hsu, "Democrats May Proceed with Caution on Immigration," *Washington Post*, November 13, 2006.

138. Jim VandeHei and Jonathan Weisman, "Bush Begins Push for Immigration Deal with Congress," *Washington Post*, April 25, 2006.

139. Quoted in Erin Billings and Ben Pershing, "Roadmap," *Roll Call*, April 25, 2006.

140. Quoted in Michael Sandler, "Immigration Overhaul Gains Ground in Senate," *CQ Weekly*, May 28, 2007, 1604.

141. Quoted in Shawn Zeller, "Guest Worker Advocates Could Get Another Chance," *CQ Weekly*, November 13, 2006, 2953.

142. See the transcript of his interview with Sean Hannity, *Hannity and Colmes*, Fox, December 1, 2006.

143. Darryl Fears and Spencer Hsu, "Democrats May Proceed with Caution on Immigration," *Washington Post*, November 13, 2006.

144. Wesley Pruden, "Killing the Coalition With Poison Pills," *Washington Times*, June 8, 2007. See also Dan Balz, "In Speech, A Balancing Act of Policy and Politics," *Washington Post*, May 16, 2006.

145. Quoted in Dan Balz, "In Speech."

146. Editorial, "A Serious Approach," *Washington Times*, June 12, 2007.

147. Dan Balz, "GOP Hopefuls Keep Distance from Bush," *Washington Post*, June 7, 2007.

148. Quoted in Manu Raju and Elana Schor, "Both Sides Blame Each Other, Trade Barbs on Immigration Legislation," *The Hill*, June 8, 2007.

149. Hugh Hewitt, "Republican Immigration Talking Points," *Free Republic* (blog), May 16, 2007, http://www.freerepublic.com/focus/f-news/1834899/posts.

150. See Fears and Hsu, "Democrats May Proceed With Caution on Immigration"; Michael Sandler, "2006 Legislative Summary: Immigration Policy Overhaul," *CQ Weekly*, December 18, 2006, 3357; and Michael Sandler, "Senate Vote 157: Immigration Policy Changes," *CQ Weekly*, January 1, 2007, 69.

151. Quoted in Erin Billings and Ben Pershing, "Roadmap," *Roll Call*, April 25, 2006.

152. Jim VandeHei and Jonathan Weisman, "Bush Begins Push for Immigration Deal with Congress," *Washington Post*, April 25, 2006. See too Billings and Pershing, "Roadmap."

153. Quoted in Balz, "In Speech."

154. Quoted in Michael Sandler, "Blue Slip Threat Stalls Immigration Measure," *CQ Weekly*, June 12, 2006, 1633 (emphasis added).

155. Michael Sandler, "GOP Move Delays Conference on Immigration Bill," *CQ Weekly*, June 26, 2006, 1785; and Patrick O'Connor, "Parties Ready Battle Plans for Recess," *The Hill*, June 29, 2006.

156. Patrick O'Connor, "Republicans Establish Immigration War Room," *The Hill*, July 18, 2006.

157. See, for instance, Rep. Tom Tancredo's appearance on the television show *Your World With Neil Cavuto*, Fox, July 28, 2006.

158. Sandler, "GOP Move Delays Conference on Immigration Bill," 1785.

159. Michael Sandler, "Chambers Still at Odds on Immigration," *CQ Weekly*, July 10, 2006, 1880.

160. Rep. Tom Tancredo, *Your World with Neil Cavuto*, Fox, September 26, 2006. See too "Washington in Brief," *Washington Post*, September 15, 2006; Michael Sandler, "House Rolls Out Revised Agenda," *CQ Weekly*, September 18, 2006, 2470; Jonathan Weisman, "With Senate Vote, Congress Passes Border Fence Bill," *Washington Post*, September 30, 2006; and Michael Sandler, "Senate Clears Border Fence Legislation," *CQ Weekly*, October 2, 2006, 2634.

161. David Nather, "Democrats Turn at Immigration Split," *CQ Weekly*, March 5, 2007, 636.

162. Ibid.

163. John Gizzi, "RNC to Swallow Martinez—Under Some Protest," *Human Events*, January 17, 2007; and "New RNC Chair Pro-Amnesty Advocate for Illegal Immigrants," *Liberally Conservative*, January 19, 2007, http://www.liberallyconservative.com/new-rnc-chair-pro-amnesty-advocate-for-illegal-immigrants/.

164. Robert Behre, "DeMint Taps Into Power of Web, " *The Post Courier*, March 23, 2008, http://www.postandcourier.com/news/2008/mar/23/demint_taps_into_power_web34711/; and Michelle Malkin, "Complete the Fence Now," March 17, 2008, http://michellemalkin.com/2008/03/17/wwwcompletethefencenowcom/.

165. Quoted in Shawn Zeller, "Broadcasting the Case for a Border Crackdown," *CQ Weekly*, April 23, 2007, 1152.

166. Nather, "Democrats' Turn at Immigration Split," 636.

167. Michael Sandler, "Reid Presses Immigration Rewrite Despite Lack of a Deal in the Senate," *CQ Weekly*, May 14, 2007, 1453; See also his articles, "Negotiators Agree on Immigration Plan," *CQ Weekly*, May 21, 2007, 1518; and "Immigration Overhaul Gains Ground in Senate," *CQ Weekly*, May 28, 2007, 1604.

168. Jonathan Weisman, "Backers of Immigration Bill More Optimistic—Lawmakers Cite Sense of Urgency," *Washington Post*, June 4, 2007.

169. Available at: http://www.house.gov/bilbray/irc/index.shtml.

170. Jonathan Weisman, "Immigrant Measure Survives Challenges," *Washington Post*, June 7, 2007.

171. See Mike Allen, "Talk Radio Helped Sink Immigration Reform," *Politico*, August 20, 2007; and "Did Talk Hosts Help Derail the Immigration Bill?," *PEJ Talk Show Index*, June 3–8, 2007, http://www.journalism.org/node/6066.

172. Greg Pierce, "Talking Loudly: Nation Inside Politics," *Washington Times*, June 8, 2007, A08.

173. Jonathan Weisman and Shailagh Murry, "Republicans Hearing Static from Conservative Radio Hosts," *Washington Post*, June 20, 2007, http://seattletimes.nwsource.com/html/nationworld/2003760421_lott24.html.

174. Dan Balz, "A Failure of Leadership in a Flawed Political Culture," *Washington Post*, June 8, 2007.

175. Lamar Smith and Peter King, "Senate Strays From Americans With Amnesty Approach," *Roll Call*, May 14, 2007.

176. Sandler, "Immigration Overhaul Gains Ground in Senate," 1604.

177. Susan Davis and John Stanton, "House GOP Firmly Against Border Bill: Measure Moving Forward in Senate," *Roll Call*, June 27, 2007.

178. Shailagh Murray, "Careful Strategy Is Used to Derail Immigration Bill," *Washington Post*, June 8, 2007.

179. Jonathan Weisman, "Immigration Overhaul Bill Stalls in Senate: Bipartisan Compromise Collapses: Reid Says Measure May Return," *Washington Post*, June 8, 2007.

180. Michael Sandler, "Reid Pulls Immigration Overhaul," *CQ Weekly*, June 11, 2007, 1746–47.

181. Ibid. The quoted opponent is Rep Brian Bilbray (R-CA).

182. Stephen Dinan, "Bush Seeks Immigration Action: Amendments Might Bring Bill Back," *Washington Times*, June 9, 2007; and Sandler, "Reid Pulls Immigration Overhaul," 1746–47.

183. Michael Sandler and Martin Kady II, "Immigration Bill Gets Second Chance," *CQ Weekly*, June 18, 2007, 1850.

184. Michael Sandler, "Senate to Take Another Stab at Immigration," *CQ Weekly*, June 25, 2007, 1939; and Editorial, "Bush Bets Again" *The Hill*, June 14, 2007.

185. Michael Sandler, "Immigration Overhaul Stymied," *CQ Weekly*, July 9, 2007, 2028.

186. Sellars, *Cycles of Spin,* 35–39.

187. Tim Groeling, *When Politicians Attack!: Party Cohesion in the Media* (Cambridge, UK: Cambridge University Press, 2010), 23–26.

Chapter 7

1. Quoted in Peter Baker, "The Education of a President: What Barack Obama Has Done and Hasn't and What Being President Has Done to Him," *New York Times Magazine*, October 17, 2010, 49.
2. Quoted in, E. J. Dionne, "Why Pelosi is Running for House Minority Leader," *Washingtonpost.com*, November 11, 2010, http://www.washingtonpost.com/wp-dyn/content/article/2010/11/05/AR2010110505285.html.
3. Fred I. Greenstein, "The Leadership Style of Barack Obama: An Early Assessment," *The Forum* 7 (2009), http://www.bepress.com/forum/vol7/iss1/art6.
4. George Edwards described it as being the "core" of Bush's approach to governing in his analysis, *Governing by Campaigning* (New York: Pearson Longman, 2008), 2.
5. Lawrence R. Jacobs, "The Presidency and the Press: The Paradox of the White House Communications War," in *The Presidency and the Political System,* 9th ed., ed. Michael Nelson (Washington, DC: CQ Press, 2010), 242.
6. Quoted in David Carr, "How Obama Tapped into Social Networks' Power," *New York Times*, November 10, 2008, http://www.nytimes.com/2008/11/10/business/media/10carr.html.
7. Brian Stelter, "The Facebooker Who Friended Obama," *New York Times*, July 7, 2008; and Matthew R. Kerbel, *Netroots: Online Progressives and the Transformation of American Politics* (Boulder, CO: Paradigm, 2009), 133–43.
8. Quoted in Frank Davies, "Obama Ready to Embrace Internet as Tool for Persuasion and Participation," *San Jose Mercury News*, November 10, 2008.
9. Eric Benderoff, "Macon Phillips: the Man Behind White House.gov," *Chicago Tribune*, February 24, 2009, http://www.chicagotribune.com/business/chi-tue-macon-phillips-new-mediafeb24,0,6751735.story.
10. Jeff Eller, "It's Time to Rewire the Bully Pulpit," *Politico*, November 18, 2008.
11. Macon Phillips, "Change Has Come to WhiteHouse.gov," *The White House Blog*, January 20, 2009, http://www.whitehouse.gov/blog/change_has_come_to_white house-gov/.
12. Sheryl Gay Stolberg, "A Rewired Bully Pulpit: Big, Bold and Unproven," *New York Times*, November 23, 2008.
13. Ibid.; and Eller, "It's Time to Rewire the Bully Pulpit."
14. "Obama to Pioneer Internet Outreach; He Sees Web as a Means to Connect, Push Agenda and Solicit Public Input," *Richmond Times Dispatch*, November 13, 2008; Christina Bellantoni, "Web Sites Foretell a YouTube Presidency," *Washington Times*, November 7, 2008; and Richard S. Dunham, Dwight Silverman, and Kyle Pendergast, "Obama's Preferred Address Begins with http, Not 1600; His Use of Technology Didn't End with Election, If New Web Site is a Clue, *The Houston Chronicle*, November 9, 2008.
15. Carr, "How Obama Tapped Into Social Networks' Power."
16. Benderoff, "Meet the Man Behind WhiteHouse.gov."
17. Adrian McCoy, "Quick Revamp of White House Web Site Follows Promise of More Transparency," *Pittsburgh Post-Gazette*, January 29, 2009. See Jose Antonio Vargas, "Web-Savvy Obama Team Hits Unexpected Bumps: Issue of Technology, Security and Privacy Slow the New Administration's Effort to Foster Instant Communication," *Washington Post,* March 2, 2009.
18. Vargas, "Web-Savvy Obama Team Hits Unexpected Bumps."
19. Devin Dwyer, "Obama's Media Machine: State Run 2.0?," *ABCNews.go.com*. http://abcnews.go.com/Politics/president-obama-white-house-media-operation-state-run/story?id=12913319.
20. Greg Hitt and Deborah Solomon, "Historic Bailout Passes As Economy Slips Further," *Wall Street Journal*, October 4, 2008.

21. Jack Healy, "U.S. Economy Posts Fastest Decline in 26 Years," *New York Times,* January 30, 2009, http://www.nytimes.com/2009/01/30/business/worldbusiness/30iht-USecon.4.19818575.html.

22. Edmund Andrews, "Fed Chairman Endorses New Round of Stimulus," *New York Times,* October 20, 2008; and Barbara Hagenbaugh, "Majority of Economists in *USA Today* Survey Back 2nd Stimulus," *USA Today,* October 28, 2008, http://www.usatoday.com/money/economy/2008-10-27-second-economic-stimulus-proposal_N.htm..

23. Jonathan Alter, *The Promise: President Obama, Year One* (New York: Simon and Shuster, 2010), chap. 6; Obama quoted on 77.

24. Ibid.

25. Quoted in Carrie Budoff Brown, "Obama: Stimulus Needed Now," *Politico,* November 7, 2008.

26. Carrie Budoff Brown, "Obama Records First Radio Address," *Politico,* November 8, 2008..

27. Alter, *The Promise,* 82–92.

28. Conducted by CBS News, October 29–31, 2008.

29. Conducted by *USA Today,* November 7–9, 2008.

30. Conducted by ABC News/*Washington Post,* December–December 14, 2008.

31. Conducted by NBC News/*Wall Street Journal.* December 4–8, 2008.

32. Conducted by Democracy Corps, October 13–16, 2008.

33. Lorraine Woellert and Hans Nichols, "Obama Uses Poll, Focus Groups to Sell Stimulus Plan to Congress," *Bloomberg,* January 8, 2009, http://www.bloomberg.com/apps/news?pid=newsarchive&sid=aHNaiptix3lk

34. Barack Obama, "Your Weekly Address from the President Elect," November 15, 2008, http://change.gov/newsroom/entry/your_weekly_address_from_the_president_elect/.

35. Based on weekly addresses posted at change.gov.

36. "President-elect Barack Obama Talks Economy, Foreign Policy, Economy on Meet the Press," http://change.gov/newsroom/entry/president_elect_barack_obama_talks_economy_foreign_policy_on_meet_the_press/; December 7, 2008; and "The President-elect on His Goals and Agenda in a Time of Crisis," http://change.gov/newsroom/entry/the_president-elect_on_his_goals_and_agenda_in_a_time_of_crisis/, December 17, 2008;

37. Postings at http://change.gov/newsroom/blog/.

38. David Clarke and Joseph J. Schatz, "The Devil's in the Stimulus Plan Details," *CQ Weekly,* January 12, 2009, 77–78.

39. "Storyline Shifts from War to Washington," *PEJ News Coverage Index,* January 5–11, 2009, http://www.journalism.org/print/14314.

40. Nia-Malika Henderson, "Obama Pushes Stimulus Plan," *Politico,* January 3, 2009.

41. Brian Knowlton, "Obama Presses for Action on the Economy," *New York Times,* January 9, 2009, http://www.nytimes.com/2009/01/09/us/politics/09obamacnd.html; and Jonathan Weisman and Greg Hitt, "Obama Seeks Fast Acton on Plan," *Wall Street Journal,* January 9, 2009, http://online.wsj.com/article/SB123141109288164019.html.

42. George Edwards notes presidents have a greater capacity to lead by "exploiting existing opinion" than by getting people to change their views. Yet even here presidents are not always successful, as Edwards makes clear in *The Strategic President: Persuasion and Opportunity in Presidential Leadership* (Princeton, NJ: Princeton University Press, 2009), chap. 3.

43. "Transcript of Obama's Speech on the Economy," *New York Times,* January 8, 2009, http://www.nytimes.com/2009/01/08/us/politics/08text-obama.html.

44. "Christina Romer Explains a New Report about Job Creation," January 11, 2009, http://change.gov/newsroom/entry/video_christna_romer_explains_a_new_report_about_job_creation/.
45. "Video: The President Elect's Plan," January 12, 2009, http://change.gov/newsroom/blog/P20/.
46. David Clarke, "Democrats Roll Out Stimulus Plan," *CQ Weekly*, January 19, 2009, 126–28. Video of Obama at Cardinal Fastener was posted at change.gov, http://www.youtube.com/watch?v=9B97zqrJSao.
47. Conducted by CBS News/*New York Times*, January 11– 15, 2009; and Conducted by NBC News and *Wall Street Journal*, January 9–12, 2009.
48. Paul M. Krawzak and Edward Epstein, "Three House Panels Move Stimulus Bill," *CQ Weekly*, January 26, 2009, 186–88.
49. Quoted in Jonathan Martin and Carol E. Lee, "Obama to GOP: 'I Won,'" *Politico*, January 23, 2009.
50. John Fund actually coined the term *Pelosi's Poodles* years earlier. See "Pelosi's Poodles," *Wall Street Journal*, November 21, 2005, http://online.wsj.com/article/SB122520429567476177.html
51. Quoted in Dave Cook, "House GOP Leader Boehner: Bullish on Obama Speech, Bearish on US Economy," *The Christian Science Monitor*, February 25, 2009, http://www.csmonitor.com/USA/Politics/2009/0225/house-gop-leader-boehner-bullish-on-obama-speech-bearish-on-us-economy.
52. Quoted in Alexis Simendinger, "An Early Test for McConnell," *National Journal*, January 31, 2009, 10.
53. Richard E. Cohen, "GOP's Dilemma: Substance Versus Spin," *National Journal*, March 7, 2009, 15.
54. Patrick O'Connor, "Cantor to Focus on GOP Message," *Politico*, January 8, 2009.
55. Quoted in Christina Bellantoni, "The Revolution Will Be Twittered: GOP Jumps on Tech Bandwagon to Rival Obama," *Washington Times*, February 17, 2009.
56. Michael Calderone, "GOP Jams the Airwaves," *Politico*, February 5, 2009.
57. Cohen, "GOP's Dilemma."
58. Quoted in Alan K. Ota, "New Team Repackages the Right's Thinking," *CQ Weekly*, February 16, 2009, 340–41.
59. "House GOP Economic Stimulus Plan," http://republicanwhip.house.gov/jobs/.
60. See, for instance, "Franks Announces New Website Detailing Economic Recovery Plan, http://franks.house.gov/press_releases/313; and "House GOP Economic Stimulus Plan," http://republicanwhip.house.gov/Jobs/.
61. Patrick O'Connor, "Parties' New Battleground: Google," *Politico*, February 23, 2009.
62. "Bloggers Contemplate the Economy, Rush, and Zombies," *PEJ New Media Index*, January 26–30, 2009, http://www.journalism.org/print/14622.
63. "President Obama Delivers Your Weekly Saturday Address," January 24, 2009, http://www.whitehouse.gov/president-obama-delivers-your-weekly-address/.
64. Alter, *The Promise*, 117–19.
65. Jeanne Cummings, "Obama Losing Stimulus Message War," *Politico*, February 5, 2009.
66. Michael Hirsh, "Losing Control: Obama Needs to Reassert Command of the Agenda in Washington," *Newsweek*, February 4, 2009, http://www.newsweek.com/2009/02/03/losing-control.html. For a discussion of the "soft sell" approach, see Edwards, *The Strategic President*.
67. Sam Stein, "Stimulus Spin War: Obama to Go on Media Offensive," *Huffington Post*, February 2, 2009, http://www.huffingtonpost.com/2009/02/02/stimulus-spin-war-obama-t_n_163305.html.

68. "A 40-Year Wish List." *Wall Street Journal*, January 28, 2009, http://online.wsj.com/article/SB123310466514522309.html.

69. Linda Feldman, "To Sell Stimulus Plan, Obama Steps Up to Presidential Bully Pulpit," *Christian Science Monitor*, February 10, 2009, http://www.csmonitor.com/USA/Politics/2009/0210/to-sell-stimulus-plan-obama-steps-up-to-presidential-bully-pulpit.

70. Patrick O'Connor, "Boehner to GOP: Vote against Stimulus," *Politico*, January 27, 2009; and Lisa Lerer and Carrie Budoff Brown, "GOP Weapon: Obama Earmarks Pledge," *Politico*, January 26, 2009.

71. See, for instance, Rep. Frank Lucas, "The Myth of Government-Created Wealth," *The Hill Congress Blog*, February 10, 2009, http://thehill.com/blogs/congress-blog/politics/25985-the-myth-of-government-created-wealth-rep-frank-lucas.

72. Peter Wallsten, "New Era? Same as the Old One: The All-Too-Familiar Machinery of Partisan Politics Surfaces Over House Stimulus Vote," *Los Angeles Times*, January 29, 2009; and "The News Narrative Turns Bearish on Obama," *PEJ News Coverage Index*, February 2–8, 2009, http://www.journalism.org/index_report/new_coverage_index_february_2_8_2009.

73. The day after the president's address, January 25, 2009, the Speaker went on *This Week with George Stephanopolou*, ABC,to discuss the plan.

74. This blog is available at http://thehill.com/blogs/congress-blog.

75. Joseph J. Schatz and Richard Rubin, "House Democrats Pass Stimulus," *CQ Weekly*, February 2, 2009, 254–56.

76. Information on television bookings derived through a Lexis-Nexis search of television transcripts. Search carried out using member's name and "stimulus." Calculations include only transcripts in which the individual member was interviewed on the plan.

77. Quoted in Greg Sargent," Top Dems Acknowledging They're Being Outworked on TV, Vow to Fix," *The Plum Line*, February 5, 2009, http://theplumline.whorunsgov.com/political-media/top-dems-acknowledging-being-outworked-on-tv-vow-to-fix/; and Calderone, "GOP Jams the Airwaves."

78. "Report: GOP Lawmakers Outnumber Dem Lawmakers by Almost 2 to 1 in Cable News Stimulus Debate Again," *Think Progress*, February 6, 2009, http://thinkprogress.org/2009/02/06/senate-cable-stimulus-debate/; and Greg Sargent, "Republicans Outworking Dems On TV—Dems Partly to Blame?" *The Plum Line*, February 5, 2009, http://theplumline.whorunsgov.com/uncategorized/republicans-outworking-dems-on-tv.

79. S. A. Miller, "GOP Takes Its Own Message to Districts," *Washington Times*, January 30, 2009.

80. Cummings, "Obama Losing Stimulus Message War"; and Jonathan Weisman, "Emanuel Says Obama Team Lost Message on Stimulus" *Wall Street Journal*, February 12, 2009, http://online.wsj.com/article/SB123449249590080699.html.

81. "The Stimulus Debate and Daschle Dominate the Blogosphere," *PEJ New Media Index*, February 2–6, 2009, http://www.journalism.org/index_report/stimulus_debate_and_daschle_debacle_dominate_blogosphere.

82. Peter Steinhauser, "Polls Show Support for Stimulus Has Slipped," CNN, February 6, 2009, http://articles.cnn.com/2009-02-06/politics/stimulus.polls_1_stimulus-plan-cbs-news-poll-economic-recovery-bill?_s=PM:POLITICS

83. Conducted by Fox News/Opinion Dynamics, February 17–18, 2009.

84. Jonathan Martin, "Closing Argument: Change in Tone," *Politico*, February 6, 2009.

85. "DCCC Launches Radio Ads on Stimulus Vote," *Roll Call*, February 3, 2009.

86. Glenn Thrush and Patrick O'Connor, "Pelosi Dismisses Bipartisanship Calls," *Politico*, February 6, 2009.

87. Donald Lambro, "Obama, Democrats Go on Offense Over Stimulus Package," *Washington Times*, February 6, 2009.
88. Quoted in Alter, *The Promise*, 118.
89. E. J. Dionne, "Obama Losing Stimulus Fight to Defeated GOP," *Real Clear Politics*, February 5, 2009, http://www.realclearpolitics.com/articles/2009/02/obama_losing_stimulus_fight_to.html.
90. Carol E. Lee, "Team Obama Mobilizing E-Mail List," *Politico*, January 30, 2009; Sam Stein, "Organizing for America Takes First Action for Obama Agenda," *Huffington Post*, February 13, 2009, http://www.huffingtonpost.com/2009/01/30/organize-for-america-to-t_n_162519.html; and Alexandra Marks, "Obama's Backers Go to the Net for the Stimulus Bill," *Christian Science Monitor*, February 10, 2009, http://www.csmonitor.com/USA/Politics/2009/0209/obamas-backers-go-to-the-net-for-stimulus-bill. Information on the popularity of the news video taken from "Beyond Stimulus, Bloggers Focus on Pupils, Penance and Puppets," *PEJ New Media Index*, February 9–13, http://www.journalism.org/index_report/beyond_stimulus_bloggers_focus_pupils_penance_and_puppets.
91. Kirk Victor, "Honeymoon Ends Quickly For Obama," *National Journal*, February 7, 2009, 8
92. Barack Obama, "The Action Americans Need," *Washington Post*, February 5, 2009.
93. "President Obama Weekly Address, February 7, 2009, http://www.youtube.com/watch?v=WJLRyfd8zpQ.
94. Keith Koffler, "Obama Pitches to the Press," *Roll Call*, February 17, 2009; and Linda Feldmann, "To Sell Stimulus Plan, Obama Steps up to Presidential Bully Pulpit," *Christian Science Monitor*, February 11, 2009, http://www.csmonitor.com/USA/Politics/2009/0209/obamas-backers-go-to-the-net-for-stimulus-bill..
95. Victoria McGrane, "Conservative Rep. Tom Price Emerging as GOP's Bulldog," *Politico*, May 20, 2009, http://www.politico.com/news/stories/0509/22739.html.
96. Videos posted on the House Republican and Democratic Senate websites. See also, *ABC News with Diane Sawyer*, http://abcnews.go.com/Politics/Business/story?id=6870873&page=2.
97. Reid Wilson, "Stimulus Goes on the Road," *The Hill*, February 18, 2009.
98. Christopher Weaver, "Congress Brags About 'Pork' in Pork-Free Bill," *Huffington Post*, February 18, 2009, http://www.huffingtonpost.com/propublica/congress-brags-about-pork_b_167925.html?vi
99. Quoted in Andy Barr, "Pence: GOP Won Stimulus Argument," *Politico*, February 26, 2009.
100. Conducted by Pew Research Center for the People and the Press, March 9–12; and NBC News/*Wall Street Journal*, conducted February 26–March 1, 2009.
101. Mike Madden, "A Message War the Republicans Won," *Salon.com*, April 6, 2009.
102. Jared Allen, "Spring Break is Stimulus Blitz Time for Dems," *The Hill*, March 28, 2009.
103. Patrick O'Connor, "GOP Scrambles to Show It Has Ideas," *Politico*, April 14.
104. Eamon Javers, "Obama: Stimulus 'Worked as Intended,'" *Politico*, July 11, 2009.
105. "Bloodhounds," http://www.youtube.com/watch?v=tl_q0afUl0E.
106. http://www.youtube.com/watch?v=8NGEfRBzB0s; and http://www.youtube.com/watch?v=s2MjQ17kDng
107. Jackie Kucinich, "Republicans Wage Floor Games; GOP Increases Attempt to Trip Up Democrats' Agenda," *Roll Call*, July 27, 2009.
108. Available at http://www.youtube.com/watch?v=_xsqldG1huw.
109. http://www.youtube.com/user/JohnBoehner#p/search/31/RRNrzL_BtFs; http://oversight.house.gov/index.php?option=com_content&task=view&id=356&Itemid=29.
110. Conducted by *CBS/New York Times*, July 24– 28, 2009.

111. Jonathan Martin, "The White House Strikes Back," *Politico*, July 16, 2009.
112. Jonathan Martin, "DNC Targets Republican Leaders on Stimulus," *Politico*, July 28, 2009.
113. Alex Isenstadt, "Parties Launch Stimulus P.R. Offensives," *Politico*, November 28, 2009.
114. Jake Sherman, "McCain, Coburn Tag Team Stimulus," *Politico*, December 8, 2009.
115. Conducted by *NBC News/Wall Street Journal*, January 10–14, 2010; and the *Pew Research Center for the People and the Press*, February 3–February 9, 2010.
116. Patrick O'Connor, "GOP Wants Televised Jobs Debate," *Politico*, February 17, 2009; and Sheryl Gay Stolberg, "Obama and Republicans Clash Over Stimulus Bill, One Year Later," *New York Times*, February 18, 2009.
117. Posted on the House Democratic Caucus website, http://www.youtube.com/watch?v=5EWbzw64n4c.
118. Michael O'Brien, "Democrats Mark the Anniversary of the Stimulus with GOP 'Hypocrites' Video," *The Hill's Blog Briefing Room*, February 17, 2009, http://thehill.com/blogs/blog-briefing-room/news/81413-dems-note-stimulus-anniversary-with-gop-hypocrites-video.
119. Dana Milbank, "Criticizing Economic Stimulus Plan Can Be Lucrative," *Washington Post*, February 18, 2009, http://www.washingtonpost.com/wp-dyn/content/article/2010/02/17/AR2010021704055.html.
120. "Rhetoric vs. Results," February 18, 2010, http://www.youtube.com/watch?v=vzRgrDA5C7c.
121. Quoted in David Weigel, "Republicans Test 2010 Message: Cancel the Stimulus," *The Washington Independent*, July 10, 2009, http://washingtonindependent.com/50309/republicans-test-2010-message-cancel-the-stimulus.
122. Mike Allen, "Obama, Biden Declare 'Recovery Summer,'" *Politico*, June 17, 2010.
123. Coburn and McCain report http://coburn.senate.gov/public/index.cfm/press releases?ContentRecord_id=20532b9f-f9ae-46d7-b2bf-0f01cd75d90d.
124. Posted by Boehner's office, http://www.youtube.com/watch?v=QIBIRcgtiXQ.
125. Bruce Stokes, "Despite Stimulus Results, Public Relations Battle Largely Lost," *National Journal*, July 21, 2010, http://congressionalconnection.nationaljournal.com/2010/07/despite-stimulus-results-publi.php.
126. Samuel Kernell, *Going Public: New Strategies of Presidential Leadership* (Washington, DC: CQ Press, 1997), 252–53.
127. Barbara Sinclair, *Party Wars: Polarization and the Politics of National Policy Making* Norman: University of Oklahoma Press, 2006), chap. 7.
128. Edwards, *The Strategic President*, chap. 2–3.
129. Sinclair makes this same point with regard to congressional parties in *Party Wars*, 307.
130. Alter, *The Promise*, 127.
131. Samuel Kernell, *Going Public*, 260.
132. Tim Groeling, *When Politicians Attack! Party Cohesion in the Media* (New York: Cambridge University Press, 2010), 167.
133. Patrick Sellars, *Cycles of Spin: Strategic Communication in the U.S. Congress* (New York: Cambridge University Press, 2010), 72–73.
134. See David Mayhew, *Congress: The Electoral Connection* (New Haven, CT: Yale University Press, 1974).

Chapter 8

1. Quoted in Richard Cohen, "On Day Two, Eric Cantor Builds His Brand: Cantor is Clearly Gunning for Plenty of Media Coverage in His New Role," *Politico*, January 7, 2011.

2. Ibid. (emphasis added).

3. Joseph Bessette, *The Mild Voice of Reason: Deliberative Democracy and American National Government* (Chicago: University of Chicago Press, 1997); Jeffrey Tulis, *The Rhetorical Presidency* (Princeton, NJ: Princeton University Press, 1988); and Alexander Hamilton, John Jay, and James Madison, *The Federalist,* ed. George W. Carey and James McClellan (Indianapolis, IN: Liberty Fund, 2001), nos. 49–63. See Norman Ornstein, "Don't Sacrifice Deliberation for Expediency," *Roll Call,* July 9, 2003.

4. See *Federalist* no. 55.

5. This part of our argument rests in part on arguments found in Bessette, *Mild Voice of Reason* and Tulis, *Rhetorical Presidency.*

6. See Bessette, *Mild Voice of Reason,* chap. 2–3; and Tulis, *Rhetorical Presidency,* chap. 2.

7. Bessette's more restrictive definition of deliberation—"reasoning on the merits of public policy"—makes sense, given his larger goal of making the case that political scientists have underestimated the extent to which members of Congress engage in that behavior. Our goal of exploring the difference it makes when lawmakers regularly bring the larger public into their policymaking conversations shifts our focus to the larger relationship between federal constitutional officers, and so our definition is consequently broader.

8. See, for instance, Eric Uslaner, *The Decline of Comity in Congress* (Ann Arbor: University of Michigan Press, 1993), chap.1.

9. See T. R. Reid, *Congressional Odyssey: The Saga of a Senate Bill* (New York: W.H. Freeman, 1980); and Bessette, *The Mild Voice of Reason,* chap. 4.

10. A time-line tracking the development of the Sherrod episode can be found at *Mediamatters.*

11. Rep. David Obey (D-WI) observed that as the internal workings of the Congress became more visible to the public, "[w]e've lost out a lot…. Because [the media] emphasizes combat and drama rather than a thoughtful analysis of issues." David Rogers, "Obey Surveys House Then and Now," *Politico,* July 23, 2010.

12. Juliet Eilperin, *Fight Club Politics: How Partisanship is Poisoning the House of Representatives* (Lanham, MD: Rowman &Littlefield, 2006).

13. Shailagh Murray and Sam Horwitz, "Rep. Gabrielle Giffords Shot in Tucson Rampage: Federal Judge Killed," *Washington Post,* January 9, 2011, http://www.washingtonpost.com/wp-dyn/content/article/2011/01/08/AR2011010802422.html.

14. Erika Lovely, "FBI Details Surge of Threats Against Lawmakers," *Politico,* May 25, 2010.

15. See http://thinkprogress.org/2010/03/19/yankee-aggression/

16. See Ben Evans, "Lawmaker Condemns Question about Shooting Obama," *Associated Press,* February 25, 2011, http://news.yahoo.com/s/ap/20110225/ap_on_re_us/us_congressman_obama_question.

17. John McArdle, "Wilson, Grayson: Provocateurs Who Say What the Base Thinks," *Roll Call,* November 16, 2009.

18. Others have made the same point about this Congress. See Uslaner, *The Decline of Comity in Congress,* chap. 7.

19. Craig Crawford, *Attack the Messenger: How Politicians Turn You Against the Media* (Lanham, MD: Rowman & Littlefield, 2005); and David T. Z. Mindich, *Tuned Out: Why Americans Under 40 Don't Follow the News* (New York: Oxford University Press, 2004).

20. See Thomas C. Reeves, *A Question of Character: A Life of John F. Kennedy* (New York: Free Press, 1991.)

21. *Federalist* no. 10.

22. Quoted in Eilperin, *Fight Club Politics,* 37.

23. Hugh Heclo, *On Thinking Institutionally* (Boulder, CO: Paradigm, 2008).
24. The phrase pertaining to the sense of the community comes from *Federalist*, no. 63.
25. *Federalist* no. 10.
26. *Federalist* no. 1, 4.

Index